ALSO BY HRH PRINCESS MICHAEL OF KENT

The Serpent and the Moon

Cupid and the King

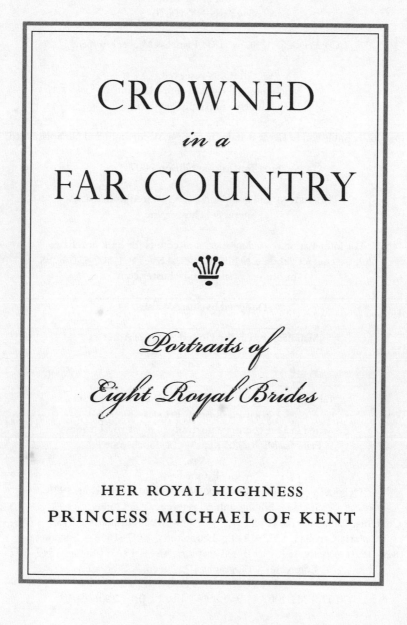

CROWNED

in a

FAR COUNTRY

Portraits of
Eight Royal Brides

HER ROYAL HIGHNESS
PRINCESS MICHAEL OF KENT

A TOUCHSTONE BOOK
PUBLISHED BY SIMON & SCHUSTER
NEW YORK   LONDON   TORONTO   SYDNEY

Touchstone
Rockefeller Center
1230 Avenue of the Americas
New York, NY 10020

Originally published in Great Britain by George Weidenfeld and Nicholson Ltd.

First Touchstone Edition 2007

TOUCHSTONE and colophon are registered trademarks
of Simon & Schuster, Inc.

For information regarding special discounts for bulk purchases,
please contact Simon & Schuster Special Sales at 1-800-456-6798
or business@simonandschuster.com.

Designed by Susan Walsh

Manufactured in the United States of America

1   3   5   7   9   10   8   6   4   2

Library of Congress Cataloging-in-Publication Data
Michael, of Kent, Princess.
Crowned in a far country : portraits of eight royal brides /
Princess Michael of Kent.—1st Touchstone ed.
p.   cm.
"A Touchstone book."
Originally published: New York : Weidenfeld & Nicolson, 1986.
Includes bibliographical references and index.
Contents: Catherine the Great, 1729–1796—Marie Antoinette, 1755–1793—
Maria Carolina, 1752–1814—Leopoldina, 1797–1814—Eugénie,
1826–1920—Vicky, 1840–1901—Alexandra, 1844–1925; Minnie, 1847–1928.
1. Empresses—Biography. 2. Queens—Biography.
3. Princesses—Biography. I. Title.
D107.3.M5 2007   940.09'9—dc22   [B]   2006050170

ISBN-13: 978-0-7432-9637-3
ISBN-10: 0-7432-9637-0

CONTENTS

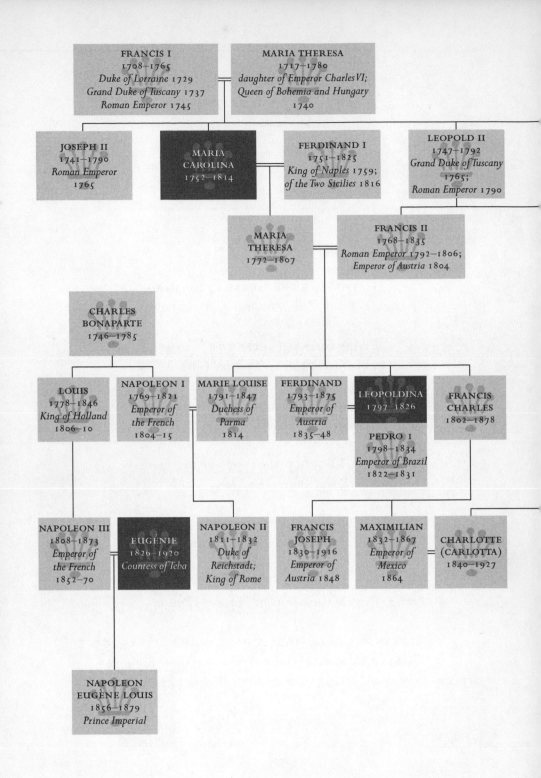

FRANCIS I
1708–1765
Duke of Lorraine 1729
Grand Duke of Tuscany 1737
Roman Emperor 1745

MARIA THERESA
1717–1780
daughter of Emperor Charles VI;
Queen of Bohemia and Hungary
1740

JOSEPH II
1741–1790
Roman Emperor
1765

MARIA
CAROLINA
1752–1814

FERDINAND I
1751–1825
King of Naples 1759;
of the Two Sicilies 1816

LEOPOLD II
1747–1792
Grand Duke of Tuscany
1765;
Roman Emperor 1790

MARIA
THERESA
1772–1807

FRANCIS II
1768–1835
Roman Emperor 1792–1806;
Emperor of Austria 1804

CHARLES
BONAPARTE
1746–1785

LOUIS
1778–1846
King of Holland
1806–10

NAPOLEON I
1769–1821
Emperor of
the French
1804–15

MARIE LOUISE
1791–1847
Duchess of
Parma
1814

FERDINAND
1793–1875
Emperor of
Austria
1835–48

LEOPOLDINA
1797–1826

PEDRO I
1798–1834
Emperor of Brazil
1822–1831

FRANCIS
CHARLES
1802–1878

NAPOLEON III
1808–1873
Emperor of
the French
1852–70

EUGÉNIE
1826–1920
Countess of Teba

NAPOLEON II
1811–1832
Duke of
Reichstadt;
King of Rome

FRANCIS
JOSEPH
1830–1916
Emperor of
Austria 1848

MAXIMILIAN
1832–1867
Emperor of
Mexico
1864

CHARLOTTE
(CARLOTTA)
1840–1927

NAPOLEON
EUGENE LOUIS
1856–1879
Prince Imperial

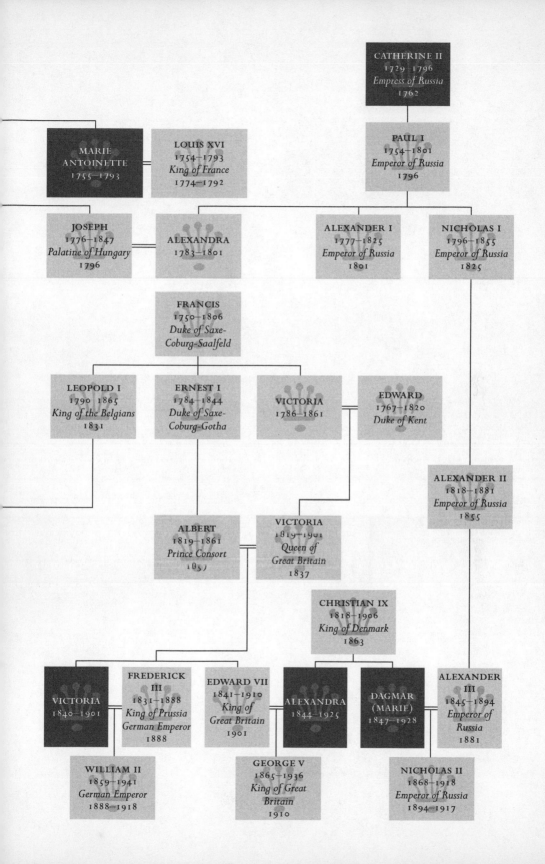

CATHERINE II
1729–1796
Empress of Russia
1762

MARIE ANTOINETTE
1755–1793

LOUIS XVI
1754–1793
King of France
1774–1792

PAUL I
1754–1801
Emperor of Russia
1796

JOSEPH
1776–1847
Palatine of Hungary
1796

ALEXANDRA
1783–1801

ALEXANDER I
1777–1825
Emperor of Russia
1801

NICHOLAS I
1796–1855
Emperor of Russia
1825

FRANCIS
1750–1806
Duke of Saxe-Coburg-Saalfeld

LEOPOLD I
1790–1865
King of the Belgians
1831

ERNEST I
1784–1844
Duke of Saxe-Coburg-Gotha

VICTORIA
1786–1861

EDWARD
1767–1820
Duke of Kent

ALEXANDER II
1818–1881
Emperor of Russia
1855

ALBERT
1819–1861
Prince Consort
1857

VICTORIA
1819–1901
Queen of Great Britain
1837

CHRISTIAN IX
1818–1906
King of Denmark
1863

VICTORIA
1840–1901

FREDERICK III
1831–1888
King of Prussia German Emperor
1888

EDWARD VII
1841–1910
King of Great Britain
1901

ALEXANDRA
1844–1925

DAGMAR (MARIE)
1847–1928

ALEXANDER III
1845–1894
Emperor of Russia
1881

WILLIAM II
1859–1941
German Emperor
1888–1918

GEORGE V
1865–1936
King of Great Britain
1910

NICHOLAS II
1868–1918
Emperor of Russia
1894–1917

Introduction

Like most children I worshipped my mother. She had courage, standing trial under the Nazis for defying them time and again in German-occupied Bohemia; she was very dashing, skiing (for Hungary) in the 1936 Olympics; but best of all, she was a wonderful storyteller. Fluent in six languages, she peppered her tales with the most poignant words of each of them, and we sat at her feet and learned to follow. Sad tales of brave Magyars singing their melancholy through the night on the eve of battle; epic accounts of Wagnerian heroes testing their chivalry; tales of how the earth began (and of how it would end if I did not hurry up and finish my homework). Blessed with a Proustian memory and a history degree, rare at that time for a woman in Vienna, my mother would paint the canvases of the past with the colors of her lyrical mind, her prodigious knowledge and anecdotes from her own exotic background. With her delicate brushwork, the great and tragic men and women of history came to life, and for endless nights I would lie awake reliving their destinies.

After I married, it is not surprising that I became intrigued by the Winter Queen. Elizabeth Stuart, elder sister of Charles I, married to Fredrick V, Elector Palatine, who reigned, briefly, as King of Bohemia. His enemies crowed he would last only one winter before ignominious defeat by the Habsburg armies. They were right, and the Thirty Years'

War began. In exile in The Hague, the Winter Queen lived on as the symbol of the Protestant cause for the next forty years, surrounded by her gifted children, her admirers—and the rats that gnawed at her tapestries as she tried to salvage some dignity in her poverty. It was inevitable that I should become fascinated by an English princess who became a Protestant Queen of Bohemia, having myself been born in Bohemia, a descendant of its great princely houses, and become a Catholic English princess. I decided to write her story, and travelled as she did—though not on a silver barge hung with palest blue velvet—down the Neckar River to Heidelberg, her husband's capital. I tried to imagine how she felt, this seventeen-year-old Jacobean girl, arriving under the rose-pink ramparts of Heidelberg, the seat of the First Elector of the Holy Roman Empire. How spartan she must have thought her new home, despite her young husband's great wealth. Hers was the first table linen seen in Germany. And how astonished the good burghers of this university town must have been at the sight of the new Electress and her English ladies, wearing their low-cut dresses and with their free and easy ways. Shakespeare had written *The Tempest* for Elizabeth's marriage festivities, and, loving the theater, she brought her troupe of players with her. Also in her suite was the great Inigo Jones, en route to Italy, who, it was said, added a wing to her palace in a style so classical and pure that it was the envy of the whole country. After the tragic death of Elizabeth's brother Henry, Prince of Wales, she engaged the service of his brilliant garden architect, Salomon de Caus, who created at Heidelberg gardens and grottoes with statues playing water-music, known then as a Wonder of the World.

Deep in admiration for this blond paragon of princely virtues, I journeyed on to Prague. There I met a wise old man, the authority on the Bohemian exiles and also on my Winter Queen. As at Heidelberg, I learned that she was loved by many, but that her English ways were misunderstood and her actions misinterpreted. I travelled on to The Hague, where the pattern repeated itself, but I had gathered boxes full of primary source material and determined to set the record straight. The Great Historian intervened and I was rushed to London for an emergency operation. In the panic, my boxes were mislaid, and the Winter Queen, like many a good actress, had to "rest" until I found the energy to repeat her journey and flight into exile. During my convalescence, I became more and more intrigued by the effect and influence a queen from another country and culture had on her new subjects. As I was unable for the time being to continue with Elizabeth, the idea for this book was born. I have not included the Winter Queen (or the Queen of Hearts, as she was also known)—if I had, she might never become my next book—and, miraculously, all my research material has since been found.

For the sake of simplicity I wanted to choose my princesses from one century, and, having decided on the nineteenth, I found I had to let Marie Antoinette slip in, and Catherine the Great *almost* qualified. In vain, I looked for some unifying traits, qualities, experiences—they were not all beautiful, nor intelligent, nor did they all have taste or dress well. They were not all victims of xenophobia: Queen Alexandra was consistently loved by the people and never blamed for being Danish; nor was this due to British forbearance—neither the people nor Society was so tolerant of the German members of their royal family. Leopoldina identified completely with her people's causes and earned the affection, and pity, of the Brazilian people. Nor were all their marriages the result of political maneuvering—Napoleon III married Eugénie for love and gained nothing from the link with Spain. But most of the marriages were arranged with political advantage as the criterion, and when the policy changed, so did the feelings toward the foreign queen who was its pawn. Marie Antoinette was decried as *Autrichienne* (*chienne,* the bitch) and Eugénie was cursed as *l'Espagnole. Die Engländerin* was spat at Vicky as she was openly accused by Bismarck of being an English spy; and Catherine buried her German origins so deep that the people eventually believed her to be Russian.

The element that does unite them is an inbred sense of duty and a genuine desire to see it performed. None fought against what she saw as her destiny, but only sought to fulfill it. Some were passionate, others cold, some were good wives, some were caring mothers; but, strangely, the thing all these queens shared was a deep and enduring love of animals, and courage and ability on horseback. Ladies had not the same social or military duty as gentlemen to learn to ride. That they did so in their youth was the result of chance and fancy; that they continued to do so after their marriages, and with more energy and enthusiasm than ever, must prove something. The freedom, the challenge, the adrenaline—wind in the face and hair—the sheer delight in exercise and the physical pleasure of controlling a powerful animal at speed must all have contributed, as well as the joy of escaping from protocol and formality. That Catherine and Marie Antoinette also derived sensual pleasure from their wild gallops cannot be in doubt, and both were virgins for many years after their marriages.

Marie Antoinette's portraitists have been remarkably successful in camouflaging her ample chest, which, coupled with her tiny waist, must have been quite a handicap on horseback. Alexandra and Eugénie were thought physically rather cold women; although Eugénie possessed a Latin temperament, her passion did not seem to extend to the boudoir. Leopoldina was the daughter of an insatiable father who loved his four wives literally to death. He was deeply religious and, regrettably for his queens, totally faithful. "The wife-killer," as he was known, passed on his religious scruples as well as his libido to Leopoldina, who tried all her life to think higher thoughts and ignore her body. Only Minnie, the beautiful Marie Feodorovna, sister of Queen Alexandra, seems to have found total conjugal happiness with her great bear of a husband, Alexander III.

The queens' shared love of animals is easier to explain. Dumb, obedient, adoring and discreet companions, animals were able to offer silent comfort and affection to homesick brides, disappointed wives or lonely widows.

I have deliberately tried to ignore politics and concentrate on the lighter side of their lives, as I myself have always felt cheated when reading biographies of such famous women without learning what they wore, or how their hair was arranged, or what they ate, particularly on some momentous day—details that would complete the picture for me. What did they read, and what was their favorite flower, or their favorite color? Did they take snuff, like Catherine, or smoke, like Minnie? She hated anyone to know, and unexpected visitors would be surprised to see a column of smoke rising behind her as the Russian empress tried to hide the cigarette behind her back.

If I were asked to state my preference, my answer would have to be qualified: Eugénie would be my model, but I admire Vicky for her intelligence and forbearance, and Alexandra and Leopoldina for their goodness and tolerance of their husbands' infidelities. As friends I would choose Marie Antoinette, who was so misunderstood, and Eugénie and Minnie because they were such fun. The one I like the least but seem to resemble the most in character is Catherine . . . and Maria Carolina would have hated me.

In writing about these women, I have learned to know and love them and I shall dearly miss them. They were all catalysts, the pivots of their worlds for a time. Some left a more lasting influence than others, but their mystique and fascination remain, for the mere mention of one of these names conjures up visions of pageantry, glamour, excitement, drama and tragedy, even if we don't know why.

Marie-Christine
HRH Princess Michael of Kent

1

Catherine the Great

——•——

PRINCESS OF ANHALT-ZERBST / EMPRESS OF ALL THE RUSSIAS

1729–1796

Peter the Great gave the Russians bodies;
Catherine gave them souls.
                    —*The poet Kherasov*

Germany

*C*atherine the Great was born Sophia Friederika Augusta,* Princess of Anhalt-Zerbst, on April 21, 1729, in Stettin, Prussia. King Frederick William of Prussia had recently acquired from Sweden this chilly gray town at the mouth of the River Oder, planning to develop it as a port for Berlin. Sophie's father, Christian August von Anhalt-Zerbst, had command of the garrison there. A man of solid virtues—a sense of duty, order, discipline, thrift, integrity, piety and a totally practical approach to life—he was promoted to governor of the town, and the family moved into the forbidding ducal castle, a sixteenth-century building of Harz granite. Here, in this cheerless town swept by winds from the Baltic, Sophie spent her first thirteen years.

In 1742, Christian August succeeded his cousin as ruler of Anhalt-Zerbst, 150 miles southeast of Stettin, in the heart of Germany. Since the house of Anhalt did not conform to the laws of primogeniture, he was obliged to share the sovereignty with his brother. Catherine wryly observed in her memoirs, "All Anhalt princes had the right to share; they have shared so much that there is almost nothing left to share."

———

* All names were given the Latin spelling at christenings.

Anhalt-Zerbst, though an independent principality for over 500 years, possessed no more than 20,000 inhabitants. Yet, as a foreign visitor observed at the time, "They live in a land of milk and honey; indeed these were the only people, considered as a state, whom before or since that time I have ever heard talk without complaining." The rich soil produced wheat, hops, potatoes, flax and tobacco. Deer and wild boar roamed the forests and the rivers were well stocked with salmon. The silk brocades produced in the principality, often flowered in gold or silver on a clear ground, were considered among the finest in Europe. Zerbst was also famous for its brewery and produced excellent beer. Christian August was devoted to the welfare of his people and greatly impressed his daughter as a ruler.

As a result of her father's new status, Sophie was now heiress in her own right to the domain of Jever in Lower Saxony. Although she was always described as coming from modest origins in comparison with the grandeur she was to come to know, Sophie's background was not without a certain style and glamour. Three or four months of the year, from her eighth to her fifteenth year, Sophie accompanied her mother to stay with the Duchess of Brunswick-Luneburg, where they attended balls, operas, hunts and dinners, met countless foreign visitors and took part in the etiquette of a well-organized court. Nor was her mother without useful family connections. The daughter of the Lutheran bishop of Lübeck, she was a member of the younger branch of the ducal house of Holstein and her brother had been chosen to marry the daughter of Peter the Great of Russia, the Grand Duchess Elizabeth. Although he had died before the marriage took place, Elizabeth never forgot her tall, handsome fiancé, and Sophie's mother never let pass any chance of fostering this relationship with the woman who, in 1740, was crowned Empress Elizabeth of All the Russias.

This was an era when every European court tried to imitate Versailles. Sophie was given a French Huguenot governess, Babet Cardel, who succeeded in inspiring her charge with a love of French language, drama and literature. Even when she was Empress of Russia, Sophie took pride in signing her letters to Diderot and Voltaire "the pupil of Babet Cardel." She remembered Babet as "patient, gentle, gay and lovable," a teacher with "a natural spiritual quality." Later, when she wanted people to forget that she was a German, she would speak to them in French.

As a girl Sophie displayed the same solid, serious virtues as her father along with the far more superficial flair and charm of her mother. Little Sophie was intelligent, lively, gay, mischievous, boisterous, relatively healthy and impudent, as well as having an instinctive love of learning and a thirst for knowledge. Although considered too thin, she always carried herself well, giving the impression of being above medium height. She possessed a natural sense of style and elegance, a mass of dark chestnut hair, sparkling blue eyes and a captivating smile with perfect teeth. Describing herself as a girl, she recalled, "I was never beautiful—but I pleased."

Few could have forecast the extraordinary future ahead. Baroness von Printzen, lady-in-waiting at the tiny court of Anhalt-Zerbst, who had been present at Sophie's birth, had watched her grow up and became her trusted friend, wrote, "I would never have guessed that she would become as famous as she did," adding that "Only through error, whimsy or flippancy could she have been called outstanding or brilliant.

"In a word," she observed candidly, "I got the impression of quite an ordinary person." But what the baroness also noticed was Sophie's ambition, noting that even as a girl she had a serious, cold and calculating mind. And as Sophie wrote of herself at this time, "I used to tell myself that to be 'something' in this world, one needs the qualities which this 'something' demands. Let us look seriously at our little inner self. Do we have these qualities or do we not? If we do not, we will develop them." Babet Cardel described her as an *esprit gauche* (perverse spirit), a mind ripe for an outside influence to give it direction. That influence was to be Russia.

The Journey

On New Year's Day 1744, a letter arrived in Zerbst marked "Secret and Confidential." Inside was an invitation from the Tsarina Elizabeth Petrovna to Her Highness the Princess Johanna Elizabeth and her daughter to come to Russia as soon as possible. Although no reason for this request was given, Sophie's mother knew exactly what it meant. Elizabeth had never married and was looking for a bride for her nephew and heir. A second letter confirmed her judgment. It came from King Frederick in Berlin and urged her to accept the tsarina's invitation in the interests of Prussia.

Sophie's father had been completely excluded from these intrigues. As a loyal subject he offered no opposition to the plan, yet it was with genuine regret that he allowed his daughter to leave—the fate of German princesses married in Russia in the past was not the future he wished for Sophie.

The princess and her party travelled incognito in the depths of winter, and there was little to alleviate either the boredom or the discomfort of the journey. It took six weeks, and Sophie long remembered her feet swelling so much that she had to be lifted in and out of the carriage. Often they travelled at night, and when they did stop at an inn it was rarely better than peasant lodgings, with little heat and no privacy.

But as soon as they reached Russia, the nightmare was over. At Riga, their incognito discarded, they received a royal welcome. The empress had sent a squadron of cavalry to escort them, grand lords and ladies to attend them, and magnificent rooms in the castle were prepared for them. Johanna Elizabeth forgot that these honors were in fact for her daughter, and from this time Sophie's real isolation began. Neglected and ignored by the one person she knew in this strange place, the future Catherine the Great hereafter kept her own counsel and relied on her inner strength. Outwardly she must have been a most unprepossessing sight to the bejeweled and gold-braided courtiers who attended her. Pale, thin and simply dressed, she passed by almost unnoticed.

They journeyed on to St. Petersburg in an imperial sledge, "scarlet, and decked with gold, and lined inside with sable." These sledges (which had been invented by Peter the Great) were pulled by six horses, and Sophie and her mother were able to lie down full length on piles of silk and satin cushions, sable rugs pulled up to their chins. So great was the contrast with the first part of their journey that Sophie instantly fell under the spell of Russia—a devotion that was to last all her life.

Russia

Her first sight of St. Petersburg revealed a city still under construction, and the only large stone building was its formidable fortress. Everywhere she came across scaffolding, hammering and noise. Yet although Petersburg was Western in appearance, fundamentally its character was Russian, utterly different from Zerbst with its medieval town hall and Gothic churches. For the rest of her life Sophie was to prefer St. Petersburg to Russia's ancient capital, Moscow. But at Moscow the tsarina was awaiting them. There, on the eve of the Grand Duke's birthday, Sophie was to undergo her first test: to meet her future husband under the watchful eye of the Empress Elizabeth.

When Sophie and her mother reached Moscow, the city was bedecked for the birthday celebrations of the Grand Duke, with Chinese lanterns and illuminations lighting up the golden domes of a thousand churches. This was a world where luxury and squalor existed side by side, whose values and standards were totally alien from those of the strict Lutheran society in which she had been brought up. Gossip and scandal, gambling, immorality and excesses of every kind—all covered by a veneer of piety—constituted the normal behavior of society. But Sophie had tired already of her Lutheran upbringing. She kept a German Bible, marked in red ink where as a child she had learned verses by heart. She had firmly decided that Martin Luther was a boor who (as she put it) "did not teach anybody anything."

Before the German princesses had time to change, Elizabeth's nephew the Grand Duke was announced, eager to see his future bride. If the fourteen-year-old girl was taken aback by the sight of this spotty, malformed youth, she gave no outward sign. As she wrote later, "I cared very little for the Grand Duke, but I cared a lot about becoming an Empress." And perhaps she thought that in this strange, barbaric land he would guide her through the labyrinth of the scheming, unfamiliar court.

Peter Feodorovich may have disappointed Sophie, but the Tsarina Elizabeth did not. Peter the Great's daughter was larger than life in every respect. Beautiful, passionate, fervently religious yet licentious too, Elizabeth was adored as a mother figure by the Russian people. She received the princesses from Zerbst with her famous dazzling smile and all her charm, treating them as relatives and spoiling them with gifts and honors.

Sustained by her ambitions to become as Russian as Elizabeth despite her German blood, Sophie set about learning not only the Russian language and the teachings of the Russian Orthodox faith but even the traditional dances of this strange land. Within two weeks she was seriously ill. Russian palaces were as primitive as conditions elsewhere throughout Russian society and in spite of huge fires, icy drafts whistled through mostly uncarpeted rooms. Sitting up in the middle of the night learning Russian in her freezing bedroom, Sophie contracted pleurisy. Her saviour as it turned out was not her mother—who had embarked on a round of mindless social entertainments and political intrigues—but the tsarina herself. Impressed with the young girl's dedication, Elizabeth nursed Sophie during the dangerous month of her near-fatal illness. Yet even when she lay at death's door, Sophie was shrewd enough to ask for an Orthodox priest rather than a Lutheran pastor.

She did not appear at court again until her fifteenth birthday. During her illness she had grown taller, thinner and certainly no prettier, but this only increased the tsarina's protective attachment to her. Elizabeth was determined her nephew should marry the German princess to ensure an heir to the Russian throne and secure the Romanov dynasty.

On June 28, 1744, Sophie was publicly received into the Orthodox faith and became the Grand Duchess Yecatarina Alexievna. Elizabeth personally dressed the child in a red and silver gown, an exact copy of her own. In carefully studied Russian, Catherine forswore her former Lutheranism, and the simplicity of her manner and bearing overcame any remaining opposition to her. The following day she was officially betrothed to the Grand Duke Peter.

Catherine was now a major figure in probably the most licentious court in Europe. Here every Tuesday transvestite balls were held, known as the "Metamorphoses"—Elizabeth adored fancy dress and with her fine legs and height she looked wonderful clothed as a man. Catherine would attend as her page—an enchanting frail figure in marked contrast to the large ladies of the court forced into men's clothes, and the eminent courtiers and generals in their hooped skirts. This was a court "where there was no conversation . . . [and] intricate intrigues were mistaken for shrewdness. Science and art were never touched on, as everybody was ignorant of those subjects; one could lay a wager that half the court could hardly read and I would be surprised if more than a third could write." Catherine became addicted to gambling and tried to win allies by giving lavish presents, but despite the large income she received from the empress, soon she was deeply in debt.

In the late summer of that year Elizabeth made a religious pilgrimage to Kiev, taking with her Catherine, the Grand Duke and Catherine's mother, along with the most entertaining members of the court. "From morning to night," Catherine recalled, "we did nothing but laugh, play and make merry." Nonetheless she was also deeply impressed by the great tsarina, dressed as a humble peasant woman, walking barefoot and carrying a cross in pilgrimage despite the crowds and the heat. Here she learned something of the importance of the Orthodox faith in the hearts and minds of her future subjects. She saw for the first time some of the many different peoples and races of the vast empire, and the bustle and significance of a seaport where so many cultures crossed. Nor could she fail to notice the squalor and misery that made up the sordid, poverty-stricken lives of those from whom ultimately the splendor and wealth of her own life at court derived.

On the way back to Moscow, Peter contracted smallpox. The disease left him hideously disfigured and also seems to have affected his already feeble brain. Despite this and the envious rumors circulating about Catherine, preparations for the wedding went ahead. The tsarina's enthusiasm for all things French now knew no bounds. French carpenters, decorators, cooks, *modistes* and tailors were all enticed to Russia at vast salaries to prepare for the great event. Elizabeth aimed to copy and outdo the recent wedding of the dauphin, and her ambassadors were instructed to study and report on the ceremonial and rules of precedence current at the courts of Europe.

On August 21, 1745, Peter and Catherine were married. Then followed nine days of festivities, a constant succession of balls, masquerades, state dinners, Italian operas, French plays and fireworks. Catherine was sixteen, her husband a year older. To her sadness, her father was not invited and, apart from her mother and a rather uncouth maternal uncle, no one else represented her family.

The little archduchess wore a dress of "silver moiré, embroidered in silver on all the hems, and of a terrific weight." The empress gave her leave to wear as many jewels as she wanted, "both hers and mine," and on her head she placed a small but heavy crown. Her hair had been curled for the wedding after a terrific argument between the hairdresser and the empress—which the hairdresser won. The religious ceremony began at ten in the morning and was not over until four o'clock that afternoon. Despite the weight of the dress, the jewels and the crown, which gave her a blinding headache, the bride was gracious, if somewhat joyless, during that interminable day of ceremonial. In the evening there was a ball. Finally, at half past one and amid much pomp, the young couple were led to bed.

Catherine's mother has left us a description of the scarlet and silver marriage bedroom, "so fine and majestic, that you cannot see it without being transfixed with admiration." Here for the first time Catherine found herself alone, waiting for the boy-husband who was to make her life a misery for the next eighteen years. One month later the Princess of Zerbst, her role as her daughter's chaperone over, was sent home.

Grand Duchess

Peter's doctors had tried to postpone the marriage as the puny Grand Duke had barely reached puberty. Despite his swaggering boasts to his bride of mistresses and liaisons, with her he was completely impotent, and for almost the next ten years Catherine remained a virgin.

It was said his impotence could have been cured by a small operation which he was too cowardly to undergo, but perhaps his inability to consummate the marriage had psychological origins. He certainly seems to have had more sexual success with experienced lower-class women.

What emerges from Catherine's memoirs is a picture of a husband who was a loutish boor, a drunkard who smelt of tobacco and alcohol, happier in the guardroom than the salon. His teachers had themselves usually been drunk and he had learned nothing from them; nor had he any experience of parental love. His mother, the elder daughter of Peter the Great, died when her son was only three months old. His father, the Duke of Holstein, neglected the boy and died when Peter was eleven. Refusing to adapt to Russian ways, Peter had remained a Lutheran and, in all essentials, a German. His character was immature, boastful, capricious and cruel. He was also the Empress Elizabeth's only male relative and her heir.

Initially he and Catherine were drawn to each other: two children linked by a common language and background. From the moment they met, Peter seems to have acknowledged her innate superiority and would run to her to solve his problems, nicknaming her "Madame la Ressource."

Catherine loved animals, especially dogs, and when Peter gave her a small English poodle, she and her ladies would spend hours combing his hair and dressing him in new clothes. Catherine allowed him to sit at table like all the other guests, and noted how he "ate very neatly from his plate" and then would "turn his head and ask for a drink, yapping at the footman who stood behind him." Some years later she became devoted to an English whippet called Tom Anderson and known as Sir Tom. He was allowed to sleep in her bedroom on a blanket she had knitted especially for him, and when he fathered a litter of puppies they were all permitted to accompany Catherine to the court theater. When Sir Tom died, she was heartbroken and ordered an Egyptian-style pyramid to be placed over his grave.

Peter's attitude to animals was callously different. To hear the howls of the dogs that he unmercifully thrashed distressed Catherine deeply. Nor was it easy to tolerate him training a pack of hounds in their bedroom. She was horrified when he solemnly court-martialed and hanged a rat for daring to eat one of his paste toy sentries. His childish love of toys was a further burden to her, for he would play with dolls till two or three in the morning, sometimes making her laugh, but more often irritating her as the whole bed was covered with heavy toys.

Careful and calculating, Catherine survived it all. Her greatest gift was the art of dissimulation, which she perfected during these miserable years of her marriage. All Russians, she decided, had "a fundamental dislike of foreigners," and were ready to spot their "weaknesses, faults and quaintness." Shrewdly she determined to give them no insight into her own sufferings.

At the age of fifteen she had drawn up three resolutions:

1. to please the Grand Duke;
2. to please the tsarina;
3. to please the nation.

"I wanted to be Russian," she wrote, "in order that the Russians should love me." The task required resolution and courage. "For eighteen years," she confessed, "I led a life which would have rendered ten women mad, and twenty others in my place would have died of a broken heart." Ten years after her marriage an observer commented that she was esteemed and loved in Russia to a high degree.

These early years of marriage forged Catherine's character. She emerged hard, disciplined and controlled, having learned to curb her temper and her pride. When her father died two years after her marriage, Catherine was only allowed one week's crying and six weeks' mourning, as he had not been a king! Although her husband made her life a misery and a degradation, she retained an overwhelming desire to love and be loved. In spite of being an egotist, she was easy to live with and easy to serve. She was indulgent toward her servants and never inordinately severe with them, so it was not surprising that they adored her.

Catherine and Elizabeth

In appearance the tsarina was all that Catherine longed to be: tall, beautiful and with perfect features—even though her excessive love of food was destroying her fine figure. Her smile was as famous as her sweet expression and her dark blue eyes. Her bearing, her manner, her gestures, her hair, hands and feet were all said to be perfect. She had an incisive intelligence and could spot falsehood immediately, and for her time she was even considered merciful. On her accession, Elizabeth had sworn that no one would be condemned to death during her reign, and she kept her promise. Her reign marked the start of a cultural renaissance in Russia. Advances were made in every field and it was she who unwittingly laid the foundations for the brilliant achievements of the young German princess who was to succeed her.

Catherine learned a great deal from her aunt. Years later she was able to recall in detail what Elizabeth had worn on any occasion and the dazzling jewelry with which she had covered her head, neck and bosom. Although Elizabeth left behind thousands of sumptuous dresses when she died, she was careful not to wear expensive dresses when travelling and wore simple clothes at home. Catherine copied this simplicity, dressing quite plainly and without jewelry even when attending the masques her husband gave at Oranienbaum, their country house, built by Peter the Great. "This won the favor of the Empress," she wrote, "who did not approve of the Oranienbaum feasts, at which the meals turned into real orgies." To Catherine, some of Elizabeth's whims for elaborate fancy dress went too far, like the occasion when the ladies of the court were all made to dress up as shepherdesses in pink and white, wearing hats "in the English style" and carrying crooks.

Elizabeth was generous to her young protégée. Soon after Catherine's arrival, she sent her 15,000 rubles and a large case of dress material (she expected her court to wear rich fabrics, which added to Catherine's burden of debts). The whole court followed Elizabeth's example and would change their clothes at least twice a day. At fifteen, Catherine found dressing up "not unpleasant." In an effort to organize her domestic affairs and bestow favors on certain of her women she liked, Catherine devised a system of privileged duties: her favorite had the key to her jewels; another looked after her lace; another her clothes; and another her ribbons. A Fräulein Schenk, who seems to be the only one of her suite from Zerbst allowed to remain, kept her linen. There was a dwarf who took care of powder and combs and another who had charge of the rouge, hairpins and *mouches* (black facial beauty patches).

Elizabeth also took care to protect this young German newcomer, to the chagrin and jealousy of many of her courtiers, who circulated stories with the aim of turning the empress against Catherine. Her protégée had become a smart young lady of fashion, and as she matured, such maliciousness grew more dangerous. Portraits of Catherine at twenty-one show a slight yet elegant figure, with dark, thick curly hair and wide-open blue eyes. Her face was too long to be considered beautiful, but she had great charm, gaiety and wit, plus a certain undercurrent of recklessness which made her company exciting. Her manners were easy and unaffected and she somehow managed to win over to her side even those set to spy on her. It is hard to believe that all her actions and relationships were contrived and the product of careful planning, as she was so natural and spontaneous in her attachments and reactions to those she met.

Rivalry between the tsarina and the ladies of her court was not encouraged. A few years after her wedding, Catherine recalled that on a great feast day she wore a beautiful white dress, embroidered in gold "with a large Spanish stitch." It provoked the tsarina's displeasure. "It is possible," Catherine noted complacently, "that the Empress found my dress more effective than her own." The same thing happened a few years later when Catherine wore a dress of mauve and silver, which the tsarina professed to dislike. On the Grand Duke's birthday, when Catherine wore an especially beautiful dress of blue velvet embroidered with gold, Elizabeth sent her chamberlain to remind her niece of the regulations forbidding the wearing of certain materials. This time Catherine fought back. She laughed in the chamberlain's face, telling him that she never wore anything Her Majesty did not like and pointing out that her quality did not reside in either her beauty or her clothing.

In spite of the tsarina's wishes, members of the court did vie to outshine each other in their appearance. On one occasion Catherine heard to what lengths of extravagance everyone was going for a particular masquerade and, fearing that she could not afford to compete, deliberately put on a bodice and skirt of "rough white cloth." She wore a tiny hoop and smoothed back her hair, tying it "with a white ribbon in the shape of a fox's tail." She placed a single rose in her long, thick hair, together with a rosebud and leaves, and another in her corsage. Around her neck, at her cuffs and as her apron, she used white gauze. When she crossed the crowded gallery, she caused a sensation. The tsarina, seeing her, exclaimed, "Good God, what simplicity!" Marvelling that Catherine had on not even a single beauty patch, she took a small box of *mouches* from her pocket and applied one to Catherine's cheek.

At court balls to which the public were not admitted, Catherine made a point of dressing very simply as the empress disliked to see anyone overdressed on these occasions. "But when the ladies were ordered to come dressed as men, I wore superb clothes, all embroidered or of an elaborate style; this did not arouse criticism—on the contrary, I do not know why, it pleased the Empress."

Elizabeth longed above all for Catherine to produce an heir, and this meant that she interfered in what would normally be regarded as the trivialities of her niece's life. Catherine's extraordinary energy found a much-needed outlet in sport and dancing. Her only real escape and pleasure, as well as exercise, was riding, especially to hounds. This she preferred to do astride the horse, but the tsarina insisted that Catherine always ride sidesaddle, since she thought that riding astride interfered with conception. Typically, Catherine devised an answer. "I invented for myself saddles on which I could sit as I wanted. They had the English crook and one could swing one's leg to sit astride; the pommel, furthermore, could be screwed off and one of the stirrups raised or lowered as one required. If the grooms were asked how I rode, they could truthfully say, 'In a lady's saddle, according to the Empress's wish.' I switched my leg only when I was sure I was not going to be observed." She cunningly designed a riding habit with a split skirt that would fall to either side of the saddle, whether sitting side or astride. These outfits were always made of silk camlet, but as this would invariably shrink in the rain or fade in the sun, they needed constant renewing.

Catherine was once asked to accompany the wife of a Saxon minister who was also a renowned "Amazon." She wore a riding habit of "rich sky blue material with silver braid and crystal buttons, which looked exactly like diamonds," as well as a black hat edged with a string of diamonds, and her horsemanship as well as her exquisite appearance far outshone her rival's, which greatly pleased the empress.

Riding also eased her intense physical frustration. At Oranienbaum she and Peter went hunting, she recalled, "every blessed day." Some days she spent thirteen out of twenty-four hours in the saddle. She recognized that "the amount of exercise I took lessened the hypochondria to which I was inclined every month around a certain period," and admitted that what passionately interested her was not hunting but riding: "the more violent the exercise, the more I enjoyed it." This was a development of a technique by which she had comforted herself in younger days. Even as a child Catherine had used up excess energy by riding her pillows in her bed in the dark. As soon as she was alone at night, instead of sleeping, "I climbed astride my pillows and galloped in my bed until I was quite worn out. I was never caught out, nor did anyone know that I travelled post-haste on my pillows."

On summer mornings at Oranienbaum, Catherine would often rise at three, dress in men's clothes, and, accompanied by an old huntsman and just a fisherman rowing the boat, she would shoot duck in the reeds that fringe the sea on both sides of the Oranienbaum Canal. Exhilarated and hungry, she would then return for a late breakfast, ride to hounds all afternoon and dance the night away. This excessive exercise routine helped to ease her tension as well as making her tough and physically fit.

Book Learning, Frustration and Practical Politics

Catherine soon found herself walking a tightrope between her husband's noisy, boring activities and the jealousy and unfounded (as she would have us believe) suspicions of the Tsarina Elizabeth. Her intellectual needs found solace in the works of the Enlightenment—for although Peter liked reading, he preferred novels and tales of highwaymen. Suffering from boredom especially during the long winters, as well as every kind of frustration at a court where immorality seemed to be condoned by its leading member, Catherine comforted herself by voracious reading. "I fell back on the books I brought with me," and by accident she came across the letters of Mme de Sévigné and "devoured them." Then she discovered the works of Voltaire. Such books, she observed, "greatly raised my standard of reading."

Catherine had a mentor, Count Gyllenborg, a member of the Swedish embassy, who had been impressed with Catherine's intelligence as a young girl in Hamburg. He warned her of the precariousness of her position—and of her need for self-knowledge, self-discipline and the nourishing of her mind and spirit. He advised her to study Tacitus and Plutarch as well as Voltaire, Baronius, Brantôme, certain French romances, and the life of Henri of France (who, like Catherine, had changed his religion to gain access to a throne, and who remained one of her heroes). Above all he recommended Montesquieu's *Spirit of Laws,* which became her bedside book.

Archduchess in Love

In the early years of Catherine's marriage, the tsarina—in spite of her own profligate ways—had the young bride carefully chaperoned at all times. When it became obvious even to Elizabeth that Catherine's childlessness was not her own fault, this strict supervision was relaxed in the hope that she might beget an heir elsewhere. With the discreet encouragement of Elizabeth's entourage, Catherine fell madly in love with Serge Saltykov, a newly appointed young chamberlain from an ancient and most distinguished family.

At twenty-three Catherine had become known as an *allumeuse,* a flirt who offered her victims no hope of satisfaction. Now that her guardians seemed to be going out of their way to encourage her trysts with Saltykov, this coldness in her changed. For the first time in her life Catherine allowed herself to respond to the advances of this handsome, spoilt young libertine. The following year she had two miscarriages. Then, in September 1754, Catherine gave birth to her son, the Grand Duke Paul. Although it is often said that he was Saltykov's son, Paul grew to resemble the Grand Duke Peter alarmingly—both physically and mentally.

In the previous year Peter had been persuaded by Saltykov to undergo an operation which cured him of his sexual infirmity. According to Catherine's own memoirs, Madame Groot, "the pretty widow of a painter" (who had painted Catherine's portrait), was then persuaded to initiate him. Thereafter Catherine had to submit to his awkward and coarse lovemaking, a duty made more difficult by her natural repugnance for Peter and her passion for Saltykov.

But Russia had an heir. Her duty done, the child was promptly taken from her. After the difficult birth she was left completely alone, with no one to care for her or even change her sheets. In the excitement over the baby she was simply forgotten.

To add to her misery, Saltykov had grown tired of Catherine's demanding and aggressive lovemaking and accepted a mission abroad. Not surprisingly, she felt abandoned and depressed. Forty days passed before Catherine was allowed to see her son, who was being smothered with love by Elizabeth. She found the child handsome; but, unlike Elizabeth, Catherine was not a natural mother. Starved of any physical relationship for so many years, surrounded by licentiousness on all sides, she threw herself into indulging her newly discovered passions—and that did not include motherhood.

Catherine needed money. Elizabeth had given her the traditional gifts as well as money after the birth of her son, but she remained deeply in debt. At this point the British ambassador in St. Petersburg, Sir Charles Hanbury-Williams, anxious to maintain the British influence in a Russia dangerously close to the court at Versailles, saw in Catherine a useful potential ally and took her onto his diplomatic payroll. She gained both cash—her first payment was £10,000—and in Hanbury-Williams an invaluable friend. This subtle and unscrupulous man gave Catherine her first lessons in diplomacy. Sir Charles soon had a very high regard for his new pupil, partly because Catherine was a master of the art of flattery.

The ambassador, himself more than a little infatuated with the ravishing Grand Duchess, also recognized in her a need even more pressing than that of money: her longing to be loved. In his suite was a Polish aristocrat, Stanislaus Poniatowski—young, charming, good-looking, widely travelled, and used to cultivated and cosmopolitan society. Poniatowski was also weak and romantic, though foremost in his mind was always the interest of his powerful maternal family, the Czartoryski. At twenty-two he was four years younger than Catherine. Obviously taken with her at their first meeting, he still took several months to muster the audacity to approach the Grand Duchess. His political aim was to establish the rule of a Polish king in his own country, a task impossible without Russian help, and to seduce the fascinating Grand Duchess might well replace such dreams with the reality of a lifetime in Siberia. So it was left to Catherine to entice him into her bed.

Poniatowski's description of her at the time of their affair leaves a clear impression of Catherine's appeal: "She had black hair, a radiant expression and a high color, large, prominent and expressive blue eyes, long dark eyelashes, a pointed nose, a kissable mouth, perfect hands and arms, a slender figure, tall rather than small. She moved quickly, yet with great nobility; she possessed an agreeable voice and a gay, good-tempered laugh, passing with ease from the most madcap childish games to arithmetic tables, undaunted either by the labours involved or by the texts themselves." This was the woman he would adore for many years and who would give him a kingdom—only to take it from him bit by bit, leaving him a broken man.

At this time Louis XV had a secret agent at the Russian court. The Chevalier d'Eon was a creature of ambiguous sexuality, for he later forswore his manhood and lived out his last years as a woman. He loathed Catherine and intriguingly described her as romantic, ardent and passionate: "Her eyes are brilliant, their look is fascinating and glassy—the expression of a wild beast." On her lofty forehead he professed to read a long and terrifying future. "She is prepossessing and affable," he noted, "but when she comes close by me I instinctively recoil, for she frightens me."

In the late 1750s the lovers became careless. Poniatowski was caught by the Grand Duke's spies as he left Catherine's apartments, disguised in a blond wig, posing as her hairdresser. Peter humiliated him by making the incident public to the whole court. By now the Grand Duke himself had taken a mistress and when Poniatowski was requested to leave the country, Catherine begged her to intervene. Delighted to have the aloof and disdainful Grand Duchess as her supplicant, she prevailed on Peter to delay Poniatowski's departure by several weeks.

On another occasion, Catherine and Poniatowski's affair was almost exposed by her small dog. After dinner, she offered to show her guests her rooms. As she approached her bedroom, the guests were alarmed by the furious yapping of Catherine's little dog, but when he saw Poniatowski he immediately stopped and ran up to him, jumping up and down with delight. Poniatowski's familiarity with the guardian of Catherine's bedroom was not lost on one of the guests, who later assured him that he was the "soul of discretion," but also advised him to always give any woman he loved a small dog, as he would then be able to tell if there was someone else in his lady's favor. "My friend, there can be nothing more treacherous than a small dog. . . ."

Catherine's devotion to Poniatowski led her to intrigue with the empress's powerful old chancellor Bestuzhev, and six months later she achieved her goal: her lover returned to Russia as Poland's official representative. When Catherine later gave birth to Poniatowski's daughter, the tsarina generously accepted the child as a Romanov, naming her Anne after Peter's mother. Once again, the child was taken from Catherine.

To conceal her amorous escapades Catherine had a small recess arranged behind her bed, "the prettiest alcove one could imagine," in which she could receive her guests in secret. There she installed a sofa, some chairs and tables and a looking glass. With the curtains of her bed drawn, nothing could be seen, and when anyone asked what the large screen in her room concealed, they were told, "the commode." Here she held intimate little parties with her friends and her lover Poniatowski. When the empress's pompous confidant Count Shuvalov came to spy on her, he could in all honesty swear that he had found Catherine in bed "all alone, while only a curtain separated my merry little crowd." After the visitor had gone, Catherine would order a huge meal, enough for six (for, she explained, childbirth had made her ravenous). "When the supper was ready and brought to my room, I had it set by my bed and dismissed the servants. My friends came out and threw themselves like wild beasts upon the food. Their gaiety had increased their appetite. I must admit that evening was one of the maddest and merriest that I had spent in my life. . . ."

The Elimination of an Emperor

It was obvious to Catherine that should her husband become emperor, his mistress and her enemies would see to her disgrace and she would end her days in a convent. Her only hope lay in persuading the chancellor Bestuzhev that Russia's best interests lay in her sharing her husband's throne and participating in the running of the country. For Bestuzhev, the prospect of the Grand Duke Peter with his Prussian sentiments ruling his beloved Russia appalled him. Secretly Catherine had no intention of sharing a throne with Peter, or of acting as regent for her son—she had already resolved "either to perish or to reign." Her first step must be to substitute her son for her husband as the future emperor; then at least she would be safe as regent. But Bestuzhev's plots regarding the succession were discovered and he was arrested; Poniatowski was once more expelled and Catherine found herself under grave suspicion and, worse, ignored by the empress. In desperation, she burned all her papers and maintained an outward appearance of calm and gaiety. Domestic co-existence with her husband had become impossible—he openly despised and humiliated her and refused to let her see her children. When the tension concerning her fate became unbearable, she threw herself on Elizabeth's mercy. It was a brave gamble, and after two momentous interviews during which she shrewdly played on Elizabeth's warm and motherly nature, begging to be allowed to return home to Zerbst rather than cause her displeasure, Catherine was forgiven and officially back in favor.

With her Polish lover banished, the whole court knew that the young, beautiful and passionate Grand Duchess was once again "available," and many well-connected aspiring suitors came forward; but Catherine's sharp political intelligence rejected even the most handsome. She chose instead an unknown but dashing young guards officer who had the unhappy commission of acting as escort to King Frederick of Prussia's favorite adjutant, a privileged prisoner of war. Peter, with his pro-Prussian sympathies, made no secret of his admiration for the prisoner and entertained him regularly in his apartments, the handsome guard remaining outside. Gregory Orlov was a brave and volatile patriot who disapproved of his Grand Duke so clearly fraternizing with the enemy. He and his three brothers were as famous for their wild behavior off the battlefield as for their great courage on it. Catherine was immediately impressed by this tall, handsome officer and she found ample opportunity to invite him to join her intimate circle. In choosing to love Gregory Orlov Catherine did well, as he was strong, handsome, virile and uncomplicated. He loved his country, had no ambition for himself, and he and his brothers had a great following in the army. As this was not a time for the Grand Duchess, and possible future regent, to be seen openly betraying her husband, she did all she could to keep their relationship totally secret.

Catherine was more than ever aware of the precariousness of her position. The Empress Elizabeth's health was deteriorating rapidly and her generals were not eager to engage in new battles against Frederick of Prussia in view of her heir's openly pro-German sympathies. The Grand Duke Peter was also scandalizing society by publicly insulting Catherine as well as privately tormenting her, and by bestowing almost royal privileges on his mistress. But just as Peter was alienating himself from the government, the army and the clergy, Catherine was cultivating the company of wise older ladies, discussing with them Russian history, culture and folklore, and deliberately avoiding court entertainments. This was not only to remind society of her husband's callous behavior toward her, but also to give the impression of serious-mindedness at a time when the empress was dying and her soldiers were fighting a war.

It was at this critical time, for which she had been waiting and scheming for years, that Catherine found herself pregnant. News that the Grand Duchess was expecting the child of a guards officer on the eve of her husband's accession would hardly help with her own ambitions. Elizabeth died on January 5, 1762. The Grand Duke became Tsar Peter III, almost immediately withdrew Russia from the war and made an alliance with the Prussians. In April, Catherine contrived to have her child in secret. Her faithful valet offered to set fire to his house, and during the excitement and commotion which Peter and his mistress hastened to watch, Catherine gave birth to a son, Count Alexis Bobrinsky. Not everyone at court was unaware of the reasons for Catherine's self-imposed withdrawal from society, and several diplomats commented on her quick recovery from her "sprain." When the French ambassador went so far as to compliment her on her sparkling looks, she replied with a mysterious smile, "You cannot imagine, sir, what it costs a woman to be beautiful."

Meanwhile Catherine's position grew more uncertain. Her husband was threatening to declare his son Paul a bastard, send Catherine to a convent and marry his ill-favored mistress. In June, when he insulted her in public, Catherine began to make her final plans. With the help of the Orlov brothers she had carefully wooed and won the army and the powerful bureaucrats in the government. On June 28, Catherine toured the Semeonovsky barracks on the eve of the army's departure to fight Denmark for Peter's Holstein territories. It was a war the soldiers did not want and which did not concern Russia, and, disaffected by the humiliating peace with Prussia, they were on the verge of mutiny. With little hesitation they threw in their lot with Catherine. On July 9, at the head of two elite regiments, the Preobrajensky and the Horse Guards, Catherine marched into St. Petersburg. With the crowds swelling the unruly procession, she entered the Cathedral of Our Lady of Kazan and was anointed Catherine II, Autocrat of All the Russias.

Although in her memoirs she tried to imply that the events of that day were a spontaneous result of the people's will, in fact she did not overlook the smallest detail. In the morning she put on a plain black dress to demonstrate her respect for the dead tsarina, and allowed her hair to hang loose on her shoulders. She looked young, fragile, heroic, and the effect was not lost on the people or the soldiers. Later, astride a white charger, wearing the uniform of a grenadier of her elite guards regiment, a sable turban surrounded by golden oak leaves resting on her long dark hair, Catherine led her army to meet her husband. The Orlovs had no difficulty in taking him prisoner and, whimpering, the pathetic figure of Tsar Peter III abdicated in favor of a little German usurper. He was incarcerated in the grim fortress of Schüsselberg, with the Orlovs as his guards. Eight days later he was dead, officially of apoplexy. In fact he had been killed and it was made to appear the result of a drunken brawl.

Catherine was neither cruel nor vindictive, but as long as Peter lived he was a threat to her position. She had not ordered his death, yet there is no doubt that it made her far more secure on the throne. Peter had neglected to have himself crowned at once, a grave error of judgment in view of the religious and traditional attitudes of the people and the clergy, and not a mistake Catherine would make. Two months after her accession she made her state entry into Moscow. Wearing the finest jewels from the imperial treasury and a train made from 4,000 ermine skins, she was crowned in the heart of the Kremlin. The ceremony took place in the fifteenth-century Uspensky Cathedral, a building steeped in history and tradition, with its high altar adorned with the medieval cross brought by Sophia Paleologue from the ruins of Constantinople. Catherine had the courage to alter the coronation ceremony by placing the crown on her own head. She also took communion and passed through the gates of the iconostasis, an area in Russian churches that women are forbidden to enter.

Empress

From the beginning, Catherine was concerned with her image. A German usurper, she had taken the throne from the lawful ruler, her husband and Peter the Great's grandson. His unpopularity had been a direct result of his German sympathies both abroad and at home, and his insensitivity to the Russian character. No wonder the little German princess who set herself up as Autocrat of All the Russias, *matouchka* to her people and who pardoned her husband's killers, felt insecure. Nor is it surprising that Catherine did all she could to suppress the memory of her own German background.

Cultural Influence

Peter the Great had begun the Westernization of Russia. He had imported technicians, tools and techniques to build a great city and port on the marshlands. Catherine continued this process by patronizing European literature in spite of her gestures toward the indigenous culture of her own empire and, above all, by adopting the style and the luminaries of the contemporary European Enlightenment.

Catherine's love of French culture and literature turned the stream of her early interest into a flood. This intelligent, articulate woman now sought to change the fundamental Russian concept of rule by hereditary right and religious sanction into the French ideal of authority based on philosophical principles. The Russian nobility welcomed her Francomania and used the French language and culture to establish a united identity. Catherine could now be a personal patron of those contemporary French writers whose works she had so avidly consumed.

She flattered and courted Montesquieu, Voltaire and Diderot (whose entire library she bought, while politely rejecting most of his liberal ideas as impractical for her country). Voltaire was by then nearly seventy, while Catherine was thirty-four. He had already written a history of Peter the Great, and she appointed him official historian of the Russian Empire. The most famous man in Europe referred to her as the Semiramis of the North—privately, he called her *la belle cateau* (the handsome wench).

The Russian aristocracy bought all his works—in the original and in translation—and no house of any standing was complete without a "Voltaire chair" of the sort in which he was always depicted sitting.

Voltaire was indeed flattered by Catherine's attention, and the opportunity of influencing so large a population equalled his pleasure at receiving her lavish gifts. Whether or not she really understood French literature and philosophy is open to conjecture. Initially she seemed willing to re-create Russia as a land of justice and education based on the models of her French mentors. She even dreamed of emancipating the serfs, and a commission set up at her command in 1767 included members of every social class (except the serfs). Its aim was to set out a completely new constitution. When it finally reported, its findings were completely ignored, and Catherine realized that her power ultimately depended on the serf owners, the nobles, and not the poor. In the end she even imposed serfdom on the Ukrainians. Montesquieu and Voltaire turned out to be dreamers, not practical philosophers, whose ideas could not really be applied to her own sprawling territories.

An active and prolific writer, she saw herself in direct competition with Frederick the Great as philosopher-king and writer-monarch. Unlike Frederick, she did her own writing and used the language of her subjects, whereas Frederick, hating the German language and culture, wrote in French. She herself described her writing as "a mania," and in her lifetime covered reams of paper in her own hand. Although most of her writing was in Russian (she lived in Russia for over fifty years), her foreign correspondence was mostly in French. She rarely corresponded in German, although she knew this language best. Fluent in the Russian spoken word, she often misspelt even simple words and made errors in written grammar.

Voltaire was the architect of her legend in the West and, as such, an essential part of her overall strategy. Early in her reign she undertook the writing of an enormous work of instructions for the Russian people, called her *Nakaz*. These consist of somewhat arbitrary maxims, inspired not only by her hero Montesquieu's *Spirit of Laws,* but also by Beccaria's *Of Crimes and Punishments,* Bielefeld's *Treatise on Jurisprudence* and Turgot's *Treatise on the Growth and Distribution of Wealth*. Catherine's *Nakaz* was hailed throughout the rest of Europe as the work of a remarkable and enlightened ruler. The authorities in France found it so radical that the work was immediately banned. Its effect in Russia was virtually nil.

This was partly because Catherine did not truly believe in it herself. For instance, the *Nakaz* urged rulers to avoid any punishment so brutally final as the death penalty. Elsewhere, however, Catherine noted that wise rulers needed to "make sure such kindness neither weakens your authority nor diminishes your people's respect."

Her attitude to freedom of expression and censorship was also ambiguous. When Catherine arrived in Russia, fewer than thirty volumes (other than church books) were published each year and foreign works were almost impossible to obtain. She founded a society to translate foreign works into Russian. These fell mostly into three categories: the classics—Homer, Plato, Virgil, Horace, Ovid and Cicero; the Enlightenment—Montesquieu, Beccaria, the *Encyclopédie* and eventually Voltaire's *Portable Philosophic Dictionary;* and, lastly, works of modern literature—such as *Robinson Crusoe, Gulliver's Travels,* Rousseau's *La Nouvelle Héloïse,* Goethe's *Werther,* and the poetry of John Milton, James Thomson and Edward Young.

Catherine personally imported into Russia 3,000 copies of Voltaire's *Dictionary,* and these sold within one week. During the 1760s she allowed her subjects considerable freedom of expression, both spoken and written. In later, more dangerous years, Catherine's attitudes hardened. Her legacy is therefore not simply or easily defined. Alongside her determination that undue freedom should not endanger the position she had fought so hard to win went a genuine stimulus to creative thought. Her anonymously published journal, *All Sorts,* for instance, inspired by *The Spectator* of Addison and Steele, made an enormous impression on the Russian satirical journals of the eighteenth century.

She was not simply trying to Europeanize her empire (even though the opening words of her *Nakaz,* which startled contemporary ears, were: "Russia is a European country"); she tried to foster its own literary culture as well. Catherine founded the Russian Academy of Letters and appointed Princess Dashkova as its president. As the Russian language lacked grammatical rules and even any precise definition of the meaning of words, the Academy's first task was to produce a dictionary and a grammar. Both Catherine and the princess contributed to the work and, though much criticized, it constitutes the first attempt at classifying concepts in the Russian language. Princess Dashkova's memoirs tell us that Catherine believed that "Russian, which blended the strength, richness and virility of German with the softness of Italian, would one day be-

come the universal language." Yet while the empress generously patron-
ized great names, Russian talent invariably went unnoticed by her.

Perhaps Catherine's greatest impact on the Russian way of life was
the severing of official culture from its religious roots. The city, not the
monastery, became the center of Russian culture. It was an ambiguous
achievement, partly brought about by her financial needs, for when she
became empress the state coffers were so depleted that Catherine reduced the clergy to state-paid functionaries by simply taking over their
land and serfs. It was perhaps a continuation of the ecclesiastical policies
of her predecessor, that other Westernizer, Peter the Great; but it was
undoubtedly a major break with the age-long traditions of the land she
had come to rule.

Although she was genuinely interested in literature, painting and architecture, the new empress was above all aware of how they related to her
all-important public image. The arts enhanced the sovereign. Like Peter
the Great and his daughter Elizabeth, Catherine believed that the Russian monarchy should not only be magnificent, it should also be seen to
be magnificent. When it came to commissioning great buildings she was
not only insatiable but also quite sincerely convinced that her building
mania was not self-indulgence. It was, she believed, a direct reflection
of the authority of the crown. The grander her buildings, the less insecure the empress felt.

Her taste in architecture altered three times during her reign. At
first there remained traces of the rococo beloved by Elizabeth, but during the second decade of her reign she greatly encouraged the innovations of three architects she had chosen to work for her: the German
Velten, the Italian Rinaldi and the Russian Bazhenov. Although the
Baroque style lingered on in several of the elevations and ground plans
of their work, Russian architecture also moved distinctly closer to classicism. Classicism totally dominated the third and last phase of Catherine's influence on Russian architecture. Once again, three architects
were her principal servants: the Scotsman Cameron,* the Italian
Quarenghi and the Russian Starov.

---

* Cameron posed as a Scotsman but was really an Englishman.

Charles Cameron was commissioned by Catherine to redecorate her summer country palace of Tsarsköe Selo in the neoclassical style. He brought to Russia a sense of color that became an inherent part of the new classicism, and his muted tones replaced the bright primary colors so loved by Elizabeth. Once Catherine had tested him on a series of guest rooms, he completely remodelled her own apartments. The result was a charming, elegant suite decorated in mauve, gold and white, with Wedgwood medallions in the marble chimneypiece. Next he rebuilt her Agate Pavilion in the grounds of Tsarsköe Selo with sixty workmen recruited from Scotland. Decorated largely in agate, it also incorporated steambaths and a marble gallery ninety yards long. She enlarged the park, as she liked to walk up to ten miles a day and, like a good German, measured the distance with a pedometer. She erected monuments and columns to her victorious generals and copied the bridge at Wilton, the classical eighteenth-century house of the Earls of Pembroke, in gray Siberian marble. Cameron then built her a chinoiserie village in the park to house oppressed serfs, where modern farming methods were taught to the children of priests and selected peasants with machinery imported from Suffolk. Peter the Great had laid out the park in the formal Dutch seventeenth-century style, with straight paths, espaliers and fish canals. Catherine imported John Bush from Hackney to change to the "English" style of rolling lawns, shady walks and unclipped trees. Bush's daughter married Charles Cameron. Joseph Cameron, their son, eventually succeeded his father as Catherine's architect.

The Italian architect Giacomo Quarenghi was employed extensively by Catherine after his arrival in Russia in 1780. He made an intensive study of antiquity and modern architecture, especially the works of Palladio, and through him Catherine acquired a more serious and less sentimental understanding of classical art. Until the end of the century he was the most influential architect in Russia.

Catherine loved flowers. "Anglomania rules my plantomania," she wrote to Voltaire, and at Tsarsköe Selo she planted flowers from all over the known world, keeping herself informed about new species and subscribing to the limited edition of the Earl of Bute's beautifully illustrated *Botanical Tables*. Her roses did well, but when her bulbs wilted after flowering for only a single day, they were simply replaced overnight by new ones in pots. The most innovative garden of its day was one she created for her lover Potemkin, Prince of Tauris, around Starov's Taurian Palace. The whole garden was heated by an immense system of hot water pipes and flues, so that in the midst of a freezing St. Petersburg winter the prince could walk in a Mediterranean garden. Following the English tradition, Catherine's gardens had endless lawns, woods and groves. It was not long before her subjects followed her lead and abandoned the geometric formality of the French style inspired by Versailles for the natural English parks.

The Empress Elizabeth had established the Academy of Fine Arts in St. Petersburg, but Catherine gave it a firmer basis, following the guidelines of the French Academy. She sent Russian artists to study in France, where many gained prominence. As young Russian artists began to interest themselves in Western techniques, she gave them special permission to enter the women's bathhouses and sketch from life. The most outstanding Russian painter of her reign was Levitski, and there were many others who were competent and pleasing, though not brilliant.

Catherine also took a personal interest in the affairs of the imperial porcelain factory, established by Elizabeth in 1744 and famous for its production of delightful tiny snuffboxes. Designs generally followed the shapes and decorations of Sèvres and Meissen as well as classical motifs. Frederick the Great had presented Catherine with a huge Berlin centerpiece, and this inspired the production of Russian peasant figures, which the empress particularly liked. She invited artists from other rival European factories to Russia, and Falconet, the modeler from Sèvres, joined her team. The factory's greatest success came toward the end of the century under the direction of Prince Youssopoff. Fine classical works in the Russian Empire style were made, especially white biscuit classical figures and huge vases covered in gilding. But her most famous porcelain commission was a 760-piece dinner service for fifty from Josiah Wedgwood. It was decorated with 1,282 views of the most remarkable buildings, ruins, parks, gardens and other natural curiosities of Britain. It was designed for her Chesme Palace, which she called the Froggery from its Finnish name, and each piece had a green painted frog in place of the imperial crest. It took three years to complete and cost £3,000.

But of all her efforts as a patron of the arts, there is one work for which the Empress Catherine is best remembered. It is the huge bronze equestrian statue of Peter the Great. Having seen his modeling at her porcelain factory, Catherine had the vision to appoint Falconet to carry out the commission. The sculptor took twelve years to complete this magnificent statue of Peter the Great reining in his horse, poised on the edge of a large rock and looking out across the River Neva, an out-stretched arm pointing at the city he had created out of the marshes; his horse meanwhile impatiently stamps on the serpent of his difficulties, now overcome. On the base she placed an inscription in gold letters forever linking her name with Peter the Great.

Although Peter enriched his country architecturally, he did little for any other branch of the arts. Catherine commissioned Yuri Velten to add a building to the Hermitage to house her priceless collection of paintings and *objets d'art,* which grew vast throughout her long reign. If she heard of a collection which might be acquired, she sent her agents to outbid her competitors. But if her taste was eclectic and quantity often out-weighed quality in her acquisitions, she did create a fashion for collecting. Elizabeth had acquired some paintings, mainly German, Dutch and Flemish, but little of first quality, and many a European duke or princeling had more important collections than imperial Russia. Cather-ine began to collect with typical intensity and, at first, a reckless disre-gard for cost. She had natural good taste, but most of her purchases were made unseen, and she had to rely on her agent's reports. Nonetheless, by instinct and good luck as well as her businesswoman's shrewdness, she made some remarkable coups. When the collection of the comte de Bau-douin came on the market, Catherine bought the best—nine Rem-brandts, six Van Dycks and a superb Claude Lorrain. She would watch excitedly as crates filled with her acquisitions from Europe were un-packed on arrival in St. Petersburg. By the end of the 1770s she had ac-quired some 400 old masters. Catherine was lucky again in buying the Walpole Collection from the Earl of Orford,* as a result of which ques-tions were asked in Parliament as to the propriety of such a famed collec-tion leaving England. The eccentric earl had a passion for hare-coursing, and with some of Catherine's money he bred a greyhound which ran

---

* Formerly Sir Robert Walpole, who was considered to have been England's first prime min-ister.

forty-seven times unbeaten. He named her Czarina, and every purebred greyhound in the world today is descended from her.

From a few dozen works at its beginning, by the end of Catherine's reign the imperial collection contained almost 4,000 first-rate paintings, testimony to Catherine's dream of civilizing Russia and inspiring her subjects to follow her lead.

Empress in Love

The Empress Elizabeth sowed the seeds of many of Catherine's cultural triumphs, and, despite Catherine's later dislike and envy of her aunt, she made a great impression on the young German princess and influenced her in a number of ways. And whereas Catherine did not follow her irregular way of life, she well exceeded even Elizabeth's mammoth sexual appetites, to the astonishment of her contemporaries. The Earl of Buckinghamshire, appointed British ambassador in the year of Catherine's coronation, wrote: "That her present favorite [1762] is the fourth [Orlov was in fact the third] person she has distinguished is as certain as that she was persuaded to receive the first by the Empress Elizabeth, who thought her nephew incapable of begetting children; and possibly anyone who is acquainted with the abandoned scenes which passed at the Court will wonder that a young, lively woman, who had long seen debauchery sanctified by usage and the highest example, should want any persuasion at all." Catherine said that she could not "live a day without love," but contrary to her reputation, the actual number of her known lovers is relatively modest. She swore to Potemkin that she had had only four before him: "the first from compulsion, the fourth from despair."

According to Catherine's memoirs, she was a complete innocent when she arrived in Russia: "I am certain most of us [ladies and maids] were extremely innocent; for myself I can testify that though I was more than sixteen years old, I had no idea what the difference [between the sexes] was. . . . I put this question to my mother and was severely scolded." She was generous and remarkably magnanimous to her favorites during their relationships, as well as at the end. They were petted and paraded, but although they were called "aides-de-camp" their only role was to be permanently "on duty," totally faithful (though some were not), and to be her escort at all official and private occasions.

Gregory Orlov, who had helped her to the throne, was created a prince and richly rewarded. Simple and rough, he was not ambitious for himself and wanted to marry her for love. She turned him into a cultivated man of the world, but eventually he was pensioned off and died raving mad. He was succeeded by a nonentity, and then she fell in love with the man who had the greatest influence on her life, Gregory Potemkin. It was often rumored that she had married him, and when they ceased to be lovers they remained close friends. Prince Potemkin fascinated her—a showman, a consummate actor, "failed mystic" and debauchee, a contradictory personality who dominated whatever stage he was on as well as dominating the empress herself. Catherine fell deeply and unequivocally in love with him. He inspired her highest achievements and won her greatest battles. He shared her dreams and made them come true with a style and bravura that matched her own. When he tired of her he turned, among others, to his fifteen-year-old niece. But he continued to satisfy Catherine's sexual needs by choosing all her subsequent lovers—except the last. He was dedicated to his country and his empress, and when he died eighteen years later, Catherine was inconsolable. "Who can I rely on now?" she cried.

All Catherine's lovers after Orlov were "tested" by her friend and confidante, Countess Prescovia Bruce. A Russian aristocrat married to the descendant of a Scottish admiral, as Catherine's *éprouveuse* she was her most discreet and trusted friend. After the candidate had been examined by Catherine's English doctor, John Rogerson, Countess Bruce would interview him for intelligence and qualities of character. She would then instruct the prospective favorite as to his more intimate "duties" and behavior with the empress. (She even dared to deceive her mistress by falling in love herself with one of them.) Next to her bedroom Catherine had two tiny rooms, each with the walls completely covered with exquisite miniatures set in gold. In one room these depicted lascivious amorous scenes, and in the other, men she had known or loved.

Fashion and Jewels

But the woman who ascended the throne of Russia in 1762 was no longer the fragile beauty who had fascinated the world's ambassadors as Grand Duchess. The British ambassador the Earl of Buckinghamshire wrote: "It is easy to discover the remains of a fine woman, but she is now no longer an object of desire." As for her clothes, he continued,

"She has the air of paying no attention to what she wears, yet she is always too well drest for a woman who is entirely indifferent to her appearance." Catherine grew quite stout and, to the fury of her court, who slavishly followed French fashions, she adopted and prescribed as formal court dress the old-style boyar lady's loose flowing gown to camouflage her figure.

A description of her daily routine has survived: she habitually rose at five in the morning and worked at her papers, wearing

a white heavy silk dressing gown or capote, and on her head a crêpe mob cap, also white, tilted slightly to the left. The empress worked at affairs of state until twelve. After that in the inner closet her hairdresser Kozoloy did her hair in a very old-fashioned style with small curls behind the ears. It was not a high style and very simple. Then she went out into the other closet where we were all waiting to see her, and by this time her company would be joined by four elderly maids who came to help the empress make her toilet. One of them handed her ice, with which she wiped her face, perhaps to show that she disdained facial cosmetics. Another put on her head a crêpe headdress and the two Zveryovuy sisters handed her pins to fasten it. Her toilet lasted not more than ten minutes, and during it the empress chatted with one of those present . . . then she would bow to the people there and retire into the bedroom with her ladies, with whose help and that of her personal maid . . . she dressed. On ordinary days she wore a silk dress, Moldavian style (characterized by wide pleated sleeves and, behind them, a second pair of sleeves which were drawn behind the back and knotted). The outer part of the dress was usually mauve or dark grey, without orders, and the underpart white.

But on official occasions, Catherine dressed with a show of majesty that would have rivalled the Empress Elizabeth. Early in her reign she had severely reprimanded a courtier for wearing a coat embroidered all over in gold thread; but by 1777, "everyone wore cloth of gold with embroidery even on ordinary days, and were now almost ashamed to have embroidery only on the edge of their garments."

In her early days at court, Catherine had followed the current fussy hair fashion, with a "kiss-me-quick" or "beau-catcher" curl glued to the dimple on the cheek. Flowers, real, artificial or bejeweled, would stand up three or four inches from the nape of the neck, "while smaller flowers were fastened in the loops [of ribbons] and hung down the neck and even as far as the waist; in all, over twenty feet of ribbon were used." Catherine later wrote that although the court and the town followed that fashion, launched by Princess Anne of Brunswick, "nothing, in fact, could have been uglier." In later life her hair was always dressed simply and neatly, and most agreed that "no head ever became a crown better than hers."

It has been said that the symbols of Catherine's imperial state were as magnificent as her claim to the throne was tenuous. Certainly the crown which she commissioned the French jeweler Posier to make for the coronation is one of the most beautiful and precious ever made. Like Peter the Great's, it is a miter crown, containing nearly 5,000 diamonds, some quite large. The edges of the miter are outlined by huge, perfectly matched pearls and a magnificent balas ruby of 414.3 metric carats is set in the center. The crown was not ready for the coronation, but was later used as the imperial crown of Russia until 1917. She also commissioned a new orb from Posier for her coronation. Despite the speed with which he was obliged to make it, this piece is magnificent— a globe of burnished gold decorated with bands of Brazilian diamonds. In the center is a large Indian diamond of 46.92 metric carats, a Ceylonese sapphire of 200 carats is set *à jour* on top of the globe, and on top of that, a cross of large diamonds. This orb was used in Russian coronations until 1896. Later in her reign Catherine commissioned a new imperial scepter with the Orlov diamond set in the center. This stone of 194.75 carats was said to have been stolen by a French soldier from a temple in Mysore, where it had been one of the eyes of a statue of Brahma. The soldier sold it to an English captain for £3,500. Eventually Prince Orlov bought it for £90,000 and gave it to Catherine.

When Orlov gave her the great diamond, Catherine, an immensely generous woman, gave him among many other wonderful gifts an exquisitely carved 19.4 carat emerald engraved with her profile and surrounded with diamonds. Considering the brittle nature of the stone, this was a great achievement. But the gift most often chosen by the empress for her friends and favorites was a snuff box. St. Petersburg was full of jewelers and goldsmiths, and one of the most celebrated was Pauzie. He created exquisitely enamelled gold and jeweled snuff boxes, one of which Catherine presented to Prince Orlov after his great victory at Chesme Bay. There were gold boxes for every occasion, even for Catherine herself to use for her own special snuff grown at home at Tsarsköe Selo. When she saw the delicious, elaborately decorated boudoir Charles Cameron made for her there, with its mirrors, semiprecious stones and glass columns, she called the little room her "snuff box." There is one circular box in her collection, covered in a delicate diamond trellis, which has a miniature portrait of Catherine's favorite greyhound Lizzie on the lid. But more often than not her presentation boxes had a portrait of herself on the lid surrounded by diamonds.

Credited with amassing 40 percent of the Russian state jewels, Catherine so enlarged the collection of Peter the Great and Elizabeth that it became known as the most magnificent collection of personal jewelry in the world. She paid particular attention to Russian sources of precious stones, and her collection contained aquamarines, her celebrated alexandrites, chrysolites, the famous amethysts from the Urals and Siberia, "gleaming by night like red fire," and many others. During her reign there was a particular fashion for diamond bows and clusters instead of the flower motifs so popular in Elizabeth's time. But all who arrived at the court in Russia were astonished at the size and quantity of diamonds and jewelry worn by the empress and her ladies. They often had large brilliants sewn onto their dresses, and even wide borders of them around the hems. Ladies of the court loved to wear diamond bracelets in flower or ribbon patterns—always in pairs—magnificent diamond necklaces and "girandole" earrings. Other than at the French court, there were no luxuries or extravagances, no amusements, arts or social entertainments to equal those of the court in Russia.

In 1789 she took her last lover, a young officer of the Horse Guards named Plato Zubov. She called him "the most innocent soul in the world" (evidently, as her biographer Vincent Cronin commented, confusing youthful freshness with moral innocence). Zubov remained Catherine's lover for the last seven years of her life. On the morning of November 5, 1796, her footman found her lying comatose on the floor, her face mottled by a stroke. The Orthodox Metropolitan performed the last rites, and she died the following evening.

To a courtier of the new tsar it seemed that in death "the pleasantness and greatness returned to her features and she seemed again to be an empress, full in the glory of her reign." Catherine's dearest friend Potemkin once gave this advice to a diplomat with an urgent mission: "Flatter her for which she ought to be, not for what she is." How well he knew that beneath the grandeur and triumphs of the empress lay the insecurity of a provincial German princess.

2

Marie Antoinette

———◆———

ARCHDUCHESS OF AUSTRIA/QUEEN OF FRANCE

1755–1793

*O*n an island in the middle of the Rhine near Strasbourg, in a sumptuous pavilion especially built for the occasion, a slim, blue-eyed girl with blond hair stood alone at a table covered with crimson velvet—symbolizing the border between France and Austria. Here the fourteen-year-old Maria Antonia Josepha Johanna, Archduchess of Austria and Lorraine, was handed over to the French.

Mercifully, the age-old custom of stripping the bride naked to rid her of all her possessions had been abandoned, and Maria Antonia simply changed, in one of the rooms on the Austrian side of the pavilion, into a ceremonial dress brought from Vienna. Her Grand Mistress of the Robes and the ladies of her suite did the same. The little bride was allowed to keep on her maiden jewelry: chain necklace, aigrettes, golden studs, fringed earrings, and a diamond comb in her hair. Taking her place on a dais in the presentation room under a canopy in an armchair, she heard a speech "of exceptional banality" read by the comte de Noailles, the Ambassador Extraordinary charged with her reception. It was May, 7, 1770. Outside, the rain poured down so heavily that the roof of the pavilion was unable to withstand the deluge and the archduchess's ladies-in-waiting were showered repeatedly.

Maria Antonia gracefully interrupted the welcoming speech: "Do not speak German, gentlemen; from this day I understand no language but

French." With that, the Archduchess Maria Antonia became Marie Antoinette, Dauphine of France.

The speeches seemed endless, but finally the ceremony was over.
With a rustle of silks the dauphine's suite retired back through the Austrian door behind her, while before her the door to France opened to
admit six elderly ladies-in-waiting, the suite of the dead Marie Leczinska, the long-neglected queen of Louis XV. Overcome, Marie Antoinette flung herself into the reluctant arms of their leader, the
comtesse de Noailles, but protocol allowed no place for emotion in this
pious lady; relentlessly she embarked on the introductions. Behind her
the walls of the pavilion were hung on all sides with tapestries depicting
the story of Jason and Medea. The young Goethe on seeing them exclaimed: "What! At the moment when the young princess was about to
step on the soil of her future husband's country, there is placed before
her eyes a picture of the most horrible marriage that can be
imagined! . . . Might one not say that the most awful spectre has been
summoned to meet the most beautiful and happy betrothed?" But as she
was so often to do during her life, Marie Antoinette rose to the occasion
and passed smiling into France. This journey was to be the only glimpse
she was to have of the country, or of the people whose queen she was
one day to be. Even so, she had seen more than the sisters of Louis XV,
who had never even been to Paris.

Austria

Born on November 2, 1755, in the Hofburg in Vienna, Maria Antonia was
the sixteenth child of the Empress Maria Theresa of Austria and the Emperor Francis I. Feeling her labor coming on, the empress nevertheless
continued working on her state boxes. When the pains became acute, she
called for her dentist and had a troublesome tooth pulled out; in the
throes of childbirth she would hardly notice the extra pain. An hour or
two after her safe delivery, the empress resumed work on her boxes.

This child was conceived at a time of great happiness for the empress—she was close to Francis; the country was at peace; its finances
were healthy; the army was in good heart and great reforms were under
way. Life at her court had a cosy, gemütlich quality unknown at other
European courts—a highly idiosyncratic mixture of glittering ceremonial and the simplest informality.

At the time of her coronation Maria Theresa abandoned her early excesses, controlled her headstrong and passionate nature and thereafter only let herself go at Carnival time. She hated the court etiquette and the traditional Spanish protocol and managed to have it virtually abolished. Her marriage to Francis of Lorraine was, by all accounts, a love match and he supported the difficult position of consort with good humor and tact. He was a connoisseur of art and good living, loving late nights and good food.

Maria Theresa possessed great energy and the highest principles. She was good-looking, and enjoyed an easy intimacy with her people without losing an unexpressed—but strongly intimate—sense of her position and authority as empress. Her court was the home of culture, art and music. An excellent horsewoman, she herself led and directed the splendid "carrousels" performed in the Imperial Riding School. Within aristocratic circles, Maria Theresa was considered the parent of society's one large family and she therefore made the rules. Rigidly virtuous in her own conduct and "faithful to the marriage bed," she made very little allowance for the indiscretions of others. "A woman of condition, if known to be frail, unless her frailty be confined to one lover, and managed with the utmost attention to privacy and decorum, is certain to receive an order to quit Vienna. . . ." The empress also made it her business, with the use of an army of spies, to know in minute and circumstantial detail the actions, amusements and pleasures of her subjects and, in particular, those of the members of her court.

And those rules extended to dress and makeup. Ladies in Habsburg society were considered elegant, graceful and pleasing, but they rarely possessed the cultivated minds of their counterparts in Britain and France. Nonetheless, they dressed well and a contemporary source at the time said there was no court in Europe where one could see such a profusion of diamonds. One absurdity, which stretched to every European court except the British, was to dress girls at seven or eight as if they were women of fifteen to eighteen.

Although married and unmarried women of fashion wore rouge, it was generally applied with moderation. Only the archduchesses were forbidden by the empress to color their cheeks. When the Emperor Francis died in 1765, she forbade anyone to wear rouge, but as her grief wore off, rouge was gradually and imperceptibly revived.

Owing to the historical enmity between Austria and France during the empress's childhood, the court had looked to Italy for its cultural inspiration. As a result of her marriage to the Archduke of Lorraine, Maria Theresa reintroduced the French language at court, French fashions, theatricals and so on. German was rarely used in mixed company and the Austrians "speak so bad a dialect of it . . . Italian is generally understood . . . English is extremely in vogue. . . . But French is indispensable."

As a child, Maria Antonia was considered lively and extremely attractive, though her features were too irregular to be thought pretty. She had fair hair, blue eyes, a high rounded forehead, slightly uneven teeth, an aquiline nose, and although her lower lip "was already full of disdain," she was universally thought adorable. Her tutor the abbé Vermond declared that "you might find faces which are more regularly beautiful, but I doubt if you could find one more attractive." As a girl, her carriage was graceful and judged even queenly, and her dazzling complexion and the whiteness of her skin were universally admired. When she walked, courtiers said, she "floated," her feet scarcely appearing to touch the ground.

But Maria Antonia's education was filled with shortcomings. In later years Maria Theresa would complain of her own poor education, but she never thought to improve that of her daughters. The only exception was her second eldest daughter, Marie Christine, who was her mother's favorite and highly intelligent, humorous, quick and shrewd. The other girls were not really taught to concentrate or to use their minds at all.

And yet the empress had extremely firm ideas about how they should be brought up. They were forced to eat everything set before them, without picking or choosing. They were given fish on Fridays, Saturdays and feast days, even though Maria Antonia heartily disliked it; they were not to eat too much sugar; all the girls had to wash properly and comb their hair. They were not to mix with the servants or to give them orders. "They are born to obey . . . and never must they be allowed to be afraid, neither of thunderstorms, fire, ghosts, witches nor any other nonsense. The servants must not talk about such things or tell horror stories." Illness, smallpox and even death were to be regarded as perfectly natural. The girls were not to show familiarity with servants, and were to be polite to everyone, especially strangers.

But Maria Theresa was too occupied with the business of ruling her country to oversee her daughters' education properly. Little Maria Antonia was able to wind her first governess so tightly around her finger that she would write out her pupils' exercises in pencil for Maria Antonia to trace later in ink. When this was discovered, the governess was replaced by another, with no greater success. Antonia was allowed to run wild—a young tomboy—until 1768, when her mother sent to Paris for a tutor, a hairdresser and a dentist. The abbé Vermond reported that he found a little laziness and frivolity in his pupil, even though she understood perfectly well what he put before her. "Her judgment is nearly always good," he said, "but I cannot get her into the way of exploring a question, although I know she is capable of it." He found Maria Antonia eager, engaging, intelligent, but unable to concentrate. Furthermore, her mocking nature and constant distractions counteracted her talent for learning. It is possible the abbé's verdict may be an early example of the misrepresentation of which Marie Antoinette was such a victim once in France. However, she could speak Italian fluently, having been taught by Metastasio, the court librettist and author of several classical tragedies. Under the instruction of the Parisian dancer Noverre, she learned to dance gracefully. And with Gluck as her teacher, she learned to play the harp, the spinet and the clavichord. A Parisian actor had given her some lessons in diction (until an outraged protest arrived from Versailles—he was hardly suitable company for a future dauphine), but her French was studded with Germanisms, her German was full of grammatical errors, and she wrote very slowly. Despite these little drawbacks, the imperial children enjoyed life. They either watched or took part in an endless round of comedies, operas and ballets, all elaborately mounted.

The empress's personal life might be informal, but in public she always did things in style. The iron discipline that made her rise at five in the morning and spend hours at her toilette must have impressed all her children. Only after her husband's death did she relax over her personal appearance, thereafter invariably wearing black and very little jewelry. Even so, the court maintained a certain brilliance, and Vienna to a large extent existed to serve that court. Although Maria Theresa's expenditure was considerably less than her father's had been (his court consisted of no fewer than 40,000 persons), she still employed, for example, 1,500 court chamberlains, who were nominally responsible for overseeing the economy of the palaces, the court entertainments and the countless musicians, painters and craftsmen on the imperial payroll. Their tasks included importing snow for the imperial children's sledges when there was none in the city and arranging for the empress's milk to arrive each day fresh from her dairy at Schönbrunn.

Schönbrunn was the empress's favorite palace, outside Vienna, located in a valley between two hills. The palace, as its name implies, possesses a spring of the most pure and refreshing water—so much so that the empress never drank any other. During the winter months when she resided in town, a heavily loaded mule brought her water from this spring. Schönbrunn Palace was damp, but its apartments were magnificent and maintained by the empress at great expense. As a child Maria Antonia joined her parents at entertainments of a baroque splendor, with masques and pageantry and shoots lasting as long as three days. Exhausted, the imperial family would climb into their carriages and return to Schönbrunn. To provide friends for her children, the empress allowed German and Austrian princesses to live with them, sharing their games and education.

For fifteen years negotiations took place over the marriage of Maria Antonia to the Dauphin of France. Neither of them was consulted and their approval was never sought. Louis Auguste was a year older than Maria Antonia and neither very strong nor very intelligent. Not very likable and a loner by temperament, all he cared for was the chase and he hunted as often as possible. He had little or no interest in art or music and did not dance, though he was well read in history and science. Although the ambassadors at his grandfather's court found little good to say of him, others, such as Louis XV himself, had a genuine regard for his knowledge and his sound common sense. This was the young man Maria Antonia came to France to marry.

France

At Compiègne on May 14, 1770, Marie Antoinette was met by Louis XV, his three daughters and his three grandsons, and it seems she charmed everyone except the tongue-tied dauphin. The next evening at dinner, Marie Antoinette had her first glimpse of the favorite, Madame du Barry. When she innocently asked the function of that pretty woman who sat next to the king, the aunts soon enlightened her. From that moment the young dauphine resented and despised Madame du Barry, and the court divided into two factions.

The next day, the young Louis and Marie Antoinette were married in the gilt and white chapel of Versailles. The bridegroom wore a suit of cloth of gold, spangled with diamonds; the bride wore white brocade: a "symphony of rose gold and silver and sparkling with diamonds." One observer noticed that "the corps of her robe was too small and left quite a broad strip of lacing and shift quite visible, which had a bad effect between two broader strips of diamonds."

After the ceremony Madame la Dauphine received the new members of her household, before attending a reception held by the king, followed by dinner in the new Opera House, which had been opened for the first time that evening. Rain unfortunately postponed the firework display. The young bride's only sadness stemmed from the apparent frigidity of her husband, and his grandfather the king was heard to remark, "He's not like other men."

Then the royal couple were escorted to bed. Just as the reception and the dinner were public—part of the enormous theater of Versailles, which presented the spectacle of royalty at home—so was this event. The Archbishop of Rheims blessed the bed, the king handed the dauphin his nightshirt and the duchesse de Chartres helped Marie Antoinette to put on her nightgown. The bride and groom lay down, the hangings were drawn and then suddenly, following tradition, opened again. This was the last vestige of the days when the consummation itself was witnessed.

There is still argument over the exact date when Louis and Marie Antoinette consummated their marriage. It is usually agreed that Marie Antoinette became the "true Queen of France" during an August night in 1777, some seven years after her marriage. Louis, it was said, suffered from phimosis, and before he could consummate the marriage he required surgery. Fearing an operation, he continually delayed it until 1777, when Marie Antoinette's brother, the Emperor Joseph, came especially from Vienna to persuade him to submit to the surgeon's knife for the sake of the alliance. Louis yielded, the operation was successful, and the following year Marie Antoinette bore their first child. Not all historians agree that Louis did in fact undergo the operation, but it is certain that the consummation dates from mid-1777. Marie Antoinette went on to give birth to four more children, only two of whom survived childhood.

It seemed that her sexual frustration led Marie Antoinette, a natural flirt and coquette, to seek relief in a giddy but disastrous round of pleasure and spending. Initially this thirst for pleasure did not go beyond the bounds permitted to an eighteen-year-old dauphine, but it nevertheless alarmed her mother. Physically "awakened but not satisfied," the dauphine found her only palliative in amusing herself by throwing off all constraints and seeking every possible pleasure save that of deceiving her husband. Melancholy, frivolous whims, mad gaiety and bad temper followed on each other. And her husband tolerated and even indulged her—most probably because of his own feelings of physical inadequacy.

Her day was otherwise boring enough, as she recounted in a long letter to her mother on July 12, 1770:

> I get up at ten or half past nine, dress and say my morning prayers. Then I breakfast, before going usually to my aunts, where I find the King. This lasts till half-past ten. At eleven I go to have my hair dressed. At midday the court is called, and there the whole world has the right to enter—though not the common people. I put on my rouge and wash my hands in front of everybody. Then the gentlemen leave and I dress in front of the ladies.

Next, to Mass, followed by dinner in the presence of the whole court. The dauphine then joined her husband, if he was free, or went to her own apartments.

> I read, I write or I work. I am making a waistcoat for the King. It makes little progress, but I hope that with God's grace it may be finished in some years. At three I go to my aunts; sometimes the King is there. At four the Abbé [Vermond] comes to me. At five the music master till six. At half past six again to my aunts or to take a walk. You must know that my husband almost always accompanies me to my aunts. From seven o'clock we play (at cards or some other games) till nine. Then we eat. When the King is not there then the aunts come to us; but when he is, we eat with them, where we wait

for him. He comes generally at half past ten, but I am allowed to lie down on a long couch and sleep till his arrival. If he does not come, we go to bed at eleven o'clock. That is all our day.

At the time of her marriage, Marie Antoinette was enormously popular. Her years as dauphine were marked by her feud with Madame du Barry, who, as a member of the anti-Austrian faction at Versailles, had done her best to wreck the marriage. (Particularly virulent was the revelation by the du Barry faction that the marriage had not been consummated.) Most people in Paris hated Madame du Barry, and Marie Antoinette's popularity was enhanced by her stand against the king's mistress. Commoners and nobility had lost respect for the king and therefore vested all their hopes in the dauphin and his young wife. Even before the young couple made their long-deferred official entry into Paris, popular opinion was on their side.

When they did eventually enter the capital, in June 1773, they were received with wild enthusiasm. On subsequent visits to the Opéra, the Comédie Française and the Théâtre des Italiens, Marie Antoinette was spoiled and fêted.

At the same time, her thirst for pleasure was growing. Eight years later, when her brother the Emperor Joseph II visited Versailles, he even expressed surprise at his sister's virtuous ways. Her behavior was quite contrary to the prevailing licentiousness of the court (and Marie Antoinette's purity is brilliantly and accurately captured in the portraits by Mme Vigée-Lebrun). According to the prince de Ligne, "Her discretion inspired as much respect as her air of majesty. One could no more forget it than one could forget oneself." In her presence, he added, "no one dared venture an indelicate remark, a ribald story, or a marked piece of spite." She refused to meet the notorious princesse de Monaco, declaring, "I do not receive women separated from their husbands."

Kind, patient and generous to a fault with the members of her household, Marie Antoinette always interested herself in their lives and fortunes. She had among her ladies young girls from good families of the Maison de Saint-Cyr. Considering herself to be their moral guardian, she would decide whether or not a play was suitable for them. If it was an old play, she spent a whole morning reading it, rather than trust her memory, before taking her decision.

In a letter to her page, baron de Tilly, she wrote: "Behave according to your station and you will receive from me all the support you would wish for." She went on, "And dress more simply. You are rich enough, but it will fail you if your tastes outrun your means. Why this hair-style? Why these curls? Are you planning to go on the stage? Simplicity will not get you noticed, but it will bring you esteem." How Marie Antoinette had changed.

But despite her avowed intention of becoming French in thought and speech, in her heart and manner, her instincts and way of feeling and thinking, Marie Antoinette remained thoroughly Austrian. She valued feeling and spontaneity possibly more than reason. She tended to go to extremes, and discretion was not among her virtues. As an outsider she naturally saw through the conventions of French court life; what others took for granted she found funny, and being Austrian, when she found something funny, she laughed outright. Although Marie Antoinette soon lost the ability to speak fluent German, she still managed to retain what her mother approvingly called "German frankness"—not that this appealed to everyone, but others of her qualities did. Her smile charmed and attracted, her "light step," her "archduchess's bearing," and "the somewhat proud carriage of her head and shoulder" made their effect. "As one watches the Princess it is difficult to refrain from feeling a respect mingled with tenderness." All marvelled at her complexion, which was "literally a blend of lilies and roses . . . which can spare her the use of rouge," noted one lady with a hint of envy. Marie Antoinette was a fresh breeze arriving in a decaying and unhealthy society.

So where did things begin to go wrong? The fatal years occurred between her entry into Paris and Joseph II's visit to Versailles in 1781, by which time she had—alas too late—reformed. In 1774 King Louis XV died of smallpox. (The new king had been inoculated on the advice of his wife—a dangerous step, for inoculation in those days often proved fatal.) Marie Antoinette was now queen, free to behave without restraint. Initially her intentions remained sound: "I shall try to commit as few faults as I possibly can," she wrote to her mother. "Little by little I want and hope to correct myself. Without ever meddling in intrigue, I wish to be worthy of my husband's confidence." Yet the three years that followed her accession were to seal Marie Antoinette's fate.

These were the years of folly—often serious, sometimes trifling—which destroyed her public reputation. While her virtues frequently went unnoticed, every mistake—either political or personal—was seized on by her enemies and magnified. They never forgot that she was a foreigner—an Austrian—and this fact was turned against her. The mere circumstance of her nationality was presented almost as a crime. When she had been queen for no more than a month, the following ditty was circulating at court:

> *Petite reine de vingt ans,*
> *Vous, qui traitez si mal les gens,*
> *Vous repasserez la barrière,*
> *Laire, laire, aire, lanlaire, laire, lanla.*

> (Little twenty-year-old queen,
> You, who behave so badly toward people,
> Will overstep the bound of decency.
> Tra-la-la.)

Libelous pens made play with the fact that the current term for lesbianism was *le vice Allemand*: "the German vice."

Even Marie Antoinette's preference for plain materials was turned against her, for whereas plain linen was produced in the Austrian Netherlands, luxurious silks—apparently scorned by the new queen of the country—were made in Lyons. So Marie Antoinette was stigmatized as "*l'Autrichienne,*" with its convenient ending *chienne* (bitch).

In spite of her own undoubted indiscretions, Marie Antoinette was certainly ruined through slander. From the moment she set foot in France, she was the victim of a vicious and shrewdly sustained process of character assassination. Her favorites did her no good, ruthlessly exploiting her as she showered them with privileges and posts that carried considerable incomes. Beneath her outward demeanor, the queen was shy and insecure. That only made the situation worse, for as more and more of the great ladies of the time moved to their palaces in Paris, she remained aloof in Versailles, keeping within her small circle of favorites and their families and never trying to win to her side some of her more powerful, malicious enemies.

The Queen of Fashion

Queen at eighteen, Marie Antoinette was considered by many to be a great beauty. According to Mrs. Thrale,* "the Queen is far the prettiest woman at her own court." (Mrs. Thrale added, "The King is well enough—like another Frenchman.") But Marie Antoinette's beauty does seem to have been more that of youth and vivacity rather than the classic beauty depicted by great artists. Undoubtedly her coloring was wonderful. But from her mother she had inherited a poor constitution, and she suffered from a weak chest, colds and sore throats.

Yet these disabilities did not prevent the queen from becoming the leader of fashion. Every year she scrapped her old wardrobe, and the records of her inventories reveal that she wore more than 170 dresses a year. Every morning when she awoke, Marie Antoinette was given a pincushion and a book containing patterns of her dresses for day and evening. She took pins and stuck them into her choices, which included a ball dress, a dinner dress, a formal dress and a dress for gambling in her apartments. The book was then taken away, and soon baskets would appear covered with taffeta, containing everything the queen had chosen to wear during that day. Each dress had its own green taffeta cover.

Marie Antoinette greatly overspent her generous dress allowance. Often at the end of the year dresses and outfits were found that had been cast aside, never worn. Yet, in spite of this extravagance, the queen favored simple styles and rejected the fussy fashions of the time. Her dresses were often of a single color—one favorite was a particular gold known as *cheveux de la reine,* woven at Gobelin to match exactly a lock of the queen's ash-blond hair. Another new shade favored by Marie Antoinette was a purplish-brown, instantly dubbed by her husband "puce"—the color of a flea—and puce became the fashion that season, with various subshades of flea, such as "flea's belly," "flea's back" and "flea's thigh."

The inspiration—or blame—for Marie Antoinette's excessive wardrobe can be largely attributed to a shrewd young dressmaker called Rose Bertin, who had been presented to the queen a few months after

---

*Mrs. Hester Thrale, an intimate of Marie Antoinette's, wrote her excellent reminiscences of family friend Dr. Johnson, who lived with her and her husband for fifteen years.

her accession. Mlle Bertin cleverly managed to deliver her work directly to the queen, bypassing the Mistress of the Wardrobe. As she submitted her accounts only several months later, no one seemed able to check what had been supplied. Her prices were considered exorbitant. Once she charged Marie Antoinette as much as 1.2 million francs for a single dress.

But how could Marie Antoinette resist such creations as the ones Rose Bertin called "Indiscreet Pleasure," "Stifled Sighs" and "Masked Desire" or the evening shoes which came out of the Aladdin's Cave of her baskets, set with a little row of emeralds on the heel? Through her patron, Rose Bertin became known throughout Europe and even sent a fashion doll dressed in the latest French style to the northern courts. She also traded with Spain, Portugal and Russia, and it was said that her fame was bounded only by the frontiers of Europe.

The queen's taste for simplicity—whether in clothes, jewels or behavior—did nothing to reduce Mlle Bertin's accounts. When the king gave his wife the Petit Trianon, she delighted in playing the country girl, and Rose Bertin made her clothes in the peasant style. Long trains were discarded, to be replaced by what was misleadingly called "undress," with a little cap for the head, so that "a duchess could not be distinguished from an actress."

The contrast between great extravagance and an affectation of simple country styles was nowhere more apparent than at the magnificent balls the queen loved both to give and to attend. In 1775 she asked her English friend Countess Spencer to send her three or four books of English country dances (in particular, "Over the Hills and Far Away"). Wearing a mask, and with her coachmen dressed in simple gray overcoats to cover their royal blue livery, the queen delighted in attending the balls at the Paris Opéra. Though she deceived herself, everyone else was fully aware of her incognito the moment she entered.

It was the fashion at this time to wear hair piled high, using false hair, gauze and pins. This was then decorated with feathers, flowers and other objects such as stuffed birds or even model ships. Hair was piled as high as three feet and ladies had to travel to a ball with their head sticking out through the open roof of their carriages. Rose Bertin adapted this fashion for hair and called it a *pouf au sentiment* because of the number of objects that it could contain, such as "fruit, flowers, vegetables, stuffed birds, dolls, and many other things giving expression to the tastes, the preferences, and the sentiments of the wearer. . . ."

When Louis had himself inoculated, Rose Bertin celebrated the occasion with a *pouf à l'inoculation*—it represented the rising sun (the king), an olive tree laden with fruit (peace), round which a serpent was twisted holding a flower-wreathed club—all symbolizing the affection felt by everyone at the success of the inoculation the royal family had undergone. As the queen was the first to wear the *pouf à l'inoculation*, the court immediately followed.

Best of all, Marie Antoinette liked to wear ostrich feathers in her hair, and once wore as many as ten tall plumes for a ball, so that she could not get into her carriage. When Maria Theresa heard, she sharply criticized her daughter's "plumage" and returned a portrait Marie Antoinette had sent her, pretending she had thought it was the portrait of an actress and not the Queen of France: "A young and pretty Queen, full of charm, has no need of all this nonsense."

In her new role Marie Antoinette was as giddy as a young girl with a new doll. As queen she was imitated by every other lady who aspired to a fashionable role at court and in French society. She never stopped to think how her own flamboyant example was ruining the purses of the husbands and parents of her young following, and it was widely repeated that the new queen would ruin all the ladies of France.

In her very first winter as queen, Marie Antoinette also set an expensive fashion for brilliant entertainments. At one private ball, four quadrilles were given in her honor, "the first in old French costumes; the second represented mountebanks; the third, which was the Queen's, was given in Tyrolean costume, and the fourth in Indian." The masquerades were so successful that the queen desired it all to be repeated the following week.

Since the king left the organizing of entertainments to his wife, Marie Antoinette found herself offered the opportunity of establishing a new and brilliant court. For several months official mourning for the late king had deprived France—and its new queen—of balls and public amusements. During her years as dauphine, Marie Antoinette had been prevented from visiting Paris as much as she would have liked, so now the twenty-two-year-old queen set about arranging an exhausting program of endless entertainments. Once a week the court attended a production at the Opéra in Paris—allegedly to save the cost of transporting scenery to Versailles. At Versailles itself two weekly balls and two weekly theatrical productions were held—one by the Comédie Française, the other by the Comédie Italienne. On the two remaining days there were gala banquets.

Such plays and entertainments might not have appeared particularly scandalous had not the queen herself, in her early days, appeared in them. Although this behavior shocked the French, it was all part of Marie Antoinette's background. Her mother had appeared in operas; and the young Austrian archdukes and archduchesses had been shown off in an endless succession of elaborate comedies, operas and ballets.

The reaction of Madame Campan, a lady devoted to Marie Antoinette, epitomizes the different impression such behavior created outside Austria. "So long as no strangers were admitted to the performances, they were but little censured," she wrote, "but the praise obtained by the performers made them look for a larger circle of admirers." So the queen permitted officers of the royal bodyguard and equerries of the king and princes to attend. Those excluded were offended, while those who were allowed entry from time to time indiscreetly murmured unkind criticism.

Marie Antoinette's love of acting and drama resulted in her decision to build the exquisite little theater still to be seen at Trianon, and she supervised its completion down to the smallest detail. She made her debut on the stage of the papier-mâché theater in the summer of 1780, the leader of a troupe composed of her coterie, and only the king and the royal family were invited to watch from the balcony. In the boxes and the pit were those in service at Trianon—about forty in all.

Still some disapproved. When the comtesse de Provence was invited to join the troupe, she exclaimed, "It is beneath me." Astonished, the queen responded, "But if I, the Queen of France, act, you should have no scruples." The comtesse replied, "I may not be a queen, but I am the stuff of which they are made." The king allowed his brother Artois to take the romantic lead; but when he played the lover, even a kiss "given in the family" did not deter the pamphleteers from printing their insinuations. Marie Antoinette was said to be an excellent actress. Her last performance was as Rosina in *The Barber of Seville* in 1785. Perhaps it was this love of acting that encouraged the queen's public speaking, for she answered all addresses herself, something the Bourbon princesses had long ceased to take the trouble to do.

Food at court was delicious, largely because Louis XV had encouraged his ladies to invent new dishes, which they did with enthusiasm. *Bouchées à la Reine* were named for his queen, *filets de sole Pompadour* for his first mistress, and Madame du Barry invented *perdrix en chartreuse*—a heavier dish than the Pompadour's fish, cooked in champagne with truffles and mushrooms, but delicious nonetheless. It was the fashion in high society and military circles to invent dishes and name them: the maréchal de Mirepoix had a sauce named in his honor, and another made of eggs and oil was given the name of *la mahonnaise* (mayonnaise) after Port Mahon in Minorca, captured by the duc de Richelieu in 1756.

Soybeans, curry and garlic were all introduced into French cooking during the reign of Louis XVI and a chef from Strasbourg contributed *pâté de foie gras aux truffes* to French haute cuisine. Extravagant confections using ice became extremely popular, and *bombes glacées* were universally acclaimed. The king liked his food and had a generous appetite, especially after hunting. A typical menu would begin with pâté, followed by cutlets and vegetables (green beans and fried artichokes were popular at Versailles), a salad dressed solely with lemon juice, fruit and a glass of Malaga.

Marie Antoinette preferred to end her meals simply and drank only water, especially that from Ville d'Avray. When she arrived in France, she brought her own pastry chef. The Austrians had learned the delicate art of feather-light pastry from the Turks during the long siege of Vienna. In memory of this siege, the Viennese created a pastry in the shape of the Turkish emblem, the crescent moon. When Marie Antoinette introduced her Austrian breakfast pastry, the French called it a *croissant*. Years later, when the starving mob were hurling abuse at her from the gates of the Tuileries, the queen was heard to utter her famous and misunderstood cry: "Give them cake." She well knew the law—if the bakers ran out of bread, they must sell cake (or *brioche*) at the same low price as bread, and this is what she was urging them to do. Another Turkish legacy that came to France via Austria is coffee, which the Turks had left behind after the siege and the clever Viennese then introduced into Europe. The queen's breakfast consisted of hot chocolate with whipped cream, or else coffee, along with croissants, brioches or kugelhopf (a circular Austrian cake), which Marie Antoinette also made popular in Paris. She ate very little at lunch. Her favorite dish was roast duck—she disliked complicated food and once suffered severe indigestion after eating iced cheese.

Probably the most disagreeable custom Marie Antoinette had to endure was that of dining every day in public. Each branch of her family had its public dinner daily and any decently dressed person was admitted, so they could see a different member of the royal family for each course if they were quick enough, running from one apartment to another. Once queen, Marie Antoinette dispensed with this custom, along with many of the other ceremonies surrounding meals: "Nothing was presented directly to the Queen; her handkerchief or her gloves were placed upon a long salver of gold or silver gilt, which was placed as a piece of furniture of ceremony upon a side-table, and was called a gantière." But by making what appeared to her to be sensible changes in the ancient etiquette Marie Antoinette was in fact depriving members of the court of their cherished and jealously guarded privileges. After she became queen, Marie Antoinette declined to submit to the ordeal of dining in public more than once a week. On these occasions she ate nothing and dined in her private apartments afterward. Never showing much interest in food, she preferred to eat roast chicken and broth, and small biscuits which she soaked in a glass of water.

When the queen rose or went to bed she was surrounded by people whose privilege it was to be there: her chief physician, chief surgeon, physician in ordinary, reader, closet secretary, the king's four first *valets de chambre* and their reversioners,* and the king's chief physicians and surgeons. Marie Antoinette habitually awoke at eight, and usually breakfasted in bed at nine. As soon as the queen rose, the wardrobe woman was admitted to draw the curtains, take away the pillows and prepare the bed to be made by some of the *valets de chambre* after the queen had gone to Mass. Generally, except at Saint-Cloud, where the queen bathed in an apartment below her own, a slipper bath was rolled into her room, and her bathers brought everything that was necessary. The

---

* A person entitled to this lucrative position on the death of a *valet de chambre*.

queen was scrupulously modest and had her bath in a large gown of English flannel buttoned down to the bottom. When she came out of the bath the first woman held up a cloth to conceal her entirely from the sight of her women, and then threw it over her shoulders. The bathers wrapped her in it and dried her completely; then she put on a long open chemise, trimmed all round with lace, and afterward a white taffeta bed-gown and dimity slippers also trimmed with lace. The wardrobe woman warmed the bed; and so dressed the queen went to bed again, while the bathers and servants of the chamber took away the bathing apparatus. The queen, replaced in bed, took up a book of her tapestry work. On her bathing mornings she breakfasted in the bath, her tray placed on the cover.

With the birth of her first child, Marie-Thérèse Charlotte, in December 1778, Marie Antoinette was once more the victim of the tyranny of etiquette; custom decreed that any Frenchman might watch the birth and see with his own eyes that the baby really was the queen's and not a substitute. The room was crowded to suffocation with sightseers and it was just as well that Louis had had the foresight to tie the tapestry screens surrounding the queen's bed to the wall; otherwise they would have been knocked over on top of her.

The baby was mercifully not swaddled but, on the advice of Maria Theresa, dressed "naturally"—that is to say, loosely. Unlike so many of her French contemporaries, Marie Antoinette was very maternal. She suffered at her daughter's pain when her teeth were coming through, and wrote to her mother how touched she had been by the "sweetness and patience of the poor little thing in her suffering."

Royal Pleasures and Displeasures

Marie Antoinette's favorite companion was her brother-in-law, the comte d'Artois. He possessed all the graces lacking in poor Louis; delighted in amusing the queen and ignoring the king and encouraged her to gamble.

Until 1775 horse racing was carried on only at Newmarket in England. In March that year the comte d'Artois invited Marie Antoinette to preside over the first races held in France, on the outskirts of the Bois de Boulogne. Dr. Johnson was present and complained that he could not tell which horse was winning, since everyone wore the green livery of Artois. In spite of the driving rain and wind, Marie Antoinette loyally stayed to the end. Mingling with all classes of society, assessing the horses and placing bets, she found herself beset by the fishwives of Paris, who demanded—with ribald shouts and obscene gestures—that she bear France an heir to the throne.

Undeterred, the queen continued to patronize racing, and soon horse races took place every week on a Tuesday, eventually taking up the whole day. Once Louis came to watch a race. He clearly felt that his queen had lost her dignity cheering and calling out at her favorites to win, and made his point by asking the leading actors of the Comédie Italienne to present an impression of his queen and his brother at the races—which he found hilarious. The Empress Maria Theresa was less amused when she heard that her daughter neglected her royal duties, failing to "receive the ambassadors and foreign ministers, who of late have found themselves deprived of the honor of paying court to Her Majesty for three weeks," owing to her enthusiasm for racing.

Marie Antoinette's love of cards and gambling derived from her childhood in Vienna. Cards were also a traditional part of life at the French court. But by 1776 her gambling knew no limits and her losses were horrendous. Although her husband took the extraordinary step of publishing edicts to restrict betting, his queen paid no heed. On one occasion she took part in a game of cards that went on for thirty-six hours, lasting well into the morning of All Saints' Day. Possibly led on by dishonest partners, she lost all the money allocated to her by the treasury, and Louis, ever tolerant, paid her debts out of his personal funds. "As he is naturally extremely thrifty," the Austrian ambassador reported, "this generosity astonished the Queen."

In every novelty, Marie Antoinette took the lead. Artois bought her a new kind of two-wheeled carriage called a *Diable*—much faster than a cabriolet—and she delighted in driving it at speed. Tilting and jousting became the latest craze, and Marie Antoinette presented the winners with their prizes. So severe was the winter of 1776 that, remembering the fun of sleighing parties at home in Austria, she had sleighs built for herself and started another fashion at court. Soon the royal parks abounded with white and gold sleighs, and the horses were decked with white plumes and bells on their harness. Some of her courtiers even drove as far as Paris in their sleighs. As they were masked, the queen's enemies were able to claim that she herself rode through the city streets in a sleigh and criticism against yet another "Austrian custom" was severe. The following year Marie Antoinette left her sleighs in the stables. But while the queen and her court indulged themselves throughout that harsh winter, the king was seen distributing cartloads of wood among the poor. Watching noblemen preparing for another sleigh party, Louis pointed at the carts full of wood and remarked, "Gentlemen: these are *my* sleighs."

Marie Antoinette took to her pleasures all the more readily because the etiquette of the French court bored her so. From the moment she was introduced to her new country, she was instructed in the niceties of etiquette by the comtesse de Noailles. The princess discovered that the tiniest of her actions set off a complex sequence of formal behavior. The comtesse, well intentioned but severe, wearied her new charge with etiquette without teaching her its importance and Marie Antoinette spiritedly nicknamed her "Mme Etiquette." When one day she fell off her donkey, she implored two friends who ran to help her: "Leave me on the ground. We must wait for Mme Etiquette. She will show us the proper way to pick up a dauphine who has tumbled off a donkey."

Music and a Garden

In music and in ballet Marie Antoinette's preference was for simplicity and naturalness, and she encouraged lighter and more graceful costumes for the dancers. On the visit to Paris of her brother Maximilian, she indulged her own refined and simple tastes by arranging for Hungarian and Flemish country dances to be performed at his reception. As a child in Vienna she had been taught to play the clavichord by Gluck, and she invited the composer to Paris in 1774 to supervise a production of his *Iphigénie en Aulide*.

Gluck's musical style was sharply different from contemporary French opera. The French emphasized the ballet and orchestra, producing stylized, formal operas, full of ceremonial, with the chorus standing on either side of the stage throughout the performance (and the male singers, arms folded, separated from the women, who all carried fans). In Vienna, Gluck had begun to reduce the extravagant musical display that came between the audience and the story. When he first visited Paris, he was almost sixty years old, yet, musically speaking, fifty years ahead of his time.

Naturally the cast, unfamiliar with his new ideas and reforms, was somewhat out of its depth. The composer flew into terrible rages at the rehearsals and could barely be calmed down even by Marie Antoinette herself. Then the leading tenor fell ill on the eve of the first night and the performance, which was to have taken place in the presence of the royal family, was cancelled. Paris was scandalized, but Gluck insisted that the singer could not simply be replaced at the last moment. Marie Antoinette supported him, and a week later the performance took place. Although most of the audience found the music unfamiliar and were taken aback by some of the composer's innovations, the queen never ceased applauding.

The second performance was more successful. The majority of French operagoers continued to prefer the works of the Italian composer Niccolà Piccini to those of Gluck, but Marie Antoinette remained the enthusiastic champion of her fellow Austrian. For four more years she brought him back to Paris to direct his own works. In return he declared that he owed much of his success to her patronage, dedicating his masterpiece *Iphigénie en Tauride* to her, the "sensitive and enlightened Princess, who loves and protects all the arts." By championing Gluck, Marie Antoinette did much to change the course of French opera and to improve its standards of production.

Once the queen received the famous singer P. J. Garat, known as "the Bordeaux wonder," who was renowned for performing songs in his native Gascon dialect. Accompanied by the musician Antonio Salieri, he sang some of them for her, having translated the verses into French, and she was enchanted. Then she asked, "Do you know no music from the French operas?" Garat replied that he had never learned any, since "my father allowed me to waste my time studying only law." The queen laughed, but added that Garat surely knew a little contemporary opera. "Well, Madame," replied the Gascon genius, "yesterday I did go to the Opéra to hear a performance of *Armide*. I might be able to remember some of it." Salieri then sat down to play and accompanied Garat in every solo from *Armide*. Marie Antoinette was delighted. She gave Garat her hand to kiss, with the words "We shall meet again, Monsieur."

But it was not only the queen who succumbed to the attractions of what was deemed "natural" in music and the arts. Elegant simplicity was becoming fashionable. This was the age of Rousseau and pre-Romanticism, a reaction against the classicism of the seventeenth century and the era of Louis XV; against formality, luxury, elaborate clothes and etiquette. But although Marie Antoinette was more advanced than most, her wish to substitute gradually the simplicity of Viennese customs for those of Versailles did her more harm than she could possibly have foreseen. She drove herself in her cabriolet, fast and skillfully; but that a Queen of France should travel around so informally was unprecedented. Some of her breaches of the established form did become accepted patterns of behavior at court. She even enthusiastically applauded a famous dancer in the presence of the king—something that had never been done before—and thereafter audiences followed her lead.

When reminded what the previous queen, Marie Leczinska, used or used not to do, Marie Antoinette would reply, "Manage these matters as you wish, but do not imagine that a queen, born an archduchess of Austria, can give so much interest and enthusiasm to them as a Polish princess who became Queen of France."

The best example of Marie Antoinette's true self, her tastes and pleasures, was the Petit Trianon. As dauphine she had dearly longed for a place of her own in the country, and as soon as his grandfather died Louis gave her this miniature palace. France's greatest eighteenth-century architect, Ange-Jacques Gabriel, had built the Petit Trianon in the park at Versailles in the 1760s. It was his masterpiece, and had been the favorite home of Louis XV and Mme du Barry. A few minutes' ride or an easy walk from Versailles, the miniature palace became Marie Antoinette's retreat and escape from the formality and constrictions of life as queen.

When the king presented her with this exquisite house, he is reputed to have said, "You love flowers. I have a whole bouquet to give you: the Petit Trianon." She did indeed adore flowers, filling her apartments each day with fresh hyacinths, tulips and irises supplied by the gardeners of Versailles, as well as her favorite roses from the gardens of the Petit Trianon. She wrote proudly to her mother of the many varieties she grew and of the experts who would come to study them. Her enjoyment of flowers also led to the rejection by fashionable Frenchwomen of the heavier Eastern perfumes in favor of natural scents, often distilled from violets and roses.

At the Petit Trianon, Marie Antoinette decided to create a fine library. Never interested in books when she was dauphine, she now filled her library with her own choice of authors: Voltaire, Rousseau, Montesquieu, Marivaux and Diderot from among the French, and foreign writers such as Cervantes, Fielding, Swift and Goethe. Eventually she built up a library of over 2,000 volumes, over half of them novels or plays—a choice her mother found hardly suitable for the education of a sovereign. The books were bound in calf leather, inscribed on the front with the queen's arms and on the back with the letters C.T. (Château de Trianon) surmounted by a crown.

But the queen's first concern in her new home was to transform the garden. To care for her lawns, which she wanted as smooth and close-cut as the lawns of England, she brought in Sir John Eggleton, on the recommendation of Lord Southampton. He seems not to have been a great success, for Thomas Blaikie, Marie Antoinette's Scottish gardener, noted with relish that Eggleton "was soon lost and returned in disgrace to England, as he was a Man of no Genius."

Blaikie, however, did not totally approve of the queen's own tastes and changes at the Petit Trianon. Her inspiration came partly from the *Dissertation on Oriental Gardening* by Sir William Chambers, who designed the famous Pagoda at Kew. Once in charge of the Petit Trianon, Marie Antoinette did not hesitate to move its renowned botanic garden elsewhere, in order to make way for a new "Anglo-Chinese garden" on the model advocated by Chambers, thus partly destroying what Blaikie recognized as a valuable collection of "rare and curious plants."

The queen's Rousseauesque delight in country pleasures was fired by a group of rustic cottages she saw at Ermenonville. Gabriel's successor as court architect, Richard Mique, assisted by Hubert Robert, was commissioned to design a similar *hameau* for the Petit Trianon. Mique created for her a hamlet infinitely superior to the one at Ermenonville, with picturesque irregular roofs and exposed beams. A herdsman and his oxen and cows were added, as well as a water mill with the wheel turned by an artificial river, a barn, a dovecot, a gardener's cottage and a dairy. The queen and her friends could now live the life of country-folk, making butter and cheese from the milk of Swiss cows on her model farm by the lake. Mique also built her a romantic, mysterious grotto, carpeted with moss and with a stream flowing through it. The Belvedere, a summerhouse on the shores of the lake, was his expression of the queen's liking for what she imagined was Roman simplicity. He also created at the Petit Trianon a superbly delicate circular Temple of Love.

An example of the unjust criticism to which she was continually subjected is that Marie Antoinette's enemies dubbed these creative experiments in the English style and in innovative French architecture her *Petit Vienne,* or "little Vienna." It was Richard Mique who also built here the theater in which the queen indulged her much-criticized passion for acting. Even at the Petit Trianon, the queen failed to escape from the malicious tongues of her enemies.

Palaces and the Decorative Arts

Marie Antoinette's love of the Trianon can perhaps be even better understood when compared with the lack of comfort and coziness in her apartments at Versailles. According to Tobias Smollett, "Notwithstanding the gay disposition of the French, their homes are all gloomy. In spite of the ornaments that have been lavished on Versailles it is a dismal habitation. The apartments are dark, ill furnished, dirty and unprincely . . . a fantastic composition of magnificence and littleness, taste and foppery. . . ." And Mrs. Thrale had this to say: "However richly the Apartments may be furnished—they never are made convenient. The Queen for example has only two Rooms in any of her Houses—a Bed Chamber & a Drawing Room—in the first She sleeps, dresses, prays, chats, sees her Sisters or any other Person who is admitted to Intimacy, & lives by what I can understand in a Bustle hardly to be supported all the Morning long. She has no second Room to run to for Solitude, nor even a Closet to put her Close Stool in, which always stands by the Bedside. . . ." Dr. Johnson, on the other hand, described the rooms at the Trianon as "small, fit to soothe the imagination with privacy": no wonder Marie Antoinette loved it there.

But her preferences can best be judged by her achievements at Versailles, her main residence. Marie Antoinette's taste never veered from the geometrical or antique style characteristic of the Louis XVI period. The heavy formal decorations of Louis XIV and Louis XV were removed or remodelled. She loved the warm texture of carved woodwork and replaced stucco or marble facings with panelling painted pale blue or pale green, never the pale gray overpainting one sees so often today. For her curtains and furniture coverings she preferred white satin or white *gros de Tours*. Tapestries and marble busts were taken away and re-placed by slender and elegant furniture, richly upholstered. She hated the tortuous furniture styles of her predecessors as much as she hated austerity and large, monotonous areas. She hung looking glasses in dark recesses and despite the quantity of trimmings on her curtains and up-holstery and of ormolu on the furniture, the resulting effect was light, delicate and elegant. Pierre Mignard's delightful tapestries representing *The Four Seasons* replaced those depicting *The Fruits of War*.

Although she was accused of having spent vast amounts on her build-ings, Marie Antoinette did not, in fact, have a single large mansion built for herself during her fifteen-year reign. All that was built had been planned and decided on during the reign of Louis XV. But she did indulge with great enthusiasm in the strange eighteenth-century passion for tem-porary buildings—a combination of stage sets and prefabricated rooms and buildings. The queen had several houses which could be removed, re-constructed and demolished at will—with tapestries used to cover joins in the woodwork. These houses were so large and ingeniously con-structed that three of them could be transformed into a huge theater ca-pable of seating 500 spectators. At Saint-Cloud she also had a theater which could be completely dismantled. But like most of her contempo-raries, the queen had a passion for acquiring and arranging furniture and for decoration.

The Louis XVI style, characterized by its delicate and flowing de-sign, was totally dominated by Marie Antoinette, not only because of her taste and originality of choice but also because of her willingness to spend. Still, the new style evolved rather slowly in the early years of the new reign. The new themes for sculpture and carving—arabesques and antique ornaments, cameos, flowers, garlands and swags, trophies, ar-rows and quills—were all the inspiration of Versailles and the queen. (After the Revolution, without Marie Antoinette and Versailles, the style withered and diffused to become the Directoire.) With the queen's influence, flowers, landscapes, and mythological and pastoral subjects were the most frequently used decorative motifs. Furniture shapes were linear, with flat surfaces decorated with lacquer, parquetry or mar-quetry of the highest quality, and corners protected by ormolu cast in classical forms. Ormolu was also used to ornament friezes in the shape of leaf scrolls, flower swags, goats and putti, classical moldings and wave patterns. The incredibly high quality of the furniture made during her time was the result of a century of enthusiasts perfecting their taste—and the skill of generations of craftsmen. Their guilds were so tight with traditions so solid that they almost represented a closed society, and these master craftsmen and their families developed their manual skills to a degree not known again after the Revolution.

It is true that with her mother's encouragement, Marie Antoinette favored German craftsmen. But although some of the greatest cabinet-makers working for the royal palaces were Germans (Oeben and Riesener were both elected *ébenistes du roi*; Roentgen even had a special title created for him; and Weisweiller worked for Marie Antoinette at Saint-Cloud), this Teutonic influx in fact occurred earlier in the century. It is a matter of speculation why rich clients preferred German cabinet-makers to their French counterparts, but possibly they were less bound by the French guild traditions and restrictions and so more receptive of new ideas and better able to exploit the fashionable craving for novelty. It was a period when scientific discoveries and research were so highly prized that patrons had an unrestrained appetite for innovation. Every piece was individual and adapted to the patron's taste. Marie Antoinette inspired experiments in the use of different woods from all parts of the world—mahogany, kingwood, amboyna, cayenne wood, lemonwood, thuya, Brazilian rosewood, coral for inlay, ebony and violet-colored wood. Chinese and Japanese lacquer work was in demand as well as inlays of mother-of-pearl, copper and silver. (Marie Antoinette had always loved lacquered furniture and objects and was left a great number of pieces by her mother, which decorated her private apartments.) But the most popular novelty in furniture inspired by the queen was the insertion of Sèvres porcelain plaques on the flat surfaces.

From 1759 the king was the sole proprietor of the Sèvres factory, and as a result had a considerable influence on the style of the objects manufactured. Both Louis XV and Louis XVI took a personal interest in the administration and management and themselves placed numerous orders for their own use and as gifts. Marie Antoinette took a particular interest and placed the factory under her protection. Its projects were known as "*porcelaine de la reine.*" They also produced jugs modelled on Etruscan vases for the queen's dairies, often decorated with one of her favorite motifs—a cornflower sprig in green, blue or pink.

Furniture, like clothes, was made to measure; the wishes of the patron were fulfilled and invention was tailored to his or her requirements. Many pieces were invented for the queen: desks that could be changed into writing or reading tables; tables for each new game—rectangular for backgammon, circular for *brélan,* square for quadrille; a painting table with a tray for bottles and paints; and endless mechanical tables made with prodigious care to conceal their many functions. For her first confinement she had a table made so she could have meals in bed. Its height could be adjusted by touching a button. A second button converted it into a toilette table and a third into a writing table. (This must have been a favorite piece as she took it with her to the Tuileries.) Chairs and sofas were invented to suit personal needs—there was the armchair *à la reine* with a flat back; the "cabriolet" armchair with the back curving slightly inward and molded to the shape of the body; the "shepherdess" chair with a cushion; or the "convenience armchair" with an adjustable back to change the angle. Even toilette articles that were the least fit to be seen were still extremely refined—chamberpots were carefully fashioned in sculpted silver or delicately painted porcelain.

Because of Marie Antoinette's particular love of creating warm and luxuriously appointed interiors by using hangings and curtains, the French textile manufacturers found in her a true patron. But as well as the extraordinarily beautiful and inventive designs and textures produced at the Lyons silk factories, Marie Antoinette also loved printed linens—the *toiles de Jouy.* Painters created charming designs using cameos of country life, which became a feature of the decorations at Trianon. In her unique position Marie Antoinette was able to decorate her palaces for herself as Queen of France on the one hand and enjoy and play the role of a country squire's lady in her hamlet at Trianon on the other. Nothing used by a queen could be ordinary; and in Marie Antoinette's time, when decoration was possibly at its most costly, great expense was unavoidably caused by the slavish devotion given to each detail of a piece of furniture, a curtain, or any other object.

Although Marie Antoinette visited the Salon and inspected the great exhibitions, she did not single out the great painters nor did she buy masterpieces for the royal collections. Her tastes were more inclined toward good portraitists like Madame Vigée-Lebrun and decorative painters, and she particularly liked still-lifes. The most brilliant painter of this period and its most faithful witness was Jean Honoré Fragonard. His paintings seem to represent the ultimate definition of happiness at this time—paintings with anecdotal subjects with either very little meaning or importance—pretexts more than subjects. In Fragonard's world, life was a play with actors and spectators and Marie Antoinette was his star. Harsh reality was carefully avoided—life was amusing and gay. The queen and her companions were depicted as an integral part of an enchanted landscape, themselves the flowers among the over-whelming foliage, carefree and enjoying the present without a thought for the future. The world as Fragonard painted it was as Marie Antoinette wished to live it. She was the perfect inspiration for his genius, even though this romantic idyllic world could be experienced by so very few.

Despite her capriciousness, the queen's taste was sure and on the whole she employed the same craftsmen. She rarely used strong colors in her interiors (or her clothes), preferring white satin or coarse linen in green, lilac and blue. (Despite this, her servants' livery was red edged with silver.) All the craftsmen who worked for her had first to submit watercolors or sometimes small models to help her to decide or to make changes. It was in her own apartments that Marie Antoinette was at last able to exercise her taste for light and gaiety, nature and fantasy.

As Louis was passionately fond of the chase, Marie Antoinette took to following the hunt on horseback. In this too she broke with tradition as the ladies of the court always followed in coaches. She rode astride until her mother, hearing of this, insisted she ride sidesaddle as riding astride was thought to prevent pregnancy. Mrs. Thrale wrote,

> This morning we drove into the Forest . . . to see the Queen ride on Horseback. We were early enough to see her mount, which was not done as in England by a Man's hand, but the right foot is fixed in the Stirrup first & then drawn out again when the Lady is on her Saddle. The Horse on which the Queen rode was neither hand-some nor gentle, he was however confined with Martingales etc & richly caparison'd with blue Velvet and Silver Embroidery.

When Marie Antoinette left Vienna for her new life in France, she not only bade a tearful farewell to her mother and sisters, but also to her beloved pug dog, which she afterward sent for. The Austrian ambassador, comté de Mercy-Argenteau, noted, "Madame la Dauphine loves dogs very much, she has two already, which are unfortunately extremely unclean." She then asked him to procure her another one from Vienna. Mercy replied that doubtless one could be brought by the courier! When the queen left her prison cell for the guillotine, a new prisoner, the Pope's representative in Paris, was soon installed in her place. He noted in his memoirs that a little dog came into the room: "It is the Queen's pug; Richard, the Conciergerie guard, has given him a home. He comes to smell his mistress's bed. I have seen him do this every morning for three whole months."

Scandals and Their Consequences

As she had so many enemies, it is remarkable that Marie Antoinette succeeded in keeping relatively secret a liaison that they would undoubtedly have exploited to the full had it become public knowledge. Her relationship with her husband had never been of an intimate physical nature. "We have slept apart for a long time now," she wrote to her mother. "It is the usual custom here between man and wife, and I should not consider myself justified in pressing the king in a matter which goes very much against his way of life and personal tastes." Maria Theresa replied, "I confess that I did not know for certain that you did not sleep together; I only guessed. I must accept that what you tell me is right. Even so, I should have liked it better if you could have lived in the German way and enjoyed that certain intimacy which comes of being together." But then, Maria Theresa's own marriage had been a rare thing in royal circles: a love match.

Three years after this exchange of letters, Count Axel Fersen came to Paris. The son of one of the most powerful men in Sweden, Fersen was first presented to Marie Antoinette when he was finishing his education in Paris. They were the same age. He was well received at court and after his departure the Swedish ambassador reported that "of all the Swedes who have been here in my time, he is the one who has been best received in high society."

After an absence of four years, Fersen returned to France with the intention of distinguishing himself in the war against Great Britain. The queen greeted him like an old friend. As her intimates were beginning to notice her fascination with this handsome young Swedish officer, Fersen enlisted for duty in the French army that was fighting for American independence. Though dashing and courageous, even he must have been surprised at the speed of his promotion. Four years later he returned to France, adamantly resisted all pressure from his father to marry, and decided to settle in Paris. In a letter to his sister he confessed, "I cannot belong to the only person I would wish to, the only person who really loves me, and so I do not wish to belong to anyone."

Axel Fersen took care never to compromise the queen, writing to her as "Joséphine" and keeping a record of his letters in case any went astray. He bought a large house in Paris where they sometimes met, and she altered a number of small rooms in her apartments at Versailles, almost certainly to make it easier for Fersen to stay there. Inevitably censorious tongues spotted the affair. Louis XVI's minister, Saint-Priest, wrote in his memoirs: "Fersen would go riding three or four times a week in the park in the direction of the Petit Trianon; the queen, alone, did so too; and these rendezvous caused a public scandal, in spite of the modesty and reserve of the favorite, who was never outwardly remiss in any respect."

However, according to Saint-Priest, "Marie Antoinette had found the means of getting him [the king] to accept the liaison with Count Fersen." There is no doubt that the queen retained both her husband's affection and his confidence, clearly refusing to compromise her family life in spite of her relationship with the Swedish count. At the same time, Louis was said to be markedly lacking in attention to his wife, and when a son was born after she and Fersen had seen a great deal of each other, the king noted in his diary: "The Queen delivered of the Duke of Normandy; everything went off as in the case of my son." In fact the only other time Louis XVI referred to this child as "my son" was in prison, shortly before his death.

Even at the end of 1789, when the palace of Versailles was surrounded and occupied by a hostile crowd, Fersen still contrived to spend the night in the queen's private apartments. The next morning Marie Antoinette appeared on the balcony to face the armed and violent rabble. Along with a few other faithful friends, Axel Fersen tried to save the royal family and took part in their attempted flight to Varennes. But all his efforts failed, and following the queen's death he returned to Sweden. He never married, and after a brilliant career at the Swedish court, he too met a violent death, stoned by a hostile mob.

Far more damaging to Marie Antoinette's reputation was the disastrous "Affair of the Diamond Necklace." She had a passion for jewelry. On her marriage she was delighted to receive from Louis XV a casket containing the jewels of the Queens of France and, as a personal present, a fabulous set of diamonds. She was also given the famous collar of pearls (the smallest of which was "as large as a filibert"), brought to France by Anne of Austria, and from Vienna she brought her own considerable treasure of white diamonds.

Although her taste in jewelry was considered simple by the standards of the age, she could not resist beautiful pieces. In 1776 she bought on impulse a pair of earrings costing 348,000 livres (perhaps $450,000 today)—which the unfortunate Louis had to pay off over the next six years out of his personal income. Another time she spent 162,000 livres on diamond bracelets. Love of exquisite jewelry landed Marie Antoinette in one of the most bizarre scandals of the eighteenth century.

Well aware of the queen's weakness for fine jewels, the court jeweler used intermediaries to bring her those he wished her to buy. Having successfully persuaded her to accept the earrings and bracelets, he hoped, now that Louis XVI had paid off her other debts, to sell Marie Antoinette a necklace he had made for the aging Louis XV to give to his mistress Mme du Barry. It was a *rivière* of diamonds of incomparable quality. Unfortunately, the court jeweler chose as intermediary an unscrupulous courtesan, Mme de la Motte-Valois, who wanted only to steal and sell the diamonds for herself, and she managed to embroil the unwitting Cardinal de Rohan in her plot. At odds with the queen since her arrival in France, the cardinal now hoped to win his way into her favor. In January 1785, without Marie Antoinette's knowledge, he bought on her behalf the celebrated diamond necklace. The price was 1,600,000 francs (perhaps the equivalent of $2,000,000 today). Mme de la Motte-Valois was to bring the necklace to the queen, but instead she disappeared with the diamonds. The jeweler demanded his money and the cardinal and the queen had to answer for it.

Cardinal de Rohan had clearly committed *lèse-majesté;* nor could there have been any doubt that Marie Antoinette had been entirely ignorant of the plot, and was innocent. And yet the scandal was immense. The cardinal, fully robed, was transported to the Bastille. Foolishly, the queen insisted not on his banishment but on a trial, and as it dragged on, all France took sides. Amazingly, Cardinal de Rohan was acquitted. But Mme de la Motte-Valois was not so fortunate. The cardinal was merely banished for his foolishness; she was condemned to be whipped and branded. As fourteen warders held her down for branding, she struggled so violently that the red-hot iron burned into her breast instead of her shoulder.

In declaring the cardinal to be a duped and innocent victim, the French parlement indirectly condemned the queen. The clear implication was that she had used unorthodox, even unscrupulous means to get her hands on coveted jewelry. Her reputation, her dignity as queen, her honor as a woman were all lost. Marie Antoinette received the news of the cardinal's acquittal as an insufferable blow. For the first time—frivolous, though sensitive as she was—she became aware of her own unpopularity, and of the extreme danger of her position. "Come and weep with me; come and console my spirit," she wrote to a friend. "The verdict just given is a frightful insult. I am bathed in tears, grief and despair." It was the beginning of the end. On July 14, 1789, the mobs stormed the Bastille. Three years later, the monarchy was brought down. The brief life that remained to Marie Antoinette was spent incarcerated in the jails of Paris. The following January, her husband was guillotined on the orders of the National Convention.

In August 1793, Marie Antoinette was placed in solitary confinement, except for her dog, in the Conciergerie. After eight weeks of humiliation, on October 14, 1793, she was condemned to death by the Revolutionary Tribunal. She managed to obtain two candles, a pen and ink and a sheet of paper. To her sister-in-law she wrote that she was condemned not so much to the horrible death reserved for criminals as to rejoining her husband, and she sent a blessing to her children. She died, she wrote, in the one Catholic, Apostolic and Roman faith: "Adieu, my good and tender sister. May this letter reach you. Think of me always. I embrace you with my whole heart, as I embrace my poor, dear children. My God, how heartbreaking it is to leave them for ever! Adieu. Adieu."

At her trial she was indicted as Marie Antoinette d'Autriche, widow of Louis Capet. In October 1793, nine months after her husband, she went to the guillotine in a tumbrel. And on her death certificate they wrote: "Marie Antoinette Lorraine d'Autriche."

3

Maria Carolina

—◦•◦◦•◦—

ARCHDUCHESS OF AUSTRIA/QUEEN OF NAPLES
AND THE TWO SICILIES

1752–1814

Austria

M aria Carolina, thirteenth child of the Empress Maria Theresa of Austria and the Emperor Francis I, became Queen of Naples only because of the untimely deaths of two of her sisters, both previously intended for the hand of her husband. Ferdinand of Naples was initially betrothed to the empress's eleventh daughter, Maria Johanna, who died of smallpox. At his request Maria Theresa had speedily arranged a substitute bride, another daughter, Maria Josephina.

A most bizarre incident then occurred. During the wedding celebrations of his son the Archduke Leopold, the Emperor Francis, who was thought to be in excellent health, fell down with an attack of apoplexy and died in Leopold's arms. The empress was deeply distressed, and a pall descended on the atmosphere of the court. A year passed and still his mother was in solemn mourning, when her son Joseph, now the emperor, lost his young wife through smallpox. She had not been beautiful or intelligent, neither the people nor for that matter her husband had loved her, and she was not greatly mourned. Nonetheless the empress insisted that court procedure be properly followed, and Maria Josephina was sent to pray before the dead woman's tomb before leaving Vienna to marry the King of Naples.

Terrified of contagion, she was even more frightened of disobeying her mother, and so she descended into the crypt. Two weeks later, Maria Josephina died of smallpox. The king immediately asked for yet another of Maria Theresa's daughters for his bride, and as the wedding arrangements were well advanced, a few weeks later the empress sent Maria Carolina.

The civilized world considered Maria Theresa to be its most enlightened monarch. Consequently it was assumed that her many children were of the same stamp. Her court in Vienna was cultured, sophisticated and—outwardly—moral. The church played an important part in the lives of the monarch and the people, and Maria Theresa expected her many children to follow her principles and her example on whatever throne she placed them. Conscious of and continually complaining about her own inadequate education, she made sure that her sons were better taught. Strangely enough, she saw no reason to give her daughters a better education than her own—their duty was to cultivate docility. "They are born to obey," she said, "and must learn to do so in good time."

But this group of high-spirited, robust young archduchesses had other ideas. They terrorized their governesses, ran riot during dancing and music lessons, and thoroughly enjoyed their childhood. Until she was fifteen Maria Carolina was brought up with her sister Maria Antonia (the future Marie Antoinette), three years her junior. Their attachment for one another was deep and lasted throughout their lives. As children they were full of mischief and intrigues, and their mother considered their closeness dangerous. "I warn you that you will be totally separated from your sister Antonia," she threatened Maria Carolina, and she deplored the young girls' "secrets," which she considered to be idle gossip about neighbors, family and court ladies. Despite her strictures their friendship was not broken, and even after her marriage Maria Carolina would still beg her old governess to write and tell her of "the little events concerning my sister Antonia—what she says, what she does, and almost what she thinks." A few months later she wrote, "Tell my sister that I love her extremely."

Carolina may have been brought up by her mother to follow a strict moral code, lectured on saying her prayers and attending to her lessons, obeying her governess and not playing tricks on her little sister; but this same mother allowed her sixteen-year-old daughter to preside as queen over the most licentious court in southern Europe. And yet, the education that the archduchess did receive was still far superior to that of most women of the time and of a much higher standard of knowledge and culture than Carolina was to find in Naples.

Nor did this young archduchess relish the thought of being packed off there anyway, declaring that they might as well have thrown her into the sea. It was no secret her future husband was a boorish, if merry, oddity.

King Ferdinand was tall for his age, with a fine head, blue eyes, very white skin and gentle features. His body was covered in herpes, a condition his doctors considered to be indicative of good health! He had a talent for mechanics, but his tutors' sole preoccupation seemed to be not their pupil's mind but his health—and his constitution was indeed robust.

Given wise tuition his few talents might have had a chance to develop, but these same tutors were unfortunately willing only to encourage the young king in his pleasures, keeping him away from those who might cultivate his mind. Their pupil, in consequence, wasted his time with servant boys and illiterates of his own age. He so disliked reading and writing that he had a stamp made of his signature and entrusted it to his prime minister, Bernardo Tanucci.

Ferdinand was high-spirited and alert, with a sharp eye, especially for the absurd. But his manners and habits were uncouth; he was rowdy at table; and for society he preferred what was termed "rough merriment." A later prime minister of Naples, Sir John Acton,* described him as "a good sort of man, because nature has not supplied him with the faculties necessary to make a bad one." Ferdinand remained a boisterous young man, with hardly any sense of decorum or responsibility, and sadly, neither age nor experience matured him. His only real interests throughout his life were hunting and fishing. Maria Josephina's sudden death disagreeably obliged him to remain in the palace on the day he received the news, and he found himself forced to occupy himself indoors. First he played billiards. Then he passed the time playing leapfrog

---

*A magnetic soldier-sailor of fortune sent to Naples by Maria Carolina's brother Leopold. His wise decisions led to his rise in power until he became prime minister.

and performing other feats of agility. Finally someone suggested that the company celebrate Maria Josephina's funeral. Far from being shocked, the "bereaved" king liked the idea.

The British envoy in Naples, Sir William Hamilton, called on Ferdinand to offer his condolences on the death of his fiancée and witnessed an extraordinary sight. One of the young chamberlains, dressed as the late archduchess, had been laid out on an open bier in the Neapolitan fashion. His face and hands had been marked with chocolate drops representing the smallpox pustules. As the shocked envoy watched, the mock funeral procession passed slowly through the principal apartments of the palace, with Ferdinand acting convincingly the part of the chief mourner.

This was the man to whom Maria Carolina was so precipitately betrothed. For the next twenty years she ruled Naples in all but name, initiating wise reforms and striving to exterminate corruption. Then came the French Revolution, which destroyed her beloved sister Marie Antoinette, and with that cruel death, Maria Carolina lost her reason.

Naples

No other European city had been ruled by so varied a succession of foreign dynasties: Greek, Roman, Norman, Hohenstaufen, Angevin, Aragonese and Spanish Bourbon. In 1733 France, Spain and Sardinia-Savoy agreed that the Spanish prince Don Carlos de Borbon should rule Naples and Sicily, provided that they could be conquered for him. Don Carlos defeated Austria, and in 1738 acquired not only the two kingdoms but also Presidi, a former Habsburg possession on the coast of Tuscany.

Spain was virtually the only European power untouched by the classical revival in art: the nude, for example, never appeared in Spanish paintings. Intolerance toward Moors and Jews and 150 years of dominance in the Peninsula had throttled all that was best in the Italian Renaissance. Cultural life in the two kingdoms had been reduced to music and opera. And yet the Neapolitans welcomed the Spaniard who took the title Charles III, as he brought independence to the kingdom and carefully reformed the political and administrative system. He endowed splendid buildings, commissioning architects of the caliber of Vanvitelli and Fuga. The palaces of Capodimonte, Pórtici and especially the great

Baroque Palazzo Reale at Caserta (which is bigger than Versailles) transformed Naples. Squares were named Piazza Dante and Piazza Plebiscite. The university was modernized, and a national library and an archeological museum were established. It was here that Carlos exhibited the Farnese collections he had inherited from Parma. Here too were displayed the pick of the treasures from newly excavated Pompeii and Herculaneum. The San Carlo Theater was built, where works by composers such as Piccini, Galuppi and Paisiello were performed.

With public life now glorified, private life also improved. Houses were more conveniently furnished and the use of glass in windows became commonplace. Naples became once more a truly royal capital, benignly ruled by its king with the aid of his great minister Bernardo Tanucci. Then in 1759 Charles III unexpectedly succeeded to the throne of Spain. In accord with the constitution, he reluctantly renounced his Italian possessions in favor of his third son, Ferdinand. The new king's titles were complicated: he was Ferdinand IV of Naples and Ferdinand III of Sicily, and in 1816 he became Ferdinand I of the Two Sicilies. Initially, the boy-king was judged too young to rule Naples and a regency council, controlled by Bernardo Tanucci and Domenico Cattaneo, held power until he came of age at sixteen. Until then, the regency council continued with the reforms instigated by Charles III. When the king came of age in 1767, these reforms abruptly ceased, even though the power remained in the hands of Tanucci.

The population of Naples at this time was around 400,000, making it the fourth largest city in Europe—equal with Madrid after London, Paris and Istanbul. For all its size, Naples was without doubt among the most backward countries in western Europe. It had a peasant economy exporting chiefly olive oil, and its wealth was concentrated among the nobility, who constituted no more than 2 percent of the people. Even these aristocrats were poorer than their English or French counterparts, furnishing their palaces with pictures and little else. The differences between the classes were astonishing—the aristocracy and the clergy living in highly privileged splendor, and the lower classes desperately poor, with 90 percent of the population illiterate. The formidable city populace, known as the *lazzaroni*, provided foreign visitors with as much color and fascination in Naples as did Vesuvius and Pompeii. Though regarded by many as ragged vermin, they needed only discriminating leadership to draw out their qualities.

When Maria Carolina's brother, the Austrian emperor, visited Ferdinand's court he was astounded by the contrast between this splendor and squalor: "The palace of Naples contains five or six frescoed and marbled rooms filled with chickens, pigeons, ducks, geese, partridges, quails, birds of all sorts, canaries, dogs and even cages full of rats and mice, which the king occasionally sets free and enjoys the pleasure of chasing." The beautiful marbled staircases were cluttered with gamekeepers, whippers-in and beaters, all of them addressed by the king with the nicknames he had given them.

This was to be the domain of the young Austrian archduchess. Having inherited the trousseau of one hundred dresses made in Paris for her two dead sisters, Maria Carolina left Vienna for Florence in a travelling dress of blue and gold. On April 7, 1768, she had married Ferdinand by proxy in the Church of the Augustines in Vienna, with her brother representing her husband. At Florence she bade a tearful farewell to her Austrian suite, and accompanied by her brother Leopold, Grand Duke of Tuscany, she set out for her new country. At Poztella, the first Neapolitan town on her route, Maria Carolina saw her husband for the first time.

Her initial response to married life was decidedly unfavorable. "It is desperation," she lamented; "one suffers a martyrdom made all the worst because one must appear pleased." She was depressed, unhappy and homesick. As for Ferdinand, asked on the morning after his wedding night how he liked his new queen, he ungallantly replied, "She sleeps like the dead and sweats like a pig."

Maria Carolina soon decided to change his mind. She reconciled herself to married life and set out to win her husband's affection. In her self-possessed way, she began first to flatter and then to dominate him. If the king displeased her, she would shut him out of her rooms, and allow him back only if he pleaded and begged for forgiveness. He was no match for his queen and her influence over him grew daily. Eventually Maria Carolina became amused rather than depressed by Ferdinand's eccentric habits, referring to him as "a really nice halfwit" (ein recht guter Narr).

Lady Anne Millar saw Maria Carolina at the age of twenty and noticed that she was developing a physical beauty that she used to charm
Ferdinand—and others. She saw a beautiful woman with "the finest and
most transparent complexion I ever saw." Maria Carolina's hair was
glossy light chestnut, her eyebrows darker than her hair. Her eyes were
large, brilliant and dark blue. Her nose inclined to aquiline, her mouth
was small, her teeth were white and even, framed with very red lips
(which were, Lady Anne Miller reported, "not of the Austrian thick-
ness"). She had dimples in her cheeks when she smiled. She was "just
plump enough not to appear lean," with a long neck, an easy deport-
ment, a majestic walk and a graceful attitude and action.

Willful, impetuous, impulsive, Maria Carolina was also convinced
that she was born to rule. The daughter of a great empress, the sister of
the co-regent of Habsburg realms, she expected to play a part in world
affairs. If she could not enlarge the Kingdom of Naples, at least she
could increase its importance.

A year after his sister's marriage to Ferdinand, the Emperor Joseph
visited Naples and decided that the king was "an indefinable being." He
judged that "Even if he had not been neglected in the past, he could
never have reached distinction." But he added a new note to the familiar
tune: he perceived that Ferdinand was deeply in love with his sister, and
that she was becoming increasingly aware of her growing influence.
"Dazzled by the grandeur of the court, the honors paid to her, the
beauty of the country and the freedom she enjoys, she will become
more and more accustomed to it," he reported. "I am quite at ease
about her fate."

He found his sister a model of intelligence and poise. "She has not
the slightest germ of coquetry or desire to fascinate, either with her fa-
miliars (although she has frequent opportunities, being surrounded by
young people) or in her dress, which is very simple and devoid of affectation," he reported. He noticed that she always wore a scarf and was
only very slightly décolleté. Her skirts were so long that you could not
even see the tip of her foot. At balls she wore a hat in the English fashion, or a plume in her hair.

The king had wanted her to display more bosom, but she objected.
Since leaving Vienna she had grown a little plumper, and her arms were
lovely and round, her hands milky, though unfortunately she had devel-

oped the habit of biting the cuticle and tearing it with a pin. Nor was Joseph pleased that she had added to her fluent Italian all sorts of Neapolitan expressions picked up from the king, many of them far from polite, and he urged her to speak the purer language of Tuscany. He wrote to his mother that his sister's behavior in public, apart from a little childishness, was excellent.

Society and the Arts

It was inevitable that Maria Carolina, with her youth, vivacity, intelligence and good looks, should transform the dull court of the Spanish-inspired Tanucci regency. She had culture and she had charm; and she made good use of both.

At the balls she gave in the theater of the Palazzo Reale, Maria Carolina would be unmasked in her box, but once she had descended into the pit, everyone wore a black mask covering half the face. Here she insisted that etiquette be relaxed, and those on the floor were permitted to dance at the same time as the king and queen. Even so, they danced at their majesties' personal invitation, and many of the nobility up to the rank of duke were only allowed to watch the dancing from their boxes. Maria Carolina introduced a fashion for English country dances, of which there were always three or four sets, followed by minuets.

When the queen entertained in her palace at Caserta, here too there was a marked relaxation in etiquette. If when supper was announced she was at the other end of the room, she might well be the last to enter the supper room. Chairs would be placed against the walls, with a double row, back to back, down the center. As Spanish etiquette debarred anyone from sitting down at the king's table, tables were simply done away with.

The food was brought round by the best-looking of the king's guardsmen, who served supper with military precision. The first would carry a basket with napkins, which a second would spread on the lap of a guest. The next officer brought a basket of silver plates. Then came a basket with knives and forks, followed by an officer carrying a great *pasticcio* of macaroni, cheese and butter. Alongside him a carver armed with a knife a foot long would cut a large slice of pie, to be placed on the lap of each seated guest. Lastly a soldier would appear with an empty basket and take away all the dirty plates. This procedure would be repeated for all the various courses, and the same routine would apply to the drinks.

After the pasta came various fish dishes, ragouts, game, fried and baked meats and pies. The desserts were carried by two soldiers on large serving platters, with pyramids of sweetmeats, biscuits, iced chocolate, and a great variety of ices, iced fruits and creams.

The queen herself ate very little, and only from dishes especially prepared for her by her Austrian cook. This wretched cook was later caught stealing the eggs of the king's pheasants (which she thought was reasonable enough) and escaped Ferdinand's wrath only because the queen covered up for her.

Maria Carolina introduced the drinking of coffee in a special room, just as her sister Marie Antoinette did at Marly and the Trianon. These coffee rooms with their separate tables were exact copies of the Viennese coffeehouses, and she dressed the footmen as waiters, in white hats and jackets.

Austrian influence crept into the royal palaces. Only German was spoken in the queen's antechamber, and all her servants were Austrian or German. Maria Carolina had at least forty-five German maids who performed the function of pages and valets. The queen appointed Johann Tischbein as head of the Academy of Painting, and together with Philip Hackert, another German who had been court painter to Ferdinand, carried out decorations at her palaces. The queen liked Hackert so much that she appointed him drawing master to her daughters, often inviting him to come in the evenings just to talk and instruct them. Ferdinand became very attached to Hackert and asked his advice about the restoration of his Farnese collections, as well as commissioning from him military and sporting works. Once the king gave the painter a gold snuff box, which prompted the queen to remark, "I fear he is at the end of his tether, for he never gives presents." She was lavish with her gifts, particularly snuff boxes, and was often accused of spending far too much on them.

Much of the palace furniture was made by Germans. Although later in her reign Maria Carolina opted for the classical revival, her early influence on the decor of the palaces was Austrian rococo. Her bathroom and the adjoining dressing room at Caserta are a delicious confection of stucco putti, flower swags, urns and gilded shells—all against ceilings of pale blue skies.

With the queen's encouragement German painters flocked to Naples. Tischbein insisted on his pupils studying the nude. He was a friend of Goethe's and also joined Sir William Hamilton's circle, drawing his famous Greek vases. Other painters attracted to the court at Naples were Angelica Kauffmann, Christopher Kniep, Henry Fuger and above all the great Raphael Mengs.

There had been a German influence at the court prior to Maria Carolina's arrival. Her mother-in-law came from Saxony and had brought with her some beautiful pieces of Meissen. This was said to have inspired Charles III to found the porcelain factory at Capodimonte, which produced exquisite work. When he left Naples, Charles completely destroyed the factory, even the furnaces, setting up a new factory in Spain. Familiar with the superb porcelain made at her mother's factory in Vienna, Maria Carolina persuaded Ferdinand to establish one of his own at Pórtici near Herculaneum. Although, sadly, nothing was produced of the quality of the Capodimonte pieces, the excavations at Pompeii did inspire some very pleasing classical revival biscuit ware.

A startling innovation that perhaps more than anything else showed the influence of the queen occurred after the death of Ferdinand's brother from smallpox. Maria Carolina arranged for her brother Leopold's doctor to inoculate herself and her family. Spain disapproved of inoculation on theological grounds; but Maria Carolina—like her sister Marie Antoinette when she had Louis and her children inoculated—had her own way.

Culture and Customs

The Grand Tour passed through Naples and the city captivated everyone. The air was pure and healthy; it was rarely cold and in summer there were refreshing breezes from the sea. The countryside was rich in corn and oil, and the wine (Lachryma Christi) was considered the best in Italy. John George Keysler, famous traveller and fellow of the Royal Society, thought Naples more beautiful than Paris or London, and the streets of Rome and Florence were "mean and contemptible" compared with Neapolitan streets. Stendhal considered the Toledo "the most populous and gayest street in the world," and even Lord Macaulay, who basically disliked everything everywhere, praised the city's vitality and compared it with English ports and cities. "Rome and Pisa are dead and gone: Florence is not dead, but sleepeth; while Naples overflows with life." Goethe thought Naples paradise and wrote, "I scarcely recognize myself. I feel like a different man. Yesterday I said to myself, 'Either you have always been mad, or you are mad now.'" He wanted to stay longer in "this school of light-hearted and happy life, and try to profit from it still more."

To some visitors it was all rather overwhelming: the streets full of urchins and pickpockets, 10,000 prostitutes and 40,000 half-naked *lazzaroni* who once a day would throw off their clothes and bathe in the sea. (Afterward they would walk and sport on the shore quite naked with the acquiescence of the authorities. Exception was ultimately taken, however, when the Prince of San Lorenzo took to sitting stark naked in the Toledo.)

Naples was as filthy as any other Italian town: people relieved themselves indiscriminately in porticoes, colonnades and the courtyards of palaces. The porches and staircases of private houses were used for the same purpose, and those in carriages would stop and get out and mix with pedestrians, all with the same intention.

The Corso provided a dazzling sight to visitors; here the Neapolitans delighted in showing off their splendor. Their coaches were thought by Lady Anne Millar to "exceed in beauty the finest in Paris: they are lined with velvet or satin, fringed with gold or silver." The Neapolitan horses were magnificent: "large, strong, high-spirited, with manes and tails as fine as flax, of a great length, and in waves"; the tops of their manes were ornamented in silk, and white ostrich feathers bobbed on their heads. The harnesses were covered in silver and gilt and sometimes were even made of silk.

Then there was the awesome spectacle of Vesuvius for the visitor; or the ruins of Pompeii; or the magnificently extravagant hospitality of such princes as Francavilla, who would make his pages ("all sweethearts of the prince") dive naked into the sea and swim about in it for the amusement of his guests; or the number and squalor of the servants snoring on the magnificent staircases of the Baroque palaces of the nobility.

Among the foreign visitors there was Casanova; the adventuress Sarah Goudar, the beautiful Irishwoman who had started life as a barmaid, and was educated, refined and transformed by Monsieur Goudar;

and, of course, the Hamiltons. Sir William Hamilton was British envoy in Naples for thirty-six years and became something of an institution. He was the ideal eighteenth-century dilettante and a most generous host, particularly to foreign visitors. Not the least of his attractions was Emma Hart. She was the daughter of a Cheshire blacksmith and, having been Charles Greville's mistress, was acquired by his uncle Sir William as part of the arrangement for settling Greville's debts. The beautiful Emma would pose naked for Hamilton and his friends, adopting her famous "attitudes," a series of *poses plastiques* representing classical figures, to the delight of the company. When Sir William married Emma, the queen graciously received Lady Hamilton since she was particularly eager for an alliance with Great Britain and therefore wished to please the ambassador. Emma fascinated Maria Carolina, and as she was rather indiscreet, the queen was able to learn some useful diplomatic secrets.

In the evenings, the city's restlessness overflowed into the theaters, where audiences were noisy even by Italian standards. The vast theater of San Carlo adjoined the palace and was made up of six tiers of boxes, each containing ten or twelve people. Owners decorated their boxes with silk and backed them with mirrors. These reflected the guests and the many large wax candles held by the statues between one box and the next. The effect was magical, especially when "the queen is present, at which time the ladies of the court, and others, are full dressed, and covered with a profusion of jewels; but the queen outshines them all, not only in magnificence of dress (for that would be nothing extraordinary) but in style and beauty, and gracefulness of air, peculiar to herself." The gentlemen paraded in and out of the boxes elaborately dressed in cut velvet embroidered suits and wearing their swords. The ladies were so covered in diamonds that "they blazed like a constellation. The seams of their gowns were even studded with diamonds," and in their hair they wore "sprays of brilliants, towering on the head like feathers, diamond nets, combs, head-dresses and fringes to the gowns. . . ."

It was the custom to pay visits among the boxes, or shout across the auditorium to friends opposite, even spitting orange peel onto the heads of the people beneath. Talking throughout the performance would cease only when a favorite aria was sung, and if the performance displeased, the artist was loudly booed.

The Neapolitans had a strange way of greeting one another with a very loud "smacking" kiss on both cheeks, which "resounds throughout the room," making quite a noise in the theater as guests moved from box to box. Gentlemen did kiss the ladies' hands but they all considered the English manner of shaking hands "the most hoity toity impudent custom." "Every lady's box is the scene of tea, cards, cavaliers, servants, lapdogs, abbés, scandal and assignations," affirmed William Beckford; and if things began to pall, there were always the gambling rooms, as in most Italian theaters.

When the king and queen were present, people had to be silent; but as the king always withdrew at the beginning of the second act, the audience did not have to suffer for long. Cold supper was served in most boxes, consisting of hams, pies, macaroni and a profusion of cakes and ices.

Italy at this time was setting the standard for European music, particularly in comic opera, and in Naples there was Piccini, who was said more than any other composer of his day to have introduced the softer, lighter, gayer music that led to Mozart.

It was the queen who invited the first company of French actors to visit Naples, and the popular enthusiasm which surrounded their visit even affected the king, who was seen weeping openly at a performance of Voltaire's *Zaïre*.

These were exceptional years of peace and prosperity for Naples—except for the fish and game harried by the king. Hamilton told his life-long friend Nathaniel William Wraxall that at the royal hunting parties he had frequently seen enormous mounds composed entirely of offal or bowels, reaching as high as his head and many feet in circumference.

In general a spirit of tolerance reigned: the university was expanding; scholars were consulted and given posts in the government; and during this period even those who ended up as revolutionaries sang the praises of Ferdinand's "paternal government," never realizing that it was the iron hand in the long white glove that really ruled.

The queen knew her husband had a fetish about women's arms, especially when covered in long white gloves. In order to get whatever she wanted, Maria Carolina had only to stroke her beautifully gloved arm. According to one reliable source, Ferdinand's brain became "exalted" at the sight. "How many affairs of the greatest importance have I seen settled by the queen's care to pull her gloves over her pretty arms while discussing the subject which engrossed her! I have seen the king take notice of this, smile, and grant her wish."

The prime minister Tanucci gloried in the sensation of being indispensable. But after many years of unchallenged power even he underrated the young queen's influence. She seemed too flippant to be taken seriously. Laughing and joking one evening as she stepped off a galley after dining *al fresco*—the king had retired early so as to hunt soon after dawn—she had fallen merrily into the sea with two Austrian brothers. The commander of the royal galleys and several sailors dove in to assist her, but the incident gave rise to malicious gossip. When the king heard of it he was furious, and Tanucci reassured himself that he had little to fear from this high-spirited young woman.

Influence at Court

With her youthful vivacity and aura of Viennese glamour, Maria Carolina rejuvenated the life of the Neapolitan court. Historians speak of an Austrian Carnival after a Spanish Lent. Her ambitions were political as well as social and cultural, and her upbringing had encouraged them. Of all Maria Theresa's children, she was the most like her mother.

Maria Theresa had carefully included in the marriage contract that her daughter would take part in the state council as soon as she gave birth to a son. Although Maria Carolina had to wait seven years to achieve this, she never lost sight of that aim. In the meantime she dazzled her husband and began to wean him from the sway of Tanucci and the Spanish influence of her father-in-law.

After three years of marriage Maria Carolina gave birth to her first child, a daughter who was baptized Maria Theresa. (She would one day marry her cousin the Emperor Francis, and their daughter Leopoldina would become Empress of Brazil.) Between 1772 and 1793 (when she was already a grandmother), Maria Carolina gave birth to seventeen children, of whom ten died in childhood, and two as young brides. But in 1777 the birth of the heir presumptive, Francis, enabled her to enter the council of state, as her marriage contract stipulated.

Her first goal was to get rid of Bernardo Tanucci, the last bulwark of Spanish influence in Naples. To achieve this she needed to enlist Ferdinand's help. At his wife's insistence he wrote letters to his father in

Spain repeatedly attacking the prime minister, even though Tanucci had served the crown for four decades. Secretly Ferdinand complained to his father about his wife, claiming that her efforts to enter the government were instigated by Austria. "I shall try to prevent her from succeeding," he wrote, and there was some truth in his allegations. "My first aim," Maria Carolina confessed, "is to render service to my adored brother the emperor, for whom I would willingly shed my blood." Every week for thirty years she had a written account sent to her from Vienna of all that went on in the city. She called it her "chronicle of lies," but nonetheless she read it compulsively. In her heart and soul Maria Carolina always remained an Austrian.

Ultimately, however, Ferdinand was unable to resist his wife, and a year after the birth of the heir presumptive, after forty-two years of service, Tanucci fell. Ferdinand had virtually no interest in affairs of state and constantly allowed Maria Carolina to take the decisions. He even had the inkstands removed from the council chamber so that he would not be obliged to write anything. Living entirely for his own pleasures at Caserta, he was incapable of either originating or carrying out any plan. Once when the council was in an important session, the king heard the crack of a whip in the courtyard below. Without hesitation he rose, asked the queen to do as she thought best as usual, and joined the hunt. As Ferdinand described in another letter to his father, his wife was capable of pressing her case in the strongest possible manner. "'For at least a year, whether you die or burst, I refuse to be pregnant,'" she cried; and later she was so angry that she bit his hand.

Guided by the policies of her two brothers, Maria Carolina endeavored to win the confidence of the cultured elite and encouraged the reform of the country's economic policies. As a result a rash of publications appeared in Naples, enquiring into the cause of the country's financial imbalance and suggesting remedies for it. Tanucci's plan to suppress the Freemasons was also reversed. Maria Carolina's family in Vienna had welcomed the movement and her father, her brother Joseph and two of her sisters were Freemasons. Though Freemasonry had been condemned by the Pope and Charles III, with Maria Carolina's open support it continued to thrive in Naples. Lodges multiplied and spread throughout the provinces, including even a feminine one.

In spite of all the protestations of Ferdinand's father, the moment

Tanucci was displaced Spanish influence disappeared from Neapolitan politics, supplanted by that of Austria and its ally Britain. To reorganize the Neapolitan navy Maria Carolina sought advice from her brother Leopold and he sent her John Acton, who so enthralled the queen that inevitably they were accused of being lovers. From Madrid, King Charles tried to use this gossip to force his son to dismiss or even expel Maria Carolina's new favorite. "They have turned you into a pasteboard king," he wrote; "you must get rid of Acton at once, or send him out of your kingdom." Ferdinand and his wife locked themselves into her rooms. When they emerged twenty-four hours later, Ferdinand was convinced that Maria Carolina was right. Despite further attempts on the part of Spain to dislodge Acton, he remained and his power steadily grew.

Acton became the queen's perfect collaborator. As efficient as he was thorough, he was appointed commander in chief of both services. Four new naval colleges were founded, staffed by the finest instructors, and one of them published the first correct chart of the Mediterranean. Soon the Neapolitan shipyards were on a par with those of the Venetians. A new enthusiasm was instilled in the merchant marine, and the skill of Neapolitan pilots became world-renowned. Under the command of French, Swiss and Austrian officers the army was reorganized and the infantry was clothed and partly equipped in the Austrian manner.

The queen's decisions became those of the king. Ferdinand invariably left his palace at sunrise to go hunting, while she regularly attended meetings of the council of state, preparing papers for her husband to sign in the evening. When he returned, weary from his exertions in the chase, he agreed to whatever she put before him.

In Spain, King Charles was beside himself with anxiety over his daughter-in-law's influence. To ease his sense of frustration, he went out hunting, caught a severe chill and tried to cure it with the old hunter's remedy of a poultice of hot deer's grease. When this failed to warm him, and not wishing to rouse a doctor in the night, he asked a faithful valet to wrap him in the covers of his parrots' cages. By morning he was dead and with his death came the end of any Spanish influence in Naples.

Even Maria Carolina's bitterest enemies conceded that for twenty or so years, until the early 1790s, she governed the kingdom wisely and absolutely—though her detractors repeatedly credited her husband with her reforms and beneficent institutions. She made enemies not simply because of her opposition to the Spanish interest but also because she was young, enthusiastic and hasty in many of her decisions. But she had a deep and genuine concern for her subjects and their welfare as well as a generous heart. Even after the French Revolution, she was chided by her prime minister, now Sir John Acton, for getting the country into debt with her charitable enterprises (particularly helping French refugees after the Revolution), and he reminded her of her sister's fate when the same accusations were levelled against her. Eager as she was to carry out reforms, she tried to do too much at once. The daughter of a powerful empress, she refused to acknowledge opposition and forced her decisions to be implemented.

The more worthy or necessary her reforms, the more they offended those groups that benefited from corruption. She infuriated judges with her desire to reform the notoriously corrupt law courts. She reduced the privileges of the nobility—to their fury. Her army and navy reforms also angered noblemen who saw foreign officers appointed to posts they regarded as their own (even though they knew that not a single Neapolitan was capable of assuming high rank). When she founded secular schools she alienated the clergy, who also resented the fact that many of the institutions she supported (museums, hospitals, the university) were funded by property confiscated from the expelled Jesuits. There were numerous other improvements and reforms, and in every case Ferdinand received the credit for the good things that had been achieved, whereas the foreign queen was castigated.

As well as working hard for the state, Maria Carolina was also a devoted mother to her numerous children, lavishing much personal attention on them and their education. And yet the years in which she bore her seventeen children were also her most productive politically. It is astonishing to consider how much she actually achieved given the backward circumstances of her country and the era in which she lived.

When the time came to find husbands for her daughters, she journeyed with Ferdinand to Austria. She encouraged him to think of Vienna as his second home, so he happily spent all day hunting at Schönbrunn just as he had done in Naples, and they remained for eight contented months in the Austrian capital.

The south of Italy was almost Oriental in its casual attitude to everything: if Maria Carolina irritated many sectors of society with her autocratic ways, she was only following the pattern of her mother and brothers, who received the love of their subjects and the approbation of all the world. She was strong, ambitious and undisciplined, but she could not have done so much for the poor and ignorant if she had not been basically a conscientious and good woman. And for many years she had been very popular except with those who sided with Spain. Maria Carolina made the court splendid and exciting and the world flocked to see the beautiful Queen of Naples.

Scandal and Exile

There was much contemporary gossip about Maria Carolina's "gallantries," as it seemed that every woman in Naples, young or old, beautiful or ugly, had a lover or more. The court was considered by visitors to be licentious and indecent, and its members to behave with "brazen familiarity." It is true that John Acton seems to have been more than a friend but it is not certain he was her lover. She also had many favorites, but she definitely appeared to be more interested in power than in passion. Perhaps she enjoyed both. Or perhaps her "gallantries" were in fact no more than flirtations . . .

The French Revolution shattered her. The executions of Louis XVI and Marie Antoinette destroyed her finest sensibilities. Her sister had been abused and treated as a common criminal by the very Enlightenment Maria Carolina had sponsored in her own country. Now she began to hate all things French. Throughout 1793 the spectacle of the guillotining of her sister preyed on her mind. Naples joined the Austro-British coalition against France, and Maria Carolina's warships joined the British fleet off Toulon.

In France the Terror ran amok, and even Naples was full of Jacobins. Confusion mingled with suspicion, conspiracy with panic, as Vesuvius erupted for the thirty-third time. Her judgment gone, Maria Carolina resorted to spies as a precaution against conspiracies. Once again she found herself pregnant, and this time her health became seriously affected by her emotions. From now on, for the queen everything was either black or white, but mostly black. At home she saw only treachery; abroad she feared the influence of the French.

As her own influence waned, her political judgment became increasingly flawed. She was accused of emptying the treasury with self-indulgent schemes. And yet she was able to write to a cardinal: "I have lived here thirty-one years. . . . I do not even own a country house, a garden (a thing I have always desired), a jewel, no capital or anything. By now everyone has been able to ascertain the non-existence of my famous millions; I have not even been able to benefit those I wished to, having resolved not to depart from the strict rule of duty even in this respect. . . ."Writing in 1793, Sir William Hamilton spoke of the king's continuing hold on the affections of his people. Of Maria Carolina he observed, "The Queen of Naples is by no means popular, but as her power is evident, she is greatly feared."

That power helped to persuade Naples to join the second coalition against the French. Then in December 1798 Napoleon's armies seized Naples, and Maria Carolina and Ferdinand were forced to flee. Returning the following June, the queen was held partly responsible for a massacre of republican supporters which flagrantly violated the peace agreement.

Undeterred, in 1805 she put her remaining political strength into securing the agreement of Naples to a third war against France. By the following January, Napoleon had again captured Naples and forced the court to move to Sicily. Years of exile followed, years when she dulled her pain and her mind with opium. She hated living in Palermo, although Sicily flourished because of the court's presence. The king blamed her for their misfortunes, and so did the people. She was unwanted, and when in 1811 she fell out with the British ambassador, Lord George Bentinck, he easily persuaded Ferdinand that she should quit the island.

The king sent her back to Vienna and their separation caused a scandal. The queen was fifty-seven, and her journey to Vienna lasted eight weary months. By now her daughter who had been Empress of Austria was dead; she had quarrelled with her allies the British; and Napoleon had given the throne of Naples to his sister Caroline.

Maria Carolina's son, who was as bovine as his father, bored the exiled queen. As her erstwhile son-in-law, the Emperor Francis, had recognized Murat and Caroline as rulers of Naples, her position in Vienna was extremely awkward. To make matters yet more painful for Maria Carolina, Francis's daughter Marie Louise had married Napoleon.

As in the case of her sister Marie Antoinette, Maria Carolina's contemporaries and politically hostile historians maligned and slandered her. The achievements of her first twenty-odd years should have given her a better place in history; her tragedy is that her later years were full of misfortunes, sorrows, and injuries received or imagined, which embittered her and exaggerated her faults for posterity. Sad and alone, Maria Carolina died on September 8, 1814. As Vienna glittered and waltzed through the Congress that marked the end of the Napoleonic Wars, few noticed her death or cared.

4

Leopoldina

——— ◆ ———

ARCHDUCHESS OF AUSTRIA / EMPRESS OF BRAZIL

1797–1826

In 1808 Napoleon invaded Portugal and, on the advice of the British and with their help, the entire court moved to Portugal's colony of Brazil.

For three centuries Portugal had kept Brazil isolated from the rest of the civilized world, both culturally and economically. Now the country began to open its doors and trade with friendly nations, and this cultured European invasion from the mother country brought increased social, commercial and cultural contacts between Brazil, Europe and the United States. Towns and cities developed; manufacturing, previously forbidden, was now permitted. A royal press was founded; a royal library established; and in Rio de Janeiro imposing public buildings were erected.

In 1815, at the Congress of Vienna, Metternich and Talleyrand advised Portugal that Brazil would receive proper recognition if raised to the status of a kingdom. The following year Dom João VI succeeded to the crown of his Portuguese mother, yet even though the French no longer occupied his country, he was reluctant to return to his troubled kingdom. The British, having driven Napoleon out of Portugal, had imposed on Dom João almost complete submission. Now, to counterbalance Britain's influence and discourage the pretensions of Spain both in the Peninsula and in America, Dom João determined to form an alliance with Austria by arranging a marriage between his heir and a daughter of the Emperor Francis I.

Once Austria would have scorned the dynastic aspirations of little Portugal. But Napoleon had humiliated the nation with a crushing defeat at Austerlitz. He abolished the Holy Roman Empire, and proud Austria no longer held its position as the leading nation in Europe. Its power now lay only in its influence, and Dom João, eager to harness such a valuable ally, sent his most able ambassador, the marques de Marialva, to Vienna, to present the Braganza suit in its most favorable light.

Austria

Maria Leopoldina Josepha Carolina, Archduchess of Austria and sister of Napoleon's Empress Marie Louise, was nineteen when she became betrothed to Dom Pedro de Alcantara, heir to the crown of Portugal. Two years her junior, Dom Pedro had lived in Brazil for the previous nine years. Handsome, bold, clever and intelligent, he had been absurdly brought up—his education totally neglected, his companions the servants and hangers-on of the palace. He was constantly involved in brawls and adventures, and his character developed into a strange mixture of good and bad qualities.

The proposed marriage came as a surprise to Dom Pedro, but the thought that it might curtail his pursuit of pleasure did not outweigh his curiosity. Napoleon was his hero, and to marry the sister of the Empress of the French appealed to his romantic imagination. Nor did the portrait of Leopoldina displease him; unfortunately the picture he saw flattered the original to a point beyond recognition.

In appearance, Leopoldina was the antithesis of the kind of woman Dom Pedro admired. Of medium height and already inclined to stoutness, she was not even particularly feminine. She took not the slightest interest in her toilette, and cosmetics in Leopoldina's eyes were used not as an enhancement of natural beauty but as an unnecessary vanity. Marialva, ever the perfect courtier, when asked about her physical appeal, tactfully limited himself to the statement that "in her presence sovereignty shines forth alongside the rarest virtue."

Yet Leopoldina, though plain, was not without fine qualities. She was kind and intelligent, and although rather plump, she had expressive blue eyes, a tiny nose and a remarkably sweet smile. She pursued all sports energetically, especially horseback riding (though even this failed to streamline her). Her father had insisted that his children become fluent in English, French, Spanish, Italian, Hungarian and Czech. From the age of eight they learned history, especially the history of the Habsburgs and the Holy Roman Empire. The imperial children's day began early, and they were punished if they did not study assiduously. To develop their powers of observation, they were taken by their young stepmother, whom they loved, on excursions to towns near the capital, visiting gardens, exhibitions and even a mine. After these educational outings they were required to summarize in writing all that they had seen.

Leopoldina was particularly inclined toward mathematics and the natural sciences: botany, mineralogy, astronomy and physics. She studied Latin, drawing and music, and although she loathed her extremely severe teacher, she loved music and later became grateful for all he had taught her. She collected coins, plants, shells, flowers and minerals. One day in Vienna she met Goethe and he awoke in her a lifelong love of German literature.

Her father, the Emperor Francis, was a man of spartan self-discipline, and he imposed a similar regime on his children. He was deeply religious, charitable, cultivated and well-read; even as a young man he had amassed a large and important collection of paintings and an impressive library. He was witty and loved joking and playing with his children, to whom, as they grew older, he became a real friend.

But he also instilled in them stern virtues: the belief that the dignity and importance of monarchy should prevail even at the expense of their own happiness; a spirit of total obedience to their parents; and the notion that the princesses would later unquestioningly obey their husbands. They were all taught a strong respect for the prevailing social and political order, and were expected to find their satisfaction in carrying out their duty.

Francis also insisted that his daughters should be virgin in mind as well as in body, and that they be completely ignorant about sex even on their wedding day. This was considered so important that the brothers and sisters were brought up in virtually separate nurseries. Books were censored of any reference to the male figure, the physical side of love or human relationships, and offending pictures of statues (even with fig leaves) were cut out with scissors. Leopoldina and her sister Marie Louise shared a passion for animals and had a small farm; but censorship applied here too: all the animals were female!

Leopoldina's mother was vivacious, gay and serene, particularly in times of crisis. She managed to bear thirteen children in seventeen years, without ever losing her composure. To Leopoldina she presented a lifelong example of self-denial, charity and goodness. Though extravagant with money and criticized for the large amounts she expended on charity and family entertainments, she spent very little on herself. Leopoldina was to be the same. Her mother died when she was ten, but the children all loved their young stepmother, Marie Louise d'Este. Intelligent, agreeable and cultivated, Marie Louise filled her stepchildren's lives with happy family gatherings involving music, games and playacting. When her stepmother died at the age of twenty-nine after a long illness, Leopoldina was profoundly affected, though now the emperor spent far more time with her, often taking her hunting with him.

Leopoldina's parents insisted on a religious education for their children and Leopoldina became deeply sensitive to the mysticism of the Catholic Church. She joined the Order of the Cross of the Star, whose ideals were "to venerate and adore the Holy Cross and to aim for the salvation of the soul." These ideals were to be realized by prayer and good deeds; she was to dress modestly and show a genuine love for Jesus Christ. Leopoldina entered the order at a traumatic time in her life: her sister Marie Louise had just married Napoleon Bonaparte, the man the whole family had come to regard as the Antichrist, for twice Napoleon had forced the imperial family out of Vienna—in 1805, when Leopoldina was eight, and again in 1809.

Austria was now a relatively poor country, so when the crown of the Braganzas was offered to the Archduchess Leopoldina, it was not Portugal that held the attraction, but Brazil, the richest country in natural resources on the face of the earth.

The arrival of the marques de Marialva in Vienna was planned down to the smallest detail, and the populace was dazzled by the ambassador's display. His entry into the city with fourteen carriages and fifty liveried footmen resembled "the retinue of a sultan and the pomp of the Holy Father." The Viennese had never seen anything like the solid gold tableware and plates at his banquets, nor the gifts of South American diamonds, sapphires, aquamarines and pearls with which he showered the imperial family and his guests. The little archduchess was instantly captivated by the features of the handsome youth she was intended to marry, who gazed levelly out at her from his portrait framed with huge Brazilian diamonds. This was surmounted by a crown of diamonds and hung from a chain of even larger diamonds, which Leopoldina immediately put around her neck. She wrote to her aunt, "A picture of my prince arrived a few days ago, I find him charming, with features that express kindness and spirit. . . ."

She had in fact been engaged to a Prince of Saxony, but after Marialva's arrival in Vienna, Metternich decided the Brazilian alliance had more to offer Austria. "Whatever Portugal may have dwindled to," said Metternich to the emperor, "Brazil must be something."

Leopoldina was being courted for her prince by the aging Ambassador Marialva, who brought her billets-doux composed in advance as well as sending her flowers and gifts. What the bride lacked in coquetry she made up for in romantic imagination. The prospect of an entirely different life in a new continent excited her. "It may be predestination," she wrote to her aunt, "but I have always had a strange curiosity about America, and as a child I always talked about visiting it." A brave spirit, she insisted that she was not afraid of the long sea journey, but repeated this so often that one suspects she protested too much. She resolved to do whatever would make her future husband happy and set about learning Portuguese, declaring that it was "a difficult language, full of Arabic words." The exquisitely mannered Marialva had assured the young archduchess that Dom Pedro was just as interested in botany and mineralogy as she was, whereas in fact, while she applied herself to studying the history and geography of Brazil, Dom Pedro was diligently applying himself to the charms of a young dancer at the ballet . . .

On May 13, 1817, amid sumptuous celebrations, Leopoldina was married by proxy, with her uncle standing in for her husband. Prince Metternich himself accompanied the bride through Italy to Leghorn, her port of embarkation. In Florence she was overjoyed to be reunited with her sister Marie Louise, now Duchess of Parma. Finally, in early August a flotilla set sail, carrying the archduchess, her party, and (in a warship) the Austrian grand ambassador. After a tearful parting with her sister, Leopoldina left Italy filled with youthful anticipation of the promised enticing future.

On board the royal corvette, her apartments were luxuriously furnished and even included a splendid bathroom. The flotilla called at Madeira, where they were welcomed with tremendous rejoicing and carefully planned festivities. This was Leopoldina's first sighting of Portuguese territory.

The ships travelled slowly and an orchestra on board played constantly to while away the tedium of the voyage. The passengers played cards and someone devised a puppet theater when they reached the tropics. The bored passengers even thought they sighted a pirate ship, but later decided it was more probably a slave trader. They crossed the equator and entered the southern hemisphere all without incident. The voyage lasted eighty-six days, and to the great relief of the "august bride" and her entourage, they encountered only two storms. On November 5, 1817, they reached Rio de Janeiro. Leopoldina could not know that she would never see Austria again.

For years European scientists had been trying to gain access to the astonishing wealth of unexplored territory in Brazil. The marriage between an Austrian archduchess and the heir to the Portuguese throne was the opportunity for which they had been waiting. Seizing that opportunity, Metternich made himself responsible for the organization of the scientific commission which was to accompany Leopoldina.

The House of Tuscany insisted that a famed botanist join the commission. The King of Bavaria, who for the past two years had been trying to arrange a way to send his scientists to South America, now took advantage of Austria's protection, adding to the wedding party two members of the Munich Academy of Sciences, the zoologist J. B. von Spix and the botanist C. F. P. von Martius. These scientists were engaged to explore the Brazilian kingdom, and to study the flora, fauna and minerals of the country as well as to examine the culture of the inhabitants.

The archduchess's varied and brilliant retinue included a librarian, a zoologist, an imperial hunter, a royal gardener, an entomologist, a mineralogist, a working miner, three drawing teachers and several artists specializing in drawing plants. The most distinguished of these was the Austrian painter Thomas Ender.

In addition the party included stewards, chamberlains, six Hungarian noblemen, six Austrian guardsmen, assorted aristocrats, a grand almoner, a chaplain, the archduchess's private doctor (who also happened to be a naturalist) and four philologically expert ladies-in-waiting! Along with this enormous suite travelled gentlemen of the Portuguese court, their wives and children, and numerous officers. Somehow they all shared the ships with a considerable number of cows, calves, pigs and sheep, 4,000 chickens, several hundred ducks and between 4,000 and 5,000 canaries. No wonder the Austrian ambassador wrote to his wife: "Noah's ark seemed like child's play in comparison with the *Dom João VI*." Most of the scientists sailed on board two frigates, preceding the imperial party by two months. Their uneventful voyage enabled von Spix and von Martius to make copious notes on the wind and the waves, analyzing the Atlantic by barometer, thermometer, areometer, hygrometer and electrometer.

Brazil

Society and customs changed dramatically in Brazil with the arrival of the Portuguese court in 1808. The Englishman was now looked on with respect, and no longer had to be sprinkled with holy water as a heretic or an "animal." Traditional customs such as dancing in church on special feast days were abandoned, and the English introduced such civilizing assets as false teeth, bread and beer.

For three centuries the country they reached had slumbered in relative isolation. Those ethnic elements already found there had blended in an extraordinary fashion. Masters and slaves, and mulatto, Asiatic, Moorish and African influences had combined to produce a distinctly Oriental, rather than Portuguese, effect in the population and its culture. Under their red roofs, houses displayed winglike projecting eaves. They boasted overhanging balconies, with windows divided into small lozenges. The fronts of the houses were decorated with painted tiles, and the courtyards within all contained fountains or wells.

Wealthy ladies travelled on palanquins and litters. The ideal Brazilian woman was plump and pretty, but never showed her face out of doors, except her eyes. At home and even in church she would sit cross-legged on a mat or a carpet. That was the Moorish influence. The china on the tables came from India and Macao; the bed hangings were imported from the Orient. Many of the dishes and seasonings in the food were Asiatic and African, as were many plants and fruit trees: Indian palms, mangoes, breadfruit, dende palms and figs.

Bright colors dominated everything—the houses and palanquins, the women's shawls and the men's ponchos. Inside the churches all was red, gold and scarlet. Furniture—even if made of rosewood—was painted red or white. More than anything else, these colors gave Brazil its Eastern look. Portugal's colony had absorbed all these native elements, which appeared most exotic to European eyes.

When Brazil opened its doors again to Europeans in the nineteenth century, it gave entry to a newly industrialized, commercial and mechanized *middle-class* invasion. The newcomers brought with them their drab urban blacks and grays—black frock coats, black boots, black top hats, black carriages—the colors of civilization, which swamped the rustic Eastern and African colors of the workingman. Brazilians soon thought it elegant slavishly to imitate their European "betters," and adopted their fashions designed for a cold climate. In the stifling heat they had previously worn loose clothing (and children little more than a linen slip). Now adults and children became martyrs to European fashions. Even five-year-old girls were obliged to wear two or three petticoats over their pantalettes, under tight dresses of silk or taffeta. On their heads they wore elaborate caps trimmed with feathers, and on their feet little black kid boots with heels.

By the time Leopoldina reached Rio de Janeiro in 1817, the Portuguese court had resided there for nine years and fashionable society undoubtedly concerned itself far more with luxury and convenience than with the arts and sciences. As von Spix drily observed, the Brazilian "was more disposed to the voluntarily offered enjoyments of so happy a climate than to those of art—which cannot be obtained without effort."

News from Europe spread to Brazil surprisingly quickly and accurately, but there were only two newspapers in the whole kingdom. There was no university, so that Brazilians had to complete their education at the Portuguese university of Coimbra. Rio boasted only two booksellers, though the upper classes imported innumerable French books, preferring French literature to any other. German literature (and the German language) was virtually unknown.

Society spoke Portuguese, for only the men spoke French and English. Women's lives were still comparatively sheltered though, following the lead of the court, Brazilian ladies began to attend the theater—a handsome building erected a few years previously and opened on Dom

Pedro's birthday. The royal box occupied the whole of the space fronting the stage, with another hundred or so extremely gloomy boxes for other important theatergoers. Most visitors found the orchestra tolerable and the performances indifferent.

The main distraction for all classes of society was music. Only the very rich possessed a piano; the favorite instrument was the guitar, to which—inside and outside polished society—everyone would dance. Dom Pedro formed a band, vocal and instrumental, of blacks and mulattoes, sometimes leading them himself. (A talented composer, he even had one of his own symphonies performed in Paris.)

Lack of culture, however, was not the greatest hardship for Europeans—especially the blond, blue-eyed, fair-skinned type like Leopoldina. Their problem was the climate. The natives were immune to yellow fever, but it attacked Europeans remorselessly. Unhappy foreigners contracted not only syphilis but also malaria, liver ailments and bubonic plague.

As Leopoldina's flotilla sailed into Rio's harbor, she was thinking of none of these hardships. She was arriving in another continent, at a country which was to be her new home, over whose people she would one day reign. For some time she had been able to see Rio's great sugarloaf mountain, and now the ships sailed into the huge amphitheater of a harbor which many contemporary travellers described as the most beautiful in the world. The luxuriance of the vegetation astonished her. Well-wooded mountains formed the backdrop, and the green banks rising out of the sea were studded with white houses, chapels, churches and forts. When the ships neared land the Germans noted "an ambrosial perfume," and as they dropped anchor, cannon boomed and a brass band played.

On a fine quayside of hewn granite, a great pavilion had been built where they were to land. Even as Leopoldina was rehearsing her speech of welcome, Dom João called out a spontaneous greeting to his new daughter-in-law, who stumbled a reply in her awkward Portuguese. And then Dom Pedro leapt on board to greet his bride, thrusting a jewel casket into her hands.

Leopoldina was overcome with awe and delight. Her husband was even more handsome than his portrait: in this wonderful place, with a warm and welcoming family, the most beautiful and romantic-looking man she could imagine stood before her. When she had left her home, shipped off to Brazil for all the world as if she were a prize filly, she had lamented her fate even while dutifully accepting it. "I admit that the sacrifice of leaving my family, perhaps for ever, is more than painful," she had declared, "but this alliance makes my father happy, and I have the consolation of knowing that I have bowed to his will, being persuaded that God has a particular way of ruling the destinies of we princes, and that submitting to our parents is submitting to his will." Archduchesses, it seemed, received even less consideration than the humblest Austrian subject. Now, as Dom Pedro stood before her, wearing a general's uniform glittering with decorations, his high embroidered collar just brushing his dark red whiskers, it was no wonder plain dumpy little Leopoldina fell irredeemably in love.

The carriages passed through triumphal arches, some made of columns with gilded capitals, others of sweet-scented flowers. Bunting and banners flapped in the breeze, and all the balconies were draped with silks and satins of varied colors. On every street corner, the heraldic shields entwining the arms of Habsburg and Braganza were displayed, and richly dressed ladies leaned from their windows, glittering with diamonds and feathers, waving their handkerchiefs and scattering flower petals on the bride and groom as they passed below. Entranced, Leopoldina rode alone with her husband in a carriage drawn by eight horses in velvet and silver harness. She was wearing a white dress embroidered in gold and silver, with a carnation in her bodice as her only decoration. What little conversation they made was in French, as he spoke no German and her Portuguese was still far from fluent. Led by a troop of cavalry, the procession of carriages reached the royal chapel, where the bridal party received benediction and a Te Deum was sung.

The royal palace was in the principal square of the city, no great distance from the quay. This attractive square had on one side the Church and Convent of the Carmelites, which also housed the royal library (open to the public for six hours a day). On the other side was the palace itself, with private houses and the fish market built uniformly with it. The fourth side opened out to the sea. The European scientists were disappointed with the palace, and indeed with most buildings in Rio. The palace, two stories high, with twenty-four windows on the southern side and nine windows on the west wing that faced the bay, was not, they judged, equal to the grand style of European palaces, or worthy of a monarch of so promising a kingdom.

Here the bridal party attended a huge banquet in the vast reception rooms, where the walls were hung with French silks and wallpapers on panels edged with gilt moldings. In the square below the crowd chanted for Dom Pedro and Leopoldina to show themselves until finally the bridal pair came out onto the balcony. It was clear from the reception she received that the people truly welcomed the first German princess to a throne in the New World. By evening the whole town was illuminated for still more festivities, which were to continue for three days and nights. Then everything returned to normal, and Rio was once again the none-too-clean country town it had been before.

At the palace, which had been redecorated and enlarged, Leopoldina, though homesick and shy, soon warmed to her new family, who presented her with wondrous gifts of precious jewelry. The king gave her a string of 400 flawless pearls, which he fastened around her neck, and her mother-in-law snapped a pair of sapphire and diamond bracelets around her wrists. Dom Miguel, her brother-in-law, presented her with a ruby brooch. From the princesses she received earrings, bangles, a gold filigree flower and a richly ornamented *trepa-moleque,* or Spanish comb headdress. Leopoldina was enchanted with her new family and touched by their kindness. When evening came, the royal family quietly left for their nearby country palace, São Cristovão.

Rio was hot, noisy and damp. During the ebb tide the marshy flats on the seaside gave off not an "ambrosial perfume" but an intolerable stench. The streets were narrow and paved with granite, with raised platforms for pedestrians, but they were filthy—and the only street cleaners were the carrion vultures, who were therefore protected. An aqueduct, built in 1740, brought fresh spring water to the fountains of the city; but the largest one in the main square was always surrounded by drinking animals and by slaves filling up their water barrels. Nearby were troughs where the washerwomen worked and chattered, close to a bench for the new slaves on sale.

Although Rio gave a first impression of being a European city, the sight of so many blacks and mulattoes who made up the working class, struggling under their burdens, dressed in filthy rags and singing their strange songs, soon distressed the visitor. Clumsy, two-wheeled carts, drawn by oxen through the city streets, creaked and rattled. At dusk the crickets, frogs and toads began their chorus. Rockets were fired almost daily at dawn to celebrate the frequent religious festivals, and cannon boomed from the fort. No wonder the royal family preferred to live a short distance from the city, away from its intolerable noise and smells.

They travelled by boat, for Dom João suffered from gout and the journey was gentler by water than by road. As they crossed the bay the water reflected the lights shining from dozens of little illuminated canoes, and the air was filled with the melancholy songs of the slaves. The short distance was soon covered, and São Cristovão appeared on the horizon.

The next day there was a reception for the diplomatic corps, and a concert in which Dom Pedro sang a small part. Dom João did everything possible to make his new daughter-in-law comfortable; he had a bust of her father placed in her room, and gave her an album with portraits of her own family. His kindness, the stunning beauty of the countryside, her new home and the attentions of her husband all combined to seduce her completely into her new life.

Living in the country, Leopoldina was in her element. She spent long afternoons in the neighboring forests, collecting rare plants and returning with her arms full of exotic orchids and other flowers. Countless specimens were sent back to her father, whose only recreation was gardening. For hours she would try to catch one of a cloud of rare blue butterflies, or quietly observe the multicolored parakeets or monkeys playing in the trees. She spent endless time gathering stones veined with porphyry or quartz to bring back to her library for classification. "It must be said that Portuguese America would be a paradise on earth, were it not for the insufferable heat of 88 degrees and the many mosquitoes which are a veritable torment. . . ."

Whenever one of the Austrian or German scientists made a strange discovery, they never forgot to let Leopoldina know. One day one of the scientists brought her a cub, "a cross between a lion and a panther," as well as "a rare bird from China, a she-mule with two colts, an ox with a Tartary hump as well as many other animals and a couple of Botocudo Indians who live near here and I should not care to part with any of them," she wrote to her father. It was not long before she made her own little zoo on an island. Later, she wrote to her European agent asking him to send her "two badger hounds and a dog that knows how to dive." Nor was her father exempt; she asked him to send her six Transylvanian horses for breeding purposes. When she wanted to make a gift to a friend in Europe she wrote to her father that she would send him "a few monkeys and other beasts to forward upon the first occasion that offers."

The following January was Leopoldina's birthday, and Rio celebrated the event with concerts, military parades, and a gala ballet at the theater. She was loath to go to town, writing afterward that in spite of the excitements of fireworks and a torchlight parade, "I am very glad to have returned with my husband to our beautiful home in São Cristovão."

When she first arrived at her country home, there was little to be proud of other than its stunning position. Surrounded by high and picturesque mountains, the palace faced a rolling plain flanked by green hills and looking toward part of the bay. On one of these hills the handsome barracks built by the Jesuits made an imposing landmark. In every direction the view was breathtaking.

São Cristovão, built on rising ground in the Moresco style, had once been a convent. Its architecture was plain, unembellished and not at all elegant and at night the lights in its many windows gave the impression of a factory rather than a palace. The imposing entrance and magnificent gates (a copy of those at Syon House outside London and a gift of the Duke of Northumberland) had fallen into disuse. Fine iron palisades made by Portuguese craftsmen had the remnants of fireworks attached to the railings, as this was the custom on religious holidays. Outside the palace wall, instead of a fine road the ground had been allowed to remain in its rough natural state. Directly in front of the palace there was a square which had neither trees nor even grass or shrubs, but deep sand instead. The general impression was of sad dilapidation.

But soon after Leopoldina's arrival, improvements began. Mr. Johnson, a builder, had come from England with the Duke of Northumberland's gates and then stayed on, and the king ordered considerable extensions to São Cristovão under Johnson's direction. Within a few years the palace was transformed. Now painted a soft yellow ocher, with new moldings around the windows picked out in white, São Cristovão looked almost like a rustic eighteenth-century Austrian *Schloss*. A beautiful new screen and a gateway of Portland stone surrounded the courtyard, which had been planted with weeping willows. At the back of the palace was a well-kept farm and a model village, with its own church for the slaves.

Within walking distance of São Cristovão and at the end of a series of interconnecting tree-lined paths, the king had built a small house in the form of a castle, with a flagstaff on the top. Comfortably furnished with chairs and sofas and with Indian matting on the floor, the Casa de Dom Pedro was charming in its simplicity. He also had a country house at Santa Cruz, built on the site of an old Jesuit college close by a village, with the horizon extending to the sea in one direction, and in every other direction views of mountains or wooded hills. The large, handsome apartments and beautiful chapel were well furnished, and the walls of the rooms were decorated in a rich creamy-white clay. The climate was far too humid here for the use of silk or paper hangings, so the walls and the cornices had borders painted on them in distemper. These were beautifully designed, and incorporated the fruits, flowers, birds and insects of the country in vivid colors. Another room was painted as if it were a garden pavilion with open pillars to show the landscape of Santa Cruz in the distance. This was more a naive effort, painted mostly by self-taught Creoles, blacks, and mulattoes.

Leopoldina had only one wish to complete her happiness. "I have no greater desire than to be a mother soon," she wrote to her aunt, "and to devote myself entirely to the education of my children, particularly in a land that is so backward in culture." Fourteen months after her arrival at Rio de Janeiro, Leopoldina was pregnant. She stopped riding and spent her time reading and drawing, driving in her carriage and going for long walks. She still suffered from the heat and rose early, since by nine o'clock the heat and humidity compelled her to stay indoors—itself unbearable enough.

A few months later her first daughter was born. Her confinement was easy and the child healthy and strong. The baby was baptized Maria da Gloria, amid great pomp and to the sound of a Te Deum specially composed for the occasion by her father. Leopoldina's disappointment at not bearing a male heir was soon forgotten in what she described to her aunt

as her "incomparable happiness in being a mother," and she spent her entire day holding Maria da Gloria in her arms. Dom Pedro was touchingly
attentive to his daughter, carrying her around and smothering her with
kisses, even holding her in his arms on long outdoor walks.

Leopoldina's letters home were full of the child and her every development, and her own contentment. "I am enjoying the completest happiness in this solitude, which suits me perfectly," she wrote, "because I
can look after my daughter and live only for my husband and my stud-
ies." To be close to Dom Pedro she began horseback riding again, but by
the end of the year she had miscarried. Determined that this should not
happen a second time, Leopoldina now gave up taking any strenuous exercise and took to painting in oils, her usual subject inevitably being the
baby. Again she became pregnant and again she miscarried. She spent a
year in prayers and supplication and in March 1821 her prayers were
answered. Prince Dom João of Braganza was born; the succession was
assured.

Meanwhile, the king still remained in Brazil, even after the French
had long been expelled from Portugal and Napoleon banished to St.
Helena. Although the parliament of Portugal, the Cortes, continually
requested his presence, he had little taste for the intrigues of the Portuguese court and he dreaded the long sea voyage; but discontent with
the absentee king grew in Portugal and his subjects were becoming jealous of Brazil. With rebellions against absolute monarchies gaining
strength throughout Europe, the liberals in Portugal forced the king's
hand: either he returned or he lost his throne. Dom João had been
happy in Brazil and now with notable reluctance he embarked for Portugal, leaving Dom Pedro behind as regent.

The thirteen years which the court had spent in Rio had done more
than just infuse new life into a colonial backwater by bringing trade and
culture. The Brazilians were growing resentful of the dictates of faraway
Portugal, whose parliament seemed to take no account of the changing
conditions of a rapidly developing colony. Revolution against Portugal
was in the air, and as Dom Pedro travelled within the country, he left
Leopoldina behind as his regent.

To the parents' great sadness their baby son died, though less than a
month later Leopoldina gave birth to another daughter. To help with her
daughters' education she appointed an Englishwoman, Mrs. Graham, as

governess. Mrs. Graham met Leopoldina in 1823 and described her then as wearing "a handsome morning dress of purple satin, with white ornaments, and looking extremely well." She also remarked how Leopoldina instantly put everyone at ease, how kindly she spoke, and the sweetness of her expression. And Mrs. Graham herself was the object of much kindness, Leopoldina even helping the governess with her Portuguese in a discussion on the various merits of English authors and Scottish novels.

Dom Pedro had identified himself totally with the aspirations of Brazil. The Cortes sought to limit his powers and force him to return to Portugal, but Leopoldina, seeing the political situation with greater clarity, persuaded him to stay. After this open break with Lisbon, she realized that there would be no going back: as she wrote to her aunt, "It is necessary to endure the sacrifice of remaining in America." Daily the inevitability of declaring independence from Portugal grew. Dom Pedro recalled his father's words as they parted: "Pedro, if Brazil must break away, I would rather see it taken by you—of whose respect I am certain—rather than some unknown adventurer."

Making no secret of her commitment to secession, Leopoldina urged her husband to action. "Brazil under your guidance will be a great country," she insisted. "Brazil wants you as its monarch." She reassured him that he had the support of the whole country, adding, "Pedro, this is the most important moment of your life." With his wife's encouragement Dom Pedro declared himself Emperor Pedro I and Brazil was to become an imperial democracy. He and Leopoldina were crowned on December 1, 1822, in a ceremony modelled on that of Dom Pedro's hero, Napoleon. The new emperor wore a mantle rather like an Indian poncho, made of green velvet lined with yellow and heavily embroidered in gold, and on his shoulders he placed a cape of orange and yellow toucan feathers. Huge, perfect Brazilian diamonds adorned his crown, and there was a winged dragon at the end of his solid gold scepter. European society was scandalized by Dom Pedro's deference to Napoleon, the man they had so recently regarded as the scourge of their continent, but the new emperor was quite indifferent to such sentiments and too far away to care.

Leopoldina proved an enormous asset to her husband, especially in the early difficult days of the empire, when her husband was fully in control only of the southern parts of the country. In all matters of state she proved his devoted collaborator. Through her father she was able to influence the Austrian court and political circles in Vienna; through Metternich she could influence all Europe. And Dom Pedro was only too well aware of the status his wife's connections gave to his fledgling empire.

Her definite support of the Brazilian struggle to separate from Portugal completely won Leopoldina the hearts of the people. Mrs. Graham noted how her charity too commanded the admiration and love of her subjects, commenting that "no distressed person ever applies to her in vain; and her conduct, both public and private, justly commands the admiration and love of her subjects." The people of Brazil always referred to Dom Pedro and Leopoldina as "our emperor" and "our empress," invariably with an epithet of affection, and to this day many towns in Brazil bear Leopoldina's name, a tribute to the Austrian princess who became their first empress.

Science, Culture and Trade

Leopoldina's marriage opened up Brazil to scientific exploration. The zoologist von Spix and the physician and botanist von Martius were among the scientists who arrived ahead of the flotilla that brought her to Rio de Janeiro. Their commission was not solely to further their own specialized disciplines in Brazil but also to note the mineralogy, history and what was dubbed its "philosophic-philology." Von Martius was especially keen to study the three races that made up the Brazilian: the Indian, the Negro and the European. They and the other scientists on board, once it was known that they came to Brazil under the protection of Austria, had no trouble with customs officials, and soon they were given a royal safe-conduct to travel throughout the entire province. Their initial stay was to be two years, but this was soon extended for another eleven months—the Austrian zoologist Johann Natterer stayed for seventeen years. The scientists worked over the country from north to south, a distance of 4,000 kilometers, and from east to west, a total of 6,500 kilometers. Von Martius collected over 300,000 species (7,000 of them plants), each drawn in its natural habitat.

Through their writings, especially those of von Spix and von Martius—Brazil became properly known to a considerable number of

German-speaking Europeans for the first time. (One effect was further immigration.) On his return to Bavaria von Martius lectured on the Indian tribes of Brazil, and in particular their constitutions, ailments and medicines. Just twenty-six when he returned, he took another sixty-six years to complete his monumental *Flora Brasiliensis,* helped by sixty-seven other botanists from many other countries, describing in 40 folio volumes, containing 3,000 engravings, 20,000 Brazilian species. Some 6,000 of these had been hitherto unknown to science. As for Natterer, he brought back to Vienna an enormous natural history collection and compiled sixty glossaries of tribal languages.

Leopoldina's marriage brought trade as well as culture to Brazil. To some extent Austrian hopes for increased trade were disappointed. Most Austrian goods were more expensive than those from Britain, and all but Portuguese and British imports suffered a 25 percent duty. Even so Austria managed to export to Brazil such varied items as watches, pianofortes, muskets, iron hoops, fishing hooks, penknives, arsenic, nails, currycombs, white and yellow wax and sal ammoniac.

The arrival of the Austrian princess undoubtedly raised the intellectual and cultural tone of the Brazilian court and gave it a badly needed touch of refinement. No one could pretend that she was a fashion leader, but Mrs. Graham's descriptions of her clothes always give an impression of dignity and majesty. "The Empress wore a white dress embroidered with gold, a corresponding cap with feathers tipped with green," she once recorded; "her diamonds were superb, her head-tire and earrings having in them opals such as I supposed the world does not contain." And on official occasions Leopoldina always wore her first gift—the emperor's portrait, surrounded by diamonds, the largest Mrs. Graham had ever seen.

Widely read, the empress accumulated the best library in Brazil. Her shopping list sent to her father included not only history, geography, belles lettres, botany and travel books but also such controversial works as Thomas Malthus' *Principles of Political Economy.* What is much harder to gauge is the political impact of the way her arrival opened up Brazil to new thinking, but without doubt Leopoldina's influence helped to make her people conscious of their own potential as an independent nation.

Love and Marriage

Leopoldina's early years with Dom Pedro were idyllically happy. After only a few months she wrote to her aunt, "I have not enough words to tell you of the happiness I feel; you well know how sweet it is to enjoy the peaceful country life at the side of a person one loves tenderly."

Her husband she described as "a most adorable friend of rare virtues" and, choosing to ignore his rough manners, she rejoiced that he could speak French, translate English and understand German, that he wrote verse with ease, had a feeling for Latin (sometimes quoting the *Aeneid*) and was passionately fond of music. She would accompany him on the piano, and both of them loved riding.

Dom Pedro was a superb horseman and often went shooting and hunting. His physique and stamina were splendid, and his new bride was determined to keep up with him, joining him on long treks on horseback exploring the countryside. Sometimes they would swim in the sea, climb the mountains of Tijuca or take a canoe and shoot the rapids, and she felt her happiness was complete just to be by his side. Leopoldina would do anything to please her husband. Knowing of his love of horses, and the lack of good breeding stock in Rio, she wrote asking her father to help. The result was not only a stable full of Pomeranians and English thoroughbreds, but also an invaluable German groom called Klotz.

When the emperor reviewed his troops, or rode in parades or out on maneuvers, the empress would ride at her husband's side, wearing a blue dragoon uniform, high boots and heavy silver spurs. She usually appeared in public on horseback, and her friendly and natural manner endeared her to the people. Dom João had looked upon his scholarly Austrian daughter-in-law as a civilizing influence not only on the barbarous court but also on his son. But it is unlikely that Dom Pedro himself had ever thought of a woman as a means of improving his mind, nor could his consuming interest—*l'amour*—be quenched by his dumpy Austrian bride. "I worship God and I am afraid of the devil," he said, "but if God or the devil were to confront me while I happened to be making love, I should kick them both into the street."

As a result, although Leopoldina's early romantic feelings for her husband developed into a deep affection, it remained difficult for a woman of her culture and background to live with a man of scarcely any education and no control over his whims or passions. Leopoldina's way of dealing with her husband was through her devotion to God. She drew up a small book of resolutions, including her prescriptions for every day, which mentioned attending Mass, devout reading and meditation. She practiced hidden mortifications, such as not eating enough or keeping silence for a while. She rejected expensive or indecent clothing and luxurious toilettes, as well as literature that might bring sensual or sexual pleasure. Her religion was practical rather than contemplative and, by abiding by these ideals, Leopoldina hoped to fulfill all her duties on earth. Yet, for all her admirable qualities, sadly she lacked the charm and physical advantages necessary to attract and hold her husband. Disdaining any beauty aids and wearing her bushy hair dressed exactly as it was the day she arrived in Rio, by the time she was twenty-five Leopoldina looked a faded matron.

The coronation year, 1822, was important in their private as well as public life, for in the same month he declared independence, Dom Pedro met Doña Domitilia de Castro Canto e Mello. With her black hair, sparkling gypsy eyes, magnolia complexion, pretty turned-up nose and sensual mouth, she was the type of woman he found irresistible. The same age as Leopoldina, Domitilia was at the peak of her beauty, and spared no effort to enhance her natural advantages, spending literally hours on her toilette. In a country where the extrovert population made a fetish of fashion, Domitilia did not follow, she initiated. She was the epitome of allure, and the emperor was her slave. Soon they were lovers.

Although the emperor had never been particularly faithful to Leopoldina, hitherto his liaisons had been discreet and his wife had probably been unaware of them. Domitilia, on the other hand, became an obsession. At first the lovers were discreet, but soon his affair became a public scandal. He was dallying with "Titilia" while Leopoldina suffered a very difficult confinement and gave birth to another daughter. When the empress became aware of her rival she chose to rise above the situation, even though her husband heaped favors on his mistress and her family, creating Domitilia a marquesa. When he asked his wife to appoint her as a lady-in-waiting, Leopoldina felt unable to refuse, and Domitilia was installed in the palace with her daughter by the emperor.

Although bewitched by this lovely siren, Dom Pedro was still very attached to his wife, so it happened that both women gave birth to his sons in the same month. Once again Brazil had an heir, and it was not very long before Dom Pedro's illegitimate children were playing in the nursery with his legitimate heirs.

Leopoldina bore all these insults heroically. The turning point came during a voyage to make an official visit to Bahia in 1825. Watching her husband flaunt his affair before her eyes and in front of her eldest daughter proved more than she could bear. The captain, seeing Dom Pedro visiting Domitilia's cabin so often, had even mistakenly addressed the mistress as "Your Majesty." It was too much, and now at last Leopoldina's attitude hardened. Her health was also deteriorating. Constant childbearing in the hot, humid climate of Rio—seven children in as many years—had worn her out, and the deep private wound and public insult inflicted on her by her adored husband's flagrant unfaithfulness must have undermined her resilience. By the end of 1826 she was pregnant yet again, and quarrelling loudly and violently with the emperor. A few days later she miscarried, and puerperal septicemia set in. Dom Pedro was called away urgently to visit another part of the empire and while he was away he heard the tragic news. On December 11, 1826, Leopoldina had died. She was twenty-nine.

Although he had never loved his wife, Dom Pedro had been very attached to her, appreciating, admiring and sometimes very much needing her. Her death—despite the gossips—by all appearances filled him with bitter remorse and left a void. A trustworthy and loyal counselor, she had been devoted to the interests of Brazil and had played an active part in the independence. Her Austrian origins gave the "constitutional emperor" prestige, while her goodness of character, her kindness and her charity made her loved by the people and contributed greatly to the popularity of the emperor. After Leopoldina's death her father, the Emperor of Austria, was heard to make the sad but true comment "What my son-in-law needs now is a bride who is both beautiful and witty." It was Leopoldina's tragedy that she had been neither.

5

Eugénie

—◦•◦—

GRANDEE OF SPAIN/EMPRESS OF FRANCE

1826–1920

A young woman, out of breath and flushed with excitement, astride a fine thoroughbred, galloped into a clearing in the forest. She was the first to arrive, and the only member of the hunting party to be in at the kill. The courage and skill of her horsemanship were instantly admired by all the company, not least her host, who promptly presented her with the horse on which she had triumphed. From that moment it was known that Louis-Napoleon, Prince-President of France, was madly in love with the beautiful Eugénie, Countess of Teba.

Spain

Maria Eugénie Ignaçia Augustina Guzmán y Palafox y Portocarrero was born on May 5, 1826, the fifth anniversary of the death of Napoleon Bonaparte. Her father, Don Cipriano, was a Spanish grandee, a younger son of the noble house of Montijo, among whose ancestors St. Dominic featured in a roll call of Peninsular history reaching back to the days of the Moors. The rest added up to an impressive record of great positions in state, army and church. Don Cipriano, a convinced Bonapartist, had fought for Napoleon I in the Peninsular War, and his courage as a liberal progressive was equalled only by his courage as a soldier. On her mother's side Eugénie's background was solid middle-class affluence, allied to Scottish efficiency. Her mother, Doña Manuela, was half Scottish and a quarter

Belgian. Doña Manuela's father, William Kirkpatrick, took American nationality and was commissioned as American consul at Malaga in 1800. He also took a Belgian wife, and their daughter was said to be "worth millions and as beautiful as the day." Ambitious and vivacious, a witty conversationalist, with a good ear for music, Doña Manuela made every effort throughout her marriage to attract politicians and diplomats to her salons—for her, "to talk politics was to live."

Eugénie was one year younger than her gentle and beautiful sister Paca. Their childhood was wild and free: when Eugénie was no more than six or seven her father would take her for long rides across the countryside, spending nights by a fire under the stars. Soon she became a familiar and fascinated visitor among the gypsies around Granada. She loved her dogs as much as her horses. The country house at Carabanchel was surrounded by huge watchdogs devoted to her, as was her lapdog and a great Newfoundland dog, which would insist on trying to rescue her from drowning if she went bathing. Eugénie had enormous energy and loved physical exercise, especially riding. Always a daring horsewoman, no wonder she caused comment by riding out alone, her wonderful red-gold hair streaming in the wind as she galloped into the mountains. There she continued to visit the gypsy encampments, where (legend has it) she was told of the emperor she would marry and the country she would one day rule.

Yet the girls were not spoiled. Don Cipriano considered economy and simplicity to be the best basis for his daughters' upbringing, and when they visited rich relatives they travelled not in carriages but on horseback or mules. Even after Don Cipriano came into the Montijo inheritance and they moved into their mansion in Madrid, his spartan standards did not lessen: he thought their silk stockings an irresponsible luxury; he wanted them to wear the same dresses winter and summer and he still disliked their driving in carriages. This dislike of waste and extravagance and a level head where money was concerned were characteristics inherited from Don Cipriano that would remain with Eugénie throughout her long life. A highly intelligent and passionate child, she followed her adored father in his politics too, becoming, like him, an ardent Bonapartist.

Eugénie was given a cosmopolitan upbringing. With her parents she spoke mostly French, she always corresponded with them in French, and she was twelve when she first began to read Spanish (though she would have heard her mother's visitors speaking Spanish and English as well as French). She was educated in France. From 1834 to 1838 she and Paca attended the Convent of the Sacré Coeur in the rue de Varenne off the faubourg Saint-Germain in Paris. It was fashionable, very Catholic and had an important influence on Eugénie. When she became empress, she was accused by the radicals of representing the extreme Catholic party at the court of Napoleon III. Although this was attributed to her Spanish background, her Catholicism was far more likely to have come from the nuns of the Sacré Coeur.

Eugénie's religious feelings were inclined more to the spiritual than to the dogmatic. To her highly emotional, imaginative nature, religion was more a consolation than an inspiration—a very necessary consolation when she had to bear so many tragedies in later life.

For their physical training, Don Cipriano insisted the girls attend a coeducational school run by a Spanish Bonapartist colonel who stressed gymnastics. Then, when Eugénie was eleven, she and Paca spent two months at an English school, near Bristol. It was not a success: Eugénie tried to run away, finally returning to France with an English governess, Miss Flower, who stayed in the service of the Montijos for the next fifty years.

Two exceptional men of letters crossed the paths of these young girls. One was Prosper Mérimée, who became a lifelong friend of Doña Manuela and Eugénie's. He introduced them to the other: the novelist Stendhal, and whenever he called, the two girls were allowed to stay up to listen to "M. Beyle," as he was really named. This was Doña Manuela's most fruitful contribution to Eugénie's education. She was twelve when she met Stendhal, who instantly became infatuated with her, just as she was fascinated by the magic web of words he spun around her and her sister. The two girls would sit adoringly at the feet of Stendhal and Mérimée, reliving history through their eyes.

When Eugénie was nearly thirteen her beloved father died in Madrid before either she or Paca could reach his bedside from Paris. Don Cipriano's death marked the end of Eugénie's childhood. All her best qualities—her values, her passion, her spirit of adventure—came from this man whom she had worshipped. Too often throughout her long life she would have to suffer the deaths of those she had loved with a passion and intensity so peculiar to her.

Eugénie's relations with her mother, however, were always difficult—Eugénie herself was difficult. It was her sister, the exquisite, gentle Paca, who was their mother's favorite. When Eugénie fell madly in
love with their childhood friend, the shy and unassuming (but immensely powerful and rich) Duke of Alba, Doña Manuela saw to it that
Alba married Paca instead. Eugénie's heart was broken. She wrote to
Alba: "I love and hate in excess, and I don't know which is better, my
love or my hate; passions mingle in me, some terrible, all of them
strong: I fight against them, but I lose the battle and in the end my life
will finish, miserably lost in a welter of passions, virtues, follies." At first
she vowed to end her days in a convent. Instead, she spent the next five
years in Spain displaying a certain defiant recklessness—riding horses
bareback through the streets of Madrid, appearing at bullfights in spectacular costumes, swimming, fencing, even smoking! And, ever generous, she transferred her love for Alba to her sister, who remained her
only real confidante all her life.

Eugénie possessed a fascinating mixture of pride, courage, diffi-
dence, self-discipline, gaiety, austerity and splendor. While her breathtaking beauty attracted countless admirers, too often her alarming
intensity frightened them away.

She was indeed beautiful. Mme Carette, who became her reader, described her regular features and extremely delicate profile, as fine as on
an antique cameo. Her eyelashes, often cast down, were like a veil cast
over her bright and deep blue eyes—"overshadowed and full of soul,
energy and sweetness." She had a proud forehead, an aristocratic nose
with finely carved nostrils, and a skin of a brilliant and transparent
whiteness so delicate it reminded Mme Carette of the blue blood of the
old Spanish nobility. "Her mouth which was small could be enlivened by
a most bewitching smile," with perfect teeth. Her whole figure was
round and small, with perfect shoulders and a swanlike neck. Her hands
were thin and her feet were smaller than those of a twelve-year-old
child. Painters, sculptors and engravers attempted to reproduce her acclaimed beauty, but "there was something in the Empress's expression
which they could not 'catch,' animated fugitiveness which defied every
interpretation."

According to Mme Carette, only two portraits remotely approached
the quality of Eugénie's beauty. One, by Winterhalter, represents her in a

white burnous (or Arabian cloak) with pearls on her neck, her hair carelessly curled behind. The other, an official portrait painted by Boulanger in 1860, shows her dressed as a female fellah, coiffed *à l'égyptienne* with a red ibis, the expression in her eyes *"mystérieux et voilé."*

Already, at seventeen, with her perfect figure and tiny waist, fair skin, extraordinary blue eyes and long golden-red hair, Eugénie bewitched. Later, society women throughout the world would dye their hair to look like hers. Surrounded by admirers, she spurned all offers of marriage and soon gained the reputation of being a cold and heartless beauty who would not grant even the smallest favor. Endless stories abounded of her attempted suicide after she herself had been scorned in love—most likely stemming from an incident when, in despair after Alba had been given to Paca, she swallowed poison made from the heads of phosphorous matches.

Her coldness to her suitors was continually blamed on an earlier broken heart. She flirted, she was a coquette, she was dashing and daring. The list of those in love with her was endless—grandees and wealthy aristocrats, handsome and even penniless officers, foreign diplomats and other visitors from abroad. Alexandre Dumas father and son both fell seriously in love with her. Her friend Prosper Mérimée continued to despair of her reluctance to marry. She even drove her little pony carriage so recklessly that many a suitor was tipped out onto the roadside. Mérimée noted drily that despite the risk, most young men would be happy to lie in a ditch with Eugénie.

As if to distract herself from any possible temptations of the heart, Eugénie flung herself into a whirl of outrageous exploits. The usual heady excitements of the bullfights were no longer enough for her. She would arrive in scarlet boots, belted like a man, sporting a fearsome dagger and a whip where other ladies carried a fan. And the gossips reported that she flirted blatantly with the matadors.

It was one thing to wear fancy dress at her mother's entertainments. It was altogether more provocative to appear in bizarre costumes in public. Once Eugénie and a woman friend dressed as gypsies for the Easter flower festival at Seville. They went so far as to set up their own tent and, believing themselves to be incognito, performed gypsy dances, making eyes at passersby when they were not dancing. Two young Englishmen were completely taken in and enchanted by the gypsy girls, discussing in English their charms and merits and whether or not they should give them some money. Finally Eugénie asked in her fluent English: "Perhaps you would like to know who we are?" and introduced herself. Naturally the Englishmen fell in love.

The episode at Seville was matched by a similarly flamboyant escapade at Toledo. This time Eugénie was accompanied by her sister, her cousin Pépé and Alba himself. The four of them rode through the streets dressed as Calabrian smugglers and even dared to enter Toledo Cathedral in their costumes.

Eugénie's theatrical nature was encouraged by the little theater that her mother had built at their country estate at Carabanchel. There she enjoyed taking part in the plays and operas put on by Doña Manuela, who encouraged her friends to perform. Eugénie adored the theater, and although in later life she claimed she could neither act nor sing, she delighted her audiences when she played the flirtatious heroine in light comedies. It was well known in her circle that she had no ear at all for classical music but liked gypsy music and the rhythm of the traditional Spanish dances.

When Eugénie was twenty-one, her mother, who at that time held the highest position in the queen mother's household, secured her permission to confer on her daughters some of their father's titles. Eugénie was made a grandee of Spain in her own right twice over and became known by the most senior of her titles, Countess of Teba. In the same year she, Paca and Alba discovered the little fishing village of Biarritz, just over the Spanish border in France. She swam in the sea and went out in fishing boats in all weathers. Later, as empress, she was to go there often, and the attention attracted by her visits turned Biarritz into a fashionable seaside resort and sadly destroyed its simplicity.

Eugénie did not, however, abandon the passion for politics that she had inherited from Don Cipriano. Bonapartists at this period were much taken with the brand of socialism preached by the French social theorist Charles Fourier. Eugénie had been interested in socialism, and especially the works of Fourier, since her school days, but this idealism had left her by the time she was twenty-five. With her generous and emotional nature, it was only to be expected that such an imaginative and unorthodox girl should become passionately involved in a variety of causes. There is a story that she persuaded her French socialist mentor Chiffrey to set free the slaves which he had inherited with a plantation in Cuba. Chiffrey did so; but as the slaves now had no work they turned to crime and terrorized the countryside. He begged them to return and work for him as free men but, fearing a trap, the former slaves burned his plantation instead. Chiffrey was ruined, and in Madrid Eugénie was not allowed to forget the results of her efforts at philanthropy.

This was the unconventional Countess of Teba who delighted in shocking society, who dined out with actors and actresses and rode bareback through the streets of Madrid smoking a cigar. (Smoking was not the custom in a lady's house in Spain, but guests could smoke at Doña Manuela's.) She first met Louis-Napoleon, the son of Bonaparte's sister Queen Hortense of Holland, when she was twenty-three years old. Eugénie and her mother were invited to supper in Paris with the prince and only one other guest, who quickly arranged for the prince to be alone with the fascinating Spanish beauty. Eugénie rejected his advances, and the evening was a failure.

Prince Louis-Napoleon had been elected President of the Second French Republic in 1848. His four-year term of office was due to come to an end in May 1852, and all attempts to pass a bill enabling him to stand for reelection were defeated in the Assembly. Although no one expected Louis-Napoleon to fade completely from public life, nonetheless his successful *coup d'état* of December 1851 took many by surprise.

Eugénie and her mother returned to Paris in September the following year. Since their first meeting with Louis-Napoleon they had been constantly on the move from one fashionable spot to another: Brussels, London for the Great Exhibition of 1851, Madrid, Les Eaux-Bonnes. As soon as they reached Paris again, Doña Manuela resumed her former political friendships, her salon and her efforts to marry off her ravishing but intimidating daughter.

At the time of her marriage to Louis-Napoleon the stories of Eugénie's wild Spanish youth were endlessly elaborated upon and hugely embellished. But what gossips so often fail to grasp is that the truth can be so much more interesting than the invention. One of the most remarkable true stories about her was a tale which she herself told years later while living in exile in Britain, and which emerged only after her death.

Top: A portrait of Catherine the Great in her coronation robes. Her crown was made for the occasion by the French jeweler Posier, containing nearly five thousand diamonds, the central ruby weighing 414 carats. The scepter contains the Orlov diamond (194¾ carats).

Bottom: The Archduchess Maria Antonia of Austria painted by Martin van Meytens

Top: Maria Carolina as Queen of Naples with one of
her children painted by Élisabeth Vigée-Lebrun

Bottom: Archduchess Leopoldina of Austria painted by Josef Kreutzinger

Top: A portrait of Eugénie as a Spanish beauty shortly before her marriage to
the Emperor Napoleon III painted by Edouard Louis Dubufe, c. 1852

Bottom: Queen Alexandra painted by François Flameng

Top: The Empress Frederick of Germany as Crown Princess of Prussia, 1882, by Heinrich von Angeli

Bottom: A family group of Catherine; her husband, Peter; and their son (the future Tsar Paul I),
1756 painted by Anna Rosita Lisiewska

Left: Gregory Orlov, who helped with his brothers to overthrow and murder Catherine's husband, Tsar Peter III. He truly loved her and was created a prince, but Catherine eventually tired of him and he died raving mad.

Right: Gregory Potemkin, created Prince of Tauris: Catherine's most influential lover and a fascinating eccentric who helped her make Russia a world power.

Catherine on horseback in the uniform of her elite Preobrajensky regiment, painted in 1762, the year of her coronation, by Vigilius Erichsen

The Château de Versailles and the Place d'Armes, 1722, by Pierre-Denis Martin

The royal château at Marly

Top: Marie Antoinette in hunting dress, painted by Krantzinger in 1771

Bottom: Marie Antoinette in 1785, walking with her son the dauphin and her daughter Madame Royale in the garden of the Petit Trianon, painted by Adolf Wertmüller

The exaggerated hairstyles made popular by Marie Antoinette's fashionable dress designer Rose Bertin

The execution of Louis XVI on January 21, 1793

Clockwise: The Habsburg imperial family:
The Emperor Francis XXI and the Empress Maria
Theresa with their children, including Marie
Antoinette and Maria Carolina. With each new birth
the painter, van Meytens, simply added another little
face to the composition.

Lady Hamilton as bacchante, mezzotint, c. 1790,
by John Raphael Smith after a painting by
Sir Joshua Reynolds

View of the Palace of Caserta from the top of the
cascade. It was built by Ferdinand's father, Charles III,
King of Spain, to rival Versailles.

Coronation of Dom Pedro, Rio de Janeiro, Brazil, December 1, 1822.
Lithograph by Thierry Frères after Jean-Baptiste Debret.

Arrival of Carolina Leopoldina, 1817.
Engraving by Simon Pradier after Jean-Baptiste Debret.

A contemporary engraving of Rio de Janiero

A slave market in Rio

Top: A portrait of Empress Eugénie in her coronation regalia by Winterhalter, who was recommended to her by Queen Victoria

Bottom: Eugène-Louis Napoleon Bonaparte, 1874, by Jules Joseph Lefevbre

The Imperial Family on Horseback, engraving, French School

The Empress Eugénie surrounded by her ladies-in-waiting, chosen for their beauty
as well as their high birth, painted by Winterhalter

A sketch by Queen Victoria of Vicky, her eldest child, with Prince
Albert's greyhound bitch, Eos, who came with him from Germany and was much loved by all the family

Left: Frederick William, Crown Prince of Prussia; Victoria, Crown Princess of Prussia;
and their younger children (*left to right*) Charlotte, Victoria, Margaret (with her father),
Sophie (with her mother) and Waldemar, in August 1874

Right: A formal photographic portrait of Victoria taken in Berlin in 1883

A painting at Sandringham of Alexandra riding on the off side surrounded by her dogs

Alexandra on the royal yacht

Top: Devoted sisters, the Princess of Wales and the Empress Marie Feodorovna of Russia often amused themselves by appearing in Society dressed alike (1874)

Bottom: Tsar Alexander III and Empress Marie Feodorovna, c. 1890

Staying in a large Spanish castle for a ball, Eugénie had retired late and gone with her maid to her room. She was about to undress when she noticed the reflection in her mirror of a man hiding under the bed. Calmly telling her maid that she had left her fan in the ballroom, she asked the girl to give a footman a note to retrieve it. The maid left with the note, which actually explained the alarming situation and was to summon help. Knowing now that the man would soon be captured, Eugénie set about torturing him by slowly undressing, all the while humming a little tune. Sitting on her bed, she swung her bare legs, her feet just occasionally brushing his face. Help arrived, and the man was apprehended and recognized as a well-known criminal. He told his captors that he had come to the castle not as a thief but merely to steal a glimpse of the exquisite Countess of Teba. The sight of her tiny feet in front of his face had driven him to such a frenzy that he begged permission to kiss them. Slowly Eugénie stretched out first one foot, then the other, and he held and kissed each foot passionately.

This, then, was the woman with whom the Prince-President of France fell so madly and suddenly in love.

France

By the time Eugénie and her mother were back in Paris in September 1852, Eugénie, at twenty-six, was a mature and confident beauty. Since mother and daughter had supported the Prince-President's *coup d'état* the previous December, they were invited to several of Louis-Napoleon's receptions. Though deeply involved in preparing his transformation from president to emperor, he still found time to woo the ravishing Countess of Teba, without trying to invite her to another intimate candlelight dinner for four.

It was November 1852 when the hunting party took place at the prince's country residence at Compiègne. By that time everyone had noticed that he had eyes only for Eugénie. She had just to admire a clover leaf glistening with dew for him to give her a clover leaf of emeralds glittering with diamonds. Another evening he placed on her head a crown of violets.

"You have no idea," wrote Eugénie after the hunting party, "what they are saying about me since I accepted that devil of a horse." But when it dawned on Parisian society that the Countess of Teba, a "notorious virgin," would not agree to be Louis-Napleon's mistress, cynical courtiers and the gossipmongers could offer only one explanation: Eugénie was a scheming adventuress intent on becoming empress; incited and briefed by her mother, she was refusing to yield to the future emperor's desires unless and until he married her.

Louis-Napoleon had always had great success with women and had been through countless affairs. Now, in middle age and to the astonishment of his closest friends, he had fallen deeply in love. Not only did he clearly admire and respect Eugénie; he also found in her someone with the ability to share his own fierce and passionate commitment to an ideal: the restoration of the Napoleonic empire.

Nevertheless, when he became the Emperor Napoleon III on December 2, 1852, Louis-Napoleon was still officially looking for a wife among the royal families of Europe. Even as he was singling out Eugénie at Compiègne and crowning her with violets—the Napoleonic flower—his request for the hand of Princess Adelaide of Hohenlohe-Langenburg was being considered. To his great relief, too much stood against him: his morals, his religion, his *parvenu* status as royalty, and the sad fate of so many Queens of France in the last sixty years. Happily, he found himself free to marry Eugénie.

Count Hübner, the Austrian ambassador, had been among the guests at Compiègne and witnessed Louis-Napoleon's growing enchantment with Eugénie. He took this new attachment seriously enough to send home an assessment of the countess's character in his diplomatic report. He described her as capricious and eccentric, passionately in love with what was new, wonderful and unforeseen. In politics he described Eugénie as "an advanced liberal and constitutionalist by taste, with a great love of contrariness." He acknowledged her force of will and physical courage, something "one meets rarely, even among women of the people." As for religion, Hübner judged her only superficially instructed in the Catholic faith (something he had grown to expect in products of the Convent of the Sacré Coeur).

When it came to affairs of the heart, Count Hübner was satisfied that Eugénie's passionate nature had never led her physically astray. She possessed, he reported, "an ardent imagination and an inflammable heart, a heart which has already undergone romantic experiences, though of a distinctly innocent kind." Other members of the court were less charitable, repeating fabricated scandalous stories about her. Some of the ladies of the court showed their resentment of this beautiful intruder by openly snubbing her.

On January 15, 1853, the emperor asked the Countess of Montijo for her daughter's hand. Three days later the people of Paris heard for the first time of the existence of the lady who was to become their empress in less than a fortnight. The stock exchange panicked. The Spanish press was delighted; for the first time since Louis XIV a French sovereign was to marry a Spanish wife.

On January 22, the emperor addressed the Senate, the Council of State and the legislative body to inform them that he would marry Eugénie. Reactions to his speech were mixed. To many it was felt that a dynastic marriage would have added prestige to the empire, whereas "to be foreign without being royal seemed the worst qualification possible for an Empress of the French." Abroad, Queen Victoria felt that in announcing the match Louis-Napoleon had spoken "in bad taste," by describing himself as *parvenu*. Lord John Russell wrote to Lord Cowley, the British ambassador in Paris, "It is a very false step. A marriage with a well-behaved young Frenchwoman would, I think, have been very politick, but to put this *intrigante* on the throne is a lowering of the Imperial dignity with a vengeance."

Louis-Napoleon's closest confidant, the Spanish ambassador Donoso Cortes, listed three clear reasons why the emperor wished to marry Eugénie: the emperor's love for her; his wish to defy the European monarchies after their offensive reluctance to accept the restored Bonaparte dynasty on equal terms; and finally "the mysterious and irresistible inner illumination" which had so far inspired his greatest successes. Louis-Napoleon was now undertaking the greatest gamble of his career: to unite his own destiny with Eugénie's so soon after proclaiming the empire in the face of inevitable opposition at home and abroad.

Eugénie moved into the Elysée Palace. Radiant and excited, she was overawed by her sense of responsibility and not unmindful of the unhappy queens who had preceded her. Napoleon was eighteen years her senior, and it is generally believed that she was not as passionately in love with him as he was with her. She was, however, touched by his devotion and romantic chivalry; her spirit responded to the dangerous challenge he was offering her in asking for her dedication to the Napoleonic cause; and she would not have been human had she not been attracted by the prospect of becoming Empress of France.

On the evening of January 29, Napoleon III and Eugénie were married at a civil ceremony in the Tuileries. The next day they were married by the Archbishop of Paris in Notre Dame. The interior of the grimy old cathedral of Paris had been overlaid—some said overdone—with flags and hangings, with the arms of France and Spain, the escutcheons of the Bonapartes and the Montijos, the shields of the cities and provinces of France.

The emperor was forty-five, the empress twenty-six. A British observer wrote of the bride that "a more lovely *coup d'oeil* could not be conceived." She wore a diamond tiara, with a belt of magnificent diamonds around her tiny waist. A similar row of diamonds was sewn onto the skirts of her gown. Her wedding dress was made of white velvet with a long train, the bodice embroidered with diamonds and sapphires, and trimmed with orange blossom. Lady Augusta Bruce observed that "a sort of cloud or mist of transparent lace enveloped her," and her skirt was draped with lace as well. On her newly famous reddish-golden hair she wore the diadem of sapphires and diamonds that Bonaparte's Empress Josephine had worn at her coronation.

Empress

After the wedding Napoleon and Eugénie spent a week's honeymoon at Villeneuve-l'Etang, visiting Versailles and the Petit Trianon.

Their "travelling" honeymoon was a preparation for Eugénie's future life as empress. The sovereigns divided their year between five imperial residences: the Tuileries, Saint-Cloud, Biarritz, Compiègne and Fontainebleau. According to Augustin Filon, Eugénie's lifelong friend and tutor to her son, the empress was "a different woman in different settings." At the Tuileries, that magnificent but hopelessly inconvenient palace, she appeared to him as "a great and noble figure," devoting body and soul to "the terrible task of sovereignty." He shows us Eugénie heavily veiled and bespectacled in a carriage whose attendants wear anonymous livery. This is Eugénie in disguise, returning from charitable visits to the poor of Paris. In the afternoon she is giving audiences, before driving out for the monotonous four o'clock carriage exercise. In the evening, she appears seated on a raised dais at a state ball, "her brow encircled with a dazzling halo of diamonds, and enveloped in the splendor of her Imperial mantle."

Saint-Cloud, too, was used for the great functions of state. Here, as at the Tuileries, Eugénie presided over the balls, grand and intimate, masked or merely *en grande tenue* during Carnival, over the concerts during Lent, over the dinners, banquets and soirées throughout the year.

Every summer from 1854, usually in August, Napoleon and Eugénie went to Biarritz for five or six weeks' holiday. Prosper Mérimée, who often stayed at the villa as Eugénie's guest, wrote: "There is not a castle in France or England where one is so perfectly at liberty and free from etiquette, or one that has such a thorough and amiable châtelaine. We go for delightful excursions into the valleys of the Pyrenees, returning home with appetites to be envied." Eugénie turned a remote and obscure fishing village on the Atlantic coast into her Osborne* (though the Villa Eugénie was destroyed by fire after the fall of the empire). Until then Biarritz had been a forgotten place, described as "the naked shingles of the world," on the edge of their realm. They left it a flourishing resort.

This was the only imperial residence where Eugénie could live an almost private life. Here, as far as was possible for a sovereign of France, she could do as she pleased, say what she thought and see whom she liked. Here, in the semi-Spanish atmosphere, she could be herself. Politics were forgotten. The only guests were people she knew and personally liked, and she banished the "fault-finders, wet blankets and sticklers for etiquette, as well as all those who refused to be merry themselves." The atmosphere was a combination of an ideal country house and a large seaside hotel. Eugénie loved the sea and went sailing and swimming—though this was considered unladylike and certainly unimperial, especially by Napoleon himself.

At the beginning of October, Eugénie and Napoleon would return from Biarritz. After a week or two at Saint-Cloud (the emperor's favorite residence) they would go to Compiègne for the autumn *série,* or season, and once again Eugénie became the empress dispensing dazzling hospitality. She selected the guests, who consisted of the most prominent persons in public life—politicians, generals, diplomats, writers and artists, distinguished foreign statesmen, and royal princes and princesses from the greater or lesser European houses who were visit-

---

*Osborne was built by Queen Victoria and Prince Albert on the Isle of Wight as a holiday residence of the British royal family.

ing France. Each group of about seventy guests was invited for a week, and it was a mark of special favor to be asked to stay longer, or to come again later in the month to a new house party.

Although Eugénie's guest lists sometimes resulted in uneasy combinations, Princess Metternich, wife of the Austrian ambassador, said of these house parties with their delightful atmosphere that only a woman of the world who had become empress could have created them—"A real princess of the blood could never have done it." Royal princesses simply did not have the knowledge of society possessed by the empress, commented Princess Metternich.

Often Eugénie arranged stag hunts on horseback for which guests were required to wear the green uniforms of the time of Louis XIV. There was shooting, too, and she also arranged excursions through the forest in open charabancs. In the evenings, after the banquets, guests might enjoy a theatrical performance, put on either by professionals or by themselves. Or there might be one of the famous *tableaux vivants* when those taking part were expected to appear in the most lavish costumes—which proved a godsend to the great couturiers. Compiègne itself became enveloped in an aura of glamour which not only achieved worldwide fame when Eugénie was its châtelaine, but has also left a nostalgic memory of elegance, the apogee of the art of gracious living.

In spring the court moved to Fontainebleau. Here the social program consisted of riding, excursions and sport. Eugénie loved Fontainebleau: like Marie Antoinette she preferred her *villégiatures,* or holiday homes, to more formal city life. The Austrian ambassador marvelled at Eugénie riding to hounds at Fontainebleau on a spirited Andalusian gray which she controlled with ease. She would organize boating parties on the lake or energetic excursions that exhilarated her and exhausted her entourage. In the evenings everyone relaxed with charades, dancing or "childish games."

Napoleon III deliberately set out to create a magnificent court. "One of the first duties of a sovereign," he would say, "is to amuse his subjects at all ranks in the social scale. He has no more right to have a dull court than he has to have a weak army or a poor navy." Attending to many of the social details himself, Napoleon based protocol and etiquette at his court on that of the First Empire. Eugénie brought it luster and charm and the result was the most brilliant court in Europe (with the possible exception of St. Petersburg); one French commentator went so far as to describe it as "probably the most brilliant court we have ever had."

Eugénie's less tangible achievement was to provide a focus for the court: she became the symbol of the Second Empire. It is her profile that one finds on so many of the books dealing with the period, and no account of the years 1852–70 seems complete without a chapter on her. It was she who made France the social capital of Europe, and the English couturier Worth the arbiter of fashion worldwide. She occupied a unique place in the imagination of Europe, and helped one of the most reserved of men to revive the panache of the *ancien régime.*

At the state balls in the Tuileries the Salle des Maréchaux blazed with the lights of a hundred crystal chandeliers, "while a softer illumination played discreetly and harmoniously over the superb toilettes, shoulders a-glitter with precious stones, the gloriously bedecked diplomatic, military and civil uniforms." Men who were not in uniform wore the blue coats and white knee-breeches of court dress. At half past nine the emperor and empress made their entry. At one such evening, the French writer Louis Sonolet remembered Eugénie wearing a white lace gown, "her beautiful shoulders exposed as was the fashion, her only jewelry a pearl necklace and pearl earrings. . . . With a typical Spanish gesture," he added, "she was manipulating a white fan."

Though Napoleon and Eugénie always left at midnight, their departure was not the signal for a general exodus, as in the days of Napoleon I. Indeed, festivities often continued until four o'clock in the morning.

Less grandiose, less ceremonious, but infinitely more appreciated by those privileged to be invited were the balls known as the "Empress's Mondays." Guests had to be known personally to Napoleon or Eugénie, and invitations were limited to 400 or 500. Etiquette and protocol were relaxed to such an extent that it seemed more like a house party. Eugénie loved to be surrounded by exquisite women and made a point of inviting those she considered to be the loveliest in Paris. More alarming from her husband's point of view was her genuinely innocent appreciation of good looks in men. She herself told the Archduke Maximilian of Austria how she had once asked Napoleon to turn back their carriage as she had caught sight of a handsome youth in the street. The emperor refused, and was surprised a few days later to see the same young man in the livery of a groom. "The Empress's gaiety and naive vivacity do not always seem to please her Imperial husband," the archduke wrote home.

It was not enough for the *parvenu* emperor simply to establish a magnificent court. Napoleon III wished to be accepted by the other crowned heads of Europe, who had by no means given him a unanimous welcome. An opportunity to improve his position was offered when he and Eugénie went to Great Britain on a state visit in 1855 to mark the alliance of the two countries during the Crimean War.

Eugénie was understandably apprehensive about her first meeting as empress with a foreign reigning family on their own soil. Queen Victoria was known to be exceptionally conscious of the exalted place to which, in her opinion, only those could aspire in whose veins flowed the blood of kings and queens. In fact the visit was a great success. Eugénie charmed Queen Victoria and made of her a lifelong friend. And when the following year the British royal family paid a return state visit to Paris for the Exhibition, Eugénie welcomed them as the brilliant star of her own glittering court.

By now, at thirty, she was a young mother. Her first duty after espousing the Napoleonic cause as the bride of Napoleon III was to provide the dynasty with an heir. This she achieved only with great difficulty. She suffered a depressing miscarriage in 1853, and the Prince Imperial was not born until March 16, 1856. His birth was complicated: labor began on the Friday and it was not until Sunday that the child was born. The contractions were so violent and painful that Eugénie's attendants had to hold her completely upright between spasms. At one point the despairing doctor asked the emperor whom he should save, the mother or the child? Without hesitation Napoleon answered, "The mother." Despite Eugénie's pain and the long labor, an exceptionally healthy boy, named Napoleon Eugène Louis Jean Joseph, was born on Palm Sunday. After the birth, the empress's doctor told her not to have another child as it would certainly cost her her life.

As Napoleon had warned Eugénie before he married her, their calling had its dangers. Several assassination attempts were made against the emperor, the most dramatic of which came to be known as the Orsini bomb plot.* On January 14, 1858, Napoleon and Eugénie were on their way to the Opéra when three bombs were thrown at their carriage. Eight peo-

---

*The plot was carried out by Felice Orsini, no relation of the great Italian family.

ple were killed and 156 wounded. Two of the emperor's carriage horses were killed, bomb splinters shattered his hat, and Eugénie's left cheek and eyelid were grazed by flying glass. She remained perfectly calm, though the emperor was visibly shaken. She called to officials to look after the wounded and not to worry about herself or the emperor, saying, "It is our business to be shot at." Napoleon wished to stay and comfort the wounded, but Eugénie, thinking that a fourth bomb might be thrown, dissuaded him. As they entered their box at the Opéra, her white dress spattered with blood, the audience greeted them with an ovation. A few weeks later it was announced that in the event of the emperor's death, the empress would become regent on the Prince Imperial's behalf. By virtue of the courage she had shown at the opera, her popularity soared. As the Austrian ambassador noted in his diary, "People here are so exalted at the picture of a beautiful woman with her baby in her arms saving France with the help of a heroic army that the Emperor, apparently about to be removed by some exploding bomb at any moment, has practically become a negligible factor."

Eugénie in fact acted as regent the following year, while Napoleon was away during the War of Italian Unification. She was regent twice more: in 1865 when Napoleon went to Algeria for a month, and during the Franco-Prussian War. This third regency ended with her dramatic flight from the Tuileries on September 4, 1870, and marked the end of the Second Empire.

Historians continue to debate the extent of her political influence on Napoleon. She inherited her lifelong interest in politics from her mother and after her marriage became Napoleon's willing pupil. It pleased her that he insisted on her presence at cabinet meetings, where her opinion, generally supporting right-wing and authoritarian policies, was welcomed. Eugénie has been bitterly criticized for "interfering" in foreign affairs, usually catastrophically and urged on by a growing *folie de grandeur*. It was assumed that her nationality would affect her politics, that her ideas of her role were governed by her Spanish training. It was further assumed that as a Spanish Catholic she would go to any lengths to defend the rights of the Holy See; and that as a Spanish royalist she listened to men from Mexico who wanted to see the vast expanses of their country linked with the thrones of Europe. She was held responsible for the presence of French troops in Rome to prop up the temporal power of the Pope. She was blamed for the disastrous results of making Archduke Maximilian of Austria Emperor of Mexico. But, worst of all, she was alleged to have said of the Franco-Prussian War, "It is my war, at last!"—even though she strongly denied this, as did the man to whom she was supposed to have said it.

All these accusations are unfair. Only in the case of Maximilian's tragic Mexican adventure can any blame be attached directly to Eugénie. This was the moment of her closest involvement in the foreign policy of the Second Empire. The final decision to try to put Maximilian on the Mexican throne was made in a conclave at Biarritz consisting of four people: herself, Napoleon, and two comparatively unimportant officials. The ill-conceived and ill-executed adventure led to the capture of Maximilian, his trial and condemnation in Mexico, and his execution by firing squad at Querétaro. According to one account, a Mexican officer gazed at the archduke's corpse and observed, "That is the work of France." Eugénie was overcome by remorse at the news of his death, especially when she brooded on the misery she had brought on his mother, the Archduchess Sophia, and his brother, the Emperor Franz Joseph. She admitted her personal guilt, confessing, "For me the most painful thing in the world would be to find myself face to face with a brother and mother to whose grief I have contributed by the instigation of the Mexican expedition." It was a brave admission. But Eugénie had not acted out of caprice in promoting the disastrous venture, nor was she responsible for the bungling incompetence of Maximilian's expedition. And in subsequent years Napoleon III continued to be willing to entrust her with the regency.

She remained utterly faithful to him, both politically and physically. She has been described as "one of nature's virgins," whereas Napoleon was "a man of strong amorous needs and desires," who "was tortured by the flesh." Eugénie generally adopted a tolerant attitude toward his affairs; she felt secure in their deep friendship and fully realized that it would be impossible to stop him pursuing other women, or for women to stop offering themselves to him.

Only two incidents shook this great friendship. The first occurred in 1860; the imperial couple were touring France's overseas territories when Eugénie's adored sister, Paca, died. Napoleon felt it best to keep the news from Eugénie until their return. She was shattered by Paca's death, and also by the fact that she should be the last to hear of it. And then her loyalty to Napoleon was severely strained by his affair with Marguerite Bellanger. That her husband had formed an alliance with a twenty-five-year-old former circus dancer and chambermaid from Boulogne proved virtually unbearable, and for a time the breach in Eugénie's relationship with Napoleon was dangerously public. She despairingly complained, "Now he has sunk down to this scum, I can stand it no longer."

Yet in spite of the painful circumstances surrounding Paca's death and the hurt she often felt at her husband's repeated infidelities, Eugénie's steadfastness and their mutual faith in the future of the Prince Imperial always made Napoleon return to her. And in her case, it was her powerful sense of loyalty and duty which prompted her tolerance.

Influence Political, Moral and Cultural

Whatever others might think of the bride of Louis-Napoleon, he himself presented her to the nation as a perfect match. "She whom I have chosen," he announced, "is of lofty birth. French by education and by memory of her father's blood shed in the cause of Empire, she has the advantage, as a Spaniard, of having no family in France to whom honours must be given." Despite her fluent French Eugénie could never have passed as a Frenchwoman. She spoke the language with a very slight foreign accent—some said it was more English than Spanish, and her admirers claimed it added a certain charm to her way of speaking.

And Eugénie could certainly charm. When Augustin Filon met her for the first time he was entranced, as well as finding her "entirely different, physically, mentally and morally," from the woman he had imagined. When he met her she was already forty, and her complexion had started to fade. She stood on the terrace of her villa at Biarritz, with neither hat nor parasol to shade her from the sun, which was almost Spanish in its intensity. Filon remembered her holding a tiny gloved hand over her eyes: "It would have been easy for her to have hidden certain marks and lines—hardly visible, perhaps—left on her face by physical and mental suffering. But she never resorted to artificial aids to beauty, and, beyond using a little rice powder, her only weakness was a pencilled line under the eyelashes." When the empire fell in 1870 and she had to flee Paris, she still insisted in pencilling in this line, even though it made her instantly recognizable and therefore much more likely to be captured by her enemies. But as Filon said, "she would not have recognized herself without the artificial shadow which changed the expression of her eyes."

Filon was also surprised to find that Eugénie was far simpler and more natural than any of the women who surrounded her. She never struck a pose: "She seemed to think no more of playing the part of a pretty woman than of assuming the role of an Empress." She spoke with a warmth and a frankness that both astonished and charmed him. She impressed him, not as "the flawless beauty who reigned like a fairy queen in the midst of theatrical splendor," but as a woman who possessed both brains and a heart and who inspired him, as she did all who surrounded her (with the notable exception of her husband), with a "passionate loyalty."

There can be little doubt that Eugénie at times gave the impression of overfamiliarity, and in consequence of dubious moral sense. To begin with there was the question of manners: "One circumstance I find has been made much of," wrote a correspondent of *The Times,* "is that the Countess of Teba has been occasionally addressed by some of her male acquaintances by her Christian name of Eugénie." This was considered to be perfectly proper in Spain, where a friend of the family, even though not related, was entitled to address members of the family of both sexes by their Christian names, either with or without the addition of Don or Doña. It was, however, difficult to convince the average middle-class Frenchman or Englishman that such familiarity did not make her an immoral woman.

In other ways the Countess of Teba, considered wild and eccentric, must have seemed strangely prudish. When Princess Mathilde Bonaparte invited her gentlemen guests to kiss the brow of the ladies present at midnight on New Year's Eve, Eugénie declined to join in, saying she preferred to adhere to the customs of her own country. In Spain a man may address a woman by her Christian name, but he may not kiss her. Eugénie's natural and easy manner, her frankness with strangers, and particularly her innocently flirtatious and coquettish ways were quite normal behavior for a lady in Spain, whereas the French understood only strict and artificial court behavior—anything else appeared to them to indicate loose morals. Where morals were concerned Eugénie abided uncompromisingly by the strict standards of her country.

It was this mixture of Spanish pride and ease which typified Eugénie, created the atmosphere of her court, and so baffled and confused those who set out to be hostile. Writing early in the reign, Prosper Mérimée noted how the empress "had learnt from her earliest youth to alternate an enjoyment of relaxation with the formalities of a Spanish noblewoman who had been much at the court." She never submerged her own character, even when imperial interests appeared to require it. Robert Sencourt, the only biographer of whom she approved, recorded that a "court dinner might commence with the bristling strictness of a new etiquette; but afterwards, especially if the Emperor were called away, it became a party between people who had known one another long and well, and finished as a Spanish *tertulia* where, all being intimate, they can call each thing by its own name and say whatever comes into their heads."

There were, however, misunderstandings on both sides. When the emperor was present, Eugénie generally maintained the dignity of her rank. But in his absence, Sencourt observed, "she would relax so much in speech and gesture as to give, even though it were only by a nuance, an impression which occasioned gossip." Sencourt admitted that Eugénie could never quite understand the French point of view. Frequently she would use an expression that shocked her entourage, and then blush, asking, "Have I said something wrong?" As Sencourt conceded, "It was easy to understand how, to those who knew nothing of Spaniards and their ways, there seemed reason to echo the gossip which had met the announcement of her engagement."

All her life Eugénie placed very little importance on sex: not as something wicked, just unimportant and cheap. "You mean," she would say in disbelief, "that men are interested in nothing but that?" when her ladies were chatting about infidelities. Perhaps her horror of sex had been brought about by the two unhappy loves of her youth and her husband's repeated infidelities. Referring to the time when she fled before the mob invading the Tuileries, Eugénie herself declared that she had no fear of death. What she feared was some sexual debasement: "All I dreaded was falling into the hands of viragos who would defile my last scene with something shameful or grotesque, who would try to dishonor me as they murdered me. I imagined them lifting my skirts. . . ." Perhaps her sexuality was of necessity powerfully repressed. She craved love; and after the early passion, Louis-Napoleon failed to give it to her. She admitted that her religion helped her to resist the temptation of finding love elsewhere. "If I were not a believer," she said, "I would have had too many lovers. To love, that is the only thing worthwhile."

How much of a believer was she? Augustin Filon wrote that because she was a Spaniard, the French took her also to be superstitious, "ever kneeling on the flagged stones of old cathedrals, telling her beads in trance-like contemplation of the lighted tapers." Filon pointed out that the picture would have been very different had these Frenchmen and women taken into account her childhood in Paris, the liberal atmosphere in which she grew up, and her store not of saintly legends but of Napoleonic memories. He himself held that Eugénie was far less superstitious than her husband. To say that she was excessively pious would be an exaggeration, he concluded, "for her religious practices were moderate, and at no time of her life did she surround herself with priests. She was just a good Catholic—and no more."

Nonetheless Eugénie's Spanish background created a gulf between her and her new countrymen. After the announcement of her engagement, for instance, she and Doña Manuela moved into the Elysée Palace until the wedding. Many people left their cards or signed the visitors' book, but in accordance with Spanish custom Eugénie neither returned calls nor accepted invitations; nor did she appear at the pre-wedding ball at the Tuileries. Needless to say, many people misunderstood this withdrawal as arrogance. There were innumerable such occasions when it seemed Eugénie gave offense without wishing to, simply by following the customs of Spain. Some unjustly accused her of imposing rigorous Spanish etiquette on her staff, whereas, according to Filon, the truth was that "she set no value on etiquette, and so often disregarded it that the emperor had constantly to recall her to a sense of the formalities befitting her exalted rank."

One of her customs did delight all who saw it: her famous curtsy, which was likened to a flower being bent and then released by the wind. The United States ambassador in Madrid described how this action entranced him, and also how Eugénie's grace even overshadowed the visiting Queen of Spain. When they took leave, Queen Isabella, wrote the ambassador, "set her whole body in motion and nodded her head as familiarly as any citizen's wife; but Eugénie turned towards them in all her graceful charm, placed her feet firmly, and then stood bending the upper part of her body back and bringing it forward again, with the easiest, prettiest movement from side to side, like a swan curving its neck; then, without turning, she slowly withdrew backwards to the doorway. In this way she copied to perfection the wonderful swaying movement of the upper part of the body in which the Andalusian danseuses are inimitable." The court used to call this single bow her *révérence circulaire,* which, combined with a single smiling glance in which she included all who were present, was "one of the empress's social triumphs, and never failed to excite admiration."

The fact that Eugénie was not royal is as important as the fact that she was a foreigner. Louis-Napoleon was to some extent an adventurer, and his ministers were dismayed that he had chosen a foreigner who to all extents and purposes appeared to be an adventuress. They felt he needed the prestige of a royal bride to give more legitimacy and credibility to his new empire. Despite Eugénie's beauty and charm, she never succeeded in winning the hearts of the Parisians, nor was she able to share in the hold her husband had over the provinces. Yet it was undeniably Eugénie who gave the Second Empire its brilliance and saved it from being commonplace. Louis-Napoleon flaunted his *parvenu* status, and it was a far greater credit to him and his choice of Eugénie as bride that they both triumphed at the foreign courts where they were guests.

They won the friendship and respect of Queen Victoria, who was initially suspicious, a friendship from which Eugénie learned much. On Queen Victoria's advice she commissioned Winterhalter to paint a number of portraits of herself and her ladies (which he did with his usual charm and lack of insight into the sitter's character). One famous Winterhalter portrait of Eugénie surrounded by her eight ladies-in-waiting, painted in 1854, is remarkable for the beauty of all its subjects. She alone among them wears no jewels; they wear bracelets and pearl necklaces, but her beauty suffices unadorned. It was as if she wished to recreate the famous gallery of beauties of Louis I of Bavaria, Marie Antoinette's godson. Eugénie had enough self-confidence to make a point of choosing her companions at court from the most beautiful ladies of the empire.

Her favorite ladies were honored by having their portraits painted on the doors of the famous Salon Bleu, the Blue Drawing Room of the Tuileries, where the arrangement of the furniture and objects shows the empress's particular touch. The word *chic* was used for the first time primarily to describe the Second Empire and particularly the court—it was simply *le chic*.

Victoria also recommended her tailor, Charles Creed, to Eugénie. The empress was so pleased with his work that soon Creed was able to open a branch in Paris. He was fortunate to work for a woman who, as far as fashion was concerned, became the cynosure of European society. French fashion invaded everywhere. In Spain, according to Mérimée, one rarely saw lace mantillas anymore—they had been replaced by Eugénie's *chic* little hats. It was the same story in London, Berlin and Vienna. In Cologne and Karlsruhe the shop windows all displayed pictures of the Empress of France. In Stuttgart the court went *à la française,* with French magazines everywhere and French spoken even in the cafés. All the women did their utmost to imitate their idol, Eugénie.

Winterhalter directed her attention to the large hats which Romney and Reynolds had so often painted on their subjects. For her next portraits, Eugénie wore a huge hat made of Italian straw and wrapped about with blue muslin. To this was added some Spanish lace, and on the wide band she pinned Parma violets, blueberries and poppies. It was a sensation, but Eugénie made it clear that this particular artist's prop was for her exclusive use. Instantly the fashion reverted to tiny *chic* hats, perched at precarious angles on the head. Winterhalter's portraits firmly place Napoleon and Eugénie among the royal families of Europe, from which he makes them quite indistinguishable. Despite accolades such as this, neither Napoleon nor Eugénie ever tried to hide or ignore their origins.

The empress's greatest contribution to fashion must surely have been her use of the crinoline. She did not invent it, however, nor was she the first to wear a crinoline at court. It was Princess Metternich whose elegant court dress of white tulle and silver lamé, trimmed with marguerites, caught Eugénie's attention, and the young designer, Worth, instantly became her protégé. Designing dresses for Europe's most elegant and beautiful sovereign made Worth's fame and fortune. The empress wore his dresses throughout the second Paris Exhibition in 1867, and as a result nearly all the queens and princesses of Europe became his customers.

In the early 1860s the silk weavers of Lyons had petitioned Eugénie to help their industry back into fashion. At that time they were near bankruptcy. Now that all Europe wore the wide-skirted crinoline, the silk industry of Lyons revived and flourished. In response to the demands of fashion Lyons produced the most exquisite materials: shot taffetas and damask—clouded, spotted, marbled, checked—at sixty francs a yard. The weavers of Lyons also made gold and silver brocades, lampas in gold and silver thread, and moiré antique in every color. The empress would call these her "political" dresses, since by wearing them she hoped to bring business to the industry.

Like most of her entourage, she much preferred the lighter fabrics: muslin, gauze, organdie, tulle, tarlatan, grenadine, jaconet and so on. But the brilliance of the 1867 season ended abruptly as the French court went into mourning after the defeat and execution of the Emperor Maximilian in Mexico. The next season Eugénie appeared in a much severer line of dress: a skirt with all the fullness at the back, ending with a short train, and straight and narrow in front. It suited her to perfection and, after nearly ten years, brought an end to the reign of the crinoline. The train was adopted by all levels of society, sweeping across the ballrooms of Europe as well as the streets and floors of the working classes.

As for color, the Napoleonic emblem of violets featured everywhere, and violet remained extremely popular. Although Eugénie herself preferred the perfume of lavender, *extrait de violettes* was the fashionable scent and, used either by high society or the demimonde, the scent of violets permeated the Second Empire. Eugénie never wore loud colors. She preferred shades of pearl-gray, mauve and maize, and for the evening only white. She adored sapphire blue, and a particular shade of blue became known as *le bleu Eugénie*. In 1869 she thrilled fashionable society with her dresses when she attended the opening ceremonies of the Suez Canal, built by her cousin Ferdinand de Lesseps. Eugénie placed a large order for the four days of balls, banquets and receptions, and among her wardrobe there was even a sailor dress! The new color became *eau de nil*, described in one contemporary journal as "an artistic blend of green and gray with a wonderful silver sheen." Silk in this color was said to resemble "the ripple of the Nile in moonlight."

Even before she became empress it was clear that Eugénie would be imitated. Her tendency to favor masculine styles—a penchant that went with her daring horsemanship—immediately influenced fashion. She in-

troduced stiff collars and cuffs; and French ladies were quick to copy
the high-heeled boots she wore at the emperor's hunting party, as well
as the tight leather belts and the embroidered Spanish bolero waistcoats
she often wore. With the outbreak of the Crimean War, fine Eastern
cashmere shawls in multicolored paisley patterns, so popular in the time
of Josephine, once again became the fashion. As they were extremely
expensive, French manufacturers immediately produced cheap copies,
and soon rich and poor alike were seen walking enveloped in a shawl.
Shawls were not only fashionable; they were also immensely practical,
as dresses were so wide at the time that no cloak could cover them.

Ladies even attempted to imitate her wonderful red-gold hair. Coif-
feurs tried by mixing endless variations of dyes to find the right shade
for their customers. Wigs, tresses, plaits, chignons and "Eugénie curls"
were exhibited in their windows and sold by the thousand—to
duchesses and milkmaids alike. To keep the elaborate hairstyles in place,
nets called *invisibles* were invented. Soon it became the custom to have
these made of one's own hair, and they were even given as gifts. In their
efforts to imitate everything Spanish, ladies also decorated their hair
with tall Spanish combs.

The empress's bedroom was a bare, impersonal room, with her huge
bed raised like a throne on a dais and hung with heavy embroidered
draperies. She used this room only for sleeping, for all the bustle and
activity took place in her dressing room next door. This was fitted with
large revolving mirrors so that she could see herself from all angles, and
the walls were lined with huge presses full of dresses and cloaks of
every design and color. There were separate rooms for hats and bon-
nets, boots and shoes, sunshades and dust cloaks. Her attendants had
rooms on the floor above which were connected to Eugénie's dressing
room by an elevator and speaking tubes. Here she installed her life-size
dolls, made according to her exact measurements. Every morning these
dolls were dressed and sent down for the empress to choose her outfit.
By day Eugénie preferred very simple dresses, choosing practical
clothes for travelling and for life in the country; but in the evening she
would wear her most sumptuous dresses and jewels. Wide-open neck-
lines were framed by a "bertha," a concoction of ribbons, ruches, laces,
embroideries, feathers and almost anything else imaginable. One of Eugénie's most spectacular creations was a bertha of rubies, sapphires,

emeralds, turquoises, amethysts, jacinths, topazes and garnets, linked together with the crown diamonds "which numbered many hundreds."*

The court invariably adopted the fashions inspired by political events abroad. Peking, Algiers and Sebastopol resulted in hatched blazers, boating jackets and the Garibaldi blouse, and after the court visited the African army at the camp at Saint-Maur the burnous came into favor. She was also credited with the introduction of the *en-tout-cas,* half umbrella, half parasol, and the wearing of colored underskirts, especially red and blue. After Eugénie's visit to Scotland, she introduced tartan cloaks, and she even dressed the Prince Imperial in a kilt.

Worth also designed a shorter skirt for walking. Not long afterward the empress and three ladies were seen skating on the lake in the Bois de Boulogne, dressed in this shorter crinoline:

As they glided smoothly in a row, they held out before them in their eight neatly gloved hands a rod covered in velvet. They were wearing extremely short crinolines, so short that they barely covered their knees, and billowed up higher in the breeze. Beneath were wide velvet knickers, fastened under the knee. Their legs were gaitered, and their flashing, silver skates were strapped on to high heeled boots. They wore short jackets, drawn in tightly at the waist and trimmed with sable and chinchilla; and small velvet toques were perched on the front of their heads.

Her influence was so widespread and her fashion authority so unquestioned that even in California and the bars of the Wild West, two months later, ladies would be copying the newest tea gown of the Empress Eugénie!

---

*In 1887 the French crown jewels were put up for auction and many of the empress's favorite pieces were seen again: "the famous vine-leaf ornament, with its wreaths of more than 3,000 larger and small diamonds . . . the comb composed of 208 large diamonds . . . the girdle of pearls, sapphires, rubies and emeralds, linked together with 2,400 diamonds . . . exquisite specimens of jewellery by Bapst, Krammer, Lemonnier . . . her diadems—the wonderful Russian tiara of 1,200 diamonds . . . the Greek scroll-like one, and others—on her flatly dressed hair, a fashion followed by others whom it did not suit." The author's ancestor Field Marshal Fürst Alfred zu Windisch-Graetz, bought the Empress Eugénie's pearls at this sale, but most of her jewels were purchased by an Indian maharaja.

But not only did the empress have a definitive influence on fashion, she also made a long-lasting impression on the women's movement. During her regency in 1866, Eugénie allowed women to be employed in the telegraph offices and so was the first employer of women in public service.

Napoleon III had a serious purpose in creating the festivities of which Eugénie was the brilliant central figure. His aim was to establish the new aristocracy in society and also to reconcile members of the old families to the new regime. Louis-Napoleon made a point of showing the greatest deference to the princes of the old regime; yet they still tended to shun the Tuileries as they had shunned the Elysée. Perhaps they resented the fact that Eugénie's court was filled with Spaniards and South Americans as well as the Mexicans and English she welcomed. She found a certain security in surrounding herself with foreigners, particularly foreign women, as (she believed) they would have less reason to conspire with the gossips and political cabals she so feared.

It was undoubtedly Eugénie who made Paris the social capital of Europe, and yet the court was constantly criticized for trying to compromise between tradition and democracy—and failing. Neither Napoleon III nor his empress wished to lose touch with their former lives. They wanted to be accessible, not protected from reality by a thick screen of protocol and etiquette. As a result the fresh liveliness and dash of their court made the other European courts appear still more stagnant. The Archduke Maximilian reproved Eugénie's court for being "irresistibly comic." "The whole thing," he mocked, "is like a court of amateurs, with its various offices filled by people who are not too sure of themselves. There can be no talk of a good or a bad tone here, for the reason that this court has no tone of any kind." "I must say," he wrote to his brother the Emperor Franz Joseph, "that I blessed the day upon which it was granted me to turn my back upon the center of civilization." Undeterred, the center of civilization continued to enjoy itself.

But Eugénie remained curiously anxious about her court and became more and more obsessed with her doomed predecessor, Marie Antoinette. From the time of her honeymoon she began to collect relics of the dead queen. She bought mementos at sales, and went to enormous lengths to find the furniture and pictures that had hung in the Petit Trianon, which she turned into a Marie Antoinette museum. To bring public attention back, she even arranged a "Marie Antoinette season," with powdered wigs worn in the old-fashioned way. For the Exhibition of 1867 she decided to put her Marie Antoinette collection on public display, encouraging anyone else with similar relics to do the same. Her efforts met with great success. Eugénie herself lent a dress sample book which Marie Antoinette had used each morning to decide what she would wear that day.

In spite of this success, the whole effect of Eugénie's devotion to the memory of Marie Antoinette had a sinister feel. Her private apartments at Saint-Cloud became a macabre reminder of the dead queen. As well as portraits of the executed queen and her family, she also possessed Marie Antoinette's famous writing desk, decorated with two bronze-gilt chimeras, a masterpiece of cabinetmaking. As a wedding gift, Louis Napoleon had given Eugénie two magnificent diamond earrings in the shape of two pears, surmounted by two large stones, which had once belonged to Marie Antoinette. But the strangest souvenir was given to her by Princess Metternich: a portrait of Marie Antoinette painted in Vienna before her marriage, at the age of about fourteen. It shows her wearing a thin red ribbon around her neck, so strangely prophetic of her fate. Before the wedding Eugénie's mother had written, "I am obsessed with the memory of Marie Antoinette and cannot help asking myself whether or not my child will share her fate." This fear tormented Eugénie too: "I think with terror," she wrote just a few months after her wedding, "of Marie Antoinette." These fears were not unjustified, and after her visit to the Suez Canal, Eugénie began to withdraw more from public life. She became more and more alarmed by the designs and attitudes of Prussia. In July 1870 France declared war on Prussia, and although Eugénie was an enthusiastic supporter of the war (as were most of her subjects) she ought not to be blamed for it. On September 1 Louis-Napoleon surrendered at Sedan. The Second Empire had fallen.

Eugénie as regent refused to leave the Tuileries until the mob had broken down the gates and no vestige of hope remained. With the help of her American dentist she escaped to England, where she was reunited with the Prince Imperial and, six months later, with the emperor. The British public had always loved Eugénie and she was greeted warmly and with great sympathy. The imperial family accepted the lease of Camden Place at Chislehurst, in Kent, and henceforth their life revolved around the education of their son. The emperor, who had suffered from kidney disease for some time, died two years later.

All hope for the Bonapartist cause now rested with the Prince Imperial. Eugénie adored him. Even in the days of her splendid court at Paris she would pass his room to say good night every evening before going down to dinner. The door would open, there would be a rustle of silks and the soft jingle of bracelets, and she would kiss him tenderly. She often longed to stay with him rather than enter the glittering court circle for an evening of gaiety, and she once lamented to Augustin Filon that *she* was not forbidden to attend a dinner, as was her son.

By the time of their exile, the Prince Imperial was remarkable in every way: handsome, intelligent, dashing and with a wisdom well beyond his years. It seemed to his supporters only a question of time before he should reclaim his throne.

In 1879 he was allowed to join the British army sent to conquer the troublesome African tribes in Zululand. There he fell into an ambush and was killed. Eugénie had moved to Farnborough, in Surrey, where she built a mausoleum to preserve the memory of Louis-Napoleon. The following year she travelled to South Africa to visit the spot where her son had fallen in battle, and brought his body back to lie next to that of the emperor his father. With her heart, though not her spirit, broken, the empress lived another forty years in seclusion in England.

6

Vicky

*O*n *a bright, bitterly cold January day in 1858* Victoria Adelaide Mary Louise, Princess Royal of Great Britain, made her state entry into Berlin. Beside her in the coach was Prince Frederick of Prussia, her new husband. Vicky marvelled at the reception the Berliners gave her, and their cheering made her forget how cold she was in the open coach with her low-cut dress and no wrap.

When they stopped at the bottom of the palace steps and Vicky saw her new family gathered at the top, she jumped down unaided and, gathering her wide skirts, ran up to meet them. Dropping a deep curtsy at the feet of her father-in-law, the Crown Prince of Prussia, Vicky expected a friendly embrace. Hesitantly she looked up, only to discover he had already passed on to greet her husband, Fritz. The usually aloof Queen Elizabeth softened and asked her if she was frozen, at which Vicky replied with characteristic fervor, "I have only one warm place, and that is in my heart."

England

The snub by the Prince of Prussia set the pattern for Vicky's relationship with her German family. From the start there had been opposition to her marriage—most notably from Otto von Bismarck. When 1856 the Adjutant General, Leopold von Gerlach, had asked his opinion about the proposed "English marriage," Bismarck replied that the *marriage* part might succeed, "for the Princess is said to be a lady of intelligence and feeling." But he greatly disliked the *English* part of it. England, he believed, possessed a far stronger feeling of nationality than his own country. In addition, Germans, from politicians, journalists, sportsmen, landowners and judges to the simple peasants, already showed a servile admiration for all things British, which Bismarck felt would only be made worse if the first lady in the land were an Englishwoman. "If she succeeds in leaving the Englishwoman at home and becomes a Prussian, she will be a blessing to the country," he announced, adding, "If our future Queen remains even only partly English, I can see the Court in danger of being surrounded by English influences."

Ironically enough, Vicky's own father, Albert the Prince Consort, had voiced exactly the same misgivings about Vicky's position as Bismarck: "The Princess Royal of England is expatriating herself and marrying Prince Frederick William of Prussia, and thereby she does not cease to be Princess Royal, and with the best will in the world to become as German as possible, she can never change her nature." Bismarck's suspicions would have been even greater had he known that Queen Victoria and Prince Albert were training their daughter as their missionary to the Prussians—to bring enlightenment from a civilized world to barbarians. Vicky was an eager pupil. Only a month after arriving in Berlin she wrote to her father, "What you say about my position is so right and is often a matter of reflection for me. If I was to lose sight of my English title and dignity I should do myself and my husband much harm, besides forgetting my duty to you and England."

Vicky's mother also never let her daughter forget what she owed to her country of origin. To Vicky, England was always "home." In her first letter after Vicky's marriage, Queen Victoria instructed her to always sign herself as a British princess first and a Prussian one second—"Victoria, Princess Royal, Princess Frederick William of Prussia"—and so she did almost invariably until she became German empress. Quite explicitly Vicky regarded her English influence on the Prussian court as a tool in her hands for doing good. Albert, for his part, had a vision of an enlightened, united Germany and saw his daughter as his instrument to further that dream. Set on such a course, Vicky would inevitably make enemies in her new home. Had she eschewed politics, she might have escaped more easily. But, as she told her father, "I think that a Princess (or any woman) who pretends to know nothing of what is going on, or takes no interest in public affairs or no pains to form her own opinions upon them, must be just as much a bore to her husband and useless to the world as one who is always mixing herself up in those matters and for them neglecting her other duties."

Vicky was an exceptional princess, having inherited her father's political acumen, and a great love and understanding of literature and the arts, combined with her mother's sharp intellect and impetuosity. She was her parents' first child, and Albert doted on his intelligent daughter, scrupulously supervising her education. She was fluent in English, French and German at an early age. She enjoyed learning: it was a case of Latin declensions before breakfast and mathematical problems before going to sleep. She devoured Gibbon's *Decline and Fall* and (as each volume was published) Macaulay's *History of England*. Precocious to the point of prodigy, she had a real talent for painting and an exceptional bent for politics.

Vicky was also rather spoilt. Despite her charm, she had a terrible temper, which she later learned to control; and her mother called her "a sly little rogue." As well as being clever and quick-witted, she could also be suddenly moved to pity and tears and was capable of great depths of emotion. At the age of ten she met her future husband.

Fritz was then twenty, visiting the Great Exhibition in London in 1851, together with his parents (then the Prince and Princess of Prussia). Her compulsive inquisitiveness ensured that by the end of the second day there was nothing about Fritz Vicky did not know. Educated at the University of Bonn, he loved reading as much as she did, and when not soldiering, spent his spare time in the library of his uncle, the king (where, to Vicky's amazement, there was not one novel). He did not share Vicky's enthusiasm for mathematics, chemistry or science, but he did enjoy poetry. He was a lonely young man with few friends and he had never kept a pet. What surprised and delighted him about the British royal children was their relaxed and loving yet respectful relations with their parents, and the parents' open affection for each other. That love could be combined with political expedient in a royal marriage was a new concept and one totally unfamiliar to Fritz's Prussian background. A bride was chosen for the concessions, bargains and advantages she had to offer, whereas "love" was something illicit and invariably extramarital. The domestic happiness he witnessed in the British royal family made a deep impression on him.

After this visit Fritz and Vicky kept up a correspondence, though that was temporarily disrupted by the Crimean War. (Relations between England and Prussia reached an all-time low during this period, since Prussian neutrality seemed incomprehensible to the British, in view of the friendship of the two royal houses.) Then, on September 14, 1855, Fritz visited Balmoral. Both his mother the Princess of Prussia and the Prince Consort felt that a marriage between him and Vicky would further plans for a liberal, united Germany and encouraged the match. Vicky had loved Fritz from the moment she first met him; it took little encouragement for him to feel the same. She was now fifteen, he was twenty-four; Fritz proposed and was accepted.

After the Crimean War, Vicky travelled with her parents to visit Emperor Napoleon III and his glamorous empress, Eugénie. That week in the Palace of Saint-Cloud opened her eyes to French sophistication and taste. Having sent Vicky a life-size "doll" in her own image, Eugénie and Napoleon then sent the doll a wardrobe and so ensured that Vicky would have suitably fashionable clothes for the visit. With her new wardrobe (and her own bedroom in Saint-Cloud) Vicky took note of everything—especially the decorations and pictures. Her room led into her own miniature garden with orange trees in tubs and a superb view of Paris. Enchanted, Vicky recorded it all in her sketchbook. She adored the Empress Eugénie, who exemplified to her young, impressionable mind all that was grace, charm and beauty.

The news of the engagement was to be kept a secret but of course it leaked out, and the Queen and Prince Albert were taken aback at the negative reaction. A leading article in *The Times* described the engagement as "unfortunate" and the Hohenzollerns as a "paltry German dynasty." In Prussia too the press headlines proclaimed, "The Marriage Is a Mistake." The animosities of the Crimean War had not been forgotten. Moreover, Parliament had to settle the tricky question of Vicky's dowry. It was resented that Vicky's household, chosen for her by the Queen of Prussia, consisted entirely of German matrons. Queen Victoria was insisting that the wedding take place in England. She won, and also stipulated that two German girls of Vicky's own age be appointed and come to Windsor as ladies-in-waiting so as to get to know Vicky before the wedding. This was a wise decision; and the choice was fortunate, for Countess Walburga Hohenthal (later Lady Paget) and Countess Marie Lynan became Vicky's instant and lifelong friends. As Vicky later wrote, "We three suited so well and were so happy, like three friends only can be who love each other truly." When Queen Victoria first met Wally (as she came to be affectionately known) before the wedding she remarked, "The Princess is seventeen, the Maid of Honour eighteen. What a respectable Court that will make!"

Meanwhile Prince Albert was using the time between the engagement and the wedding to prepare Vicky for her new life and the role in it that he envisaged for her. Each evening he spent two hours teaching her himself; he also sent her to attend a weekly lecture on chemistry at the South Kensington Museum. Albert even corresponded regularly with Fritz to open his eyes to the deplorable state of Prussian politics, and instructed both bride and groom in his vision of a unified Germany. Yet it was easy to see which of the two would take the lead. Fritz was underdeveloped for his age, and their backgrounds contrasted strikingly. "Her surroundings had been large, splendid and liberal, whilst he had been brought up in a narrow, old-fashioned and reactionary way." Lady Paget also noted that Fritz was already becoming well aware of this difference and was speaking about it openly with his friends.

Lady Paget first met Vicky when she was seventeen and found the princess young for her age, with a captivating childlike dignity and goodness. "Her eyes were what struck me most," Lady Paget remembered; "the iris was green, like the sea on a sunny day, and the white had a peculiar shimmer which gave them the fascination that, together with a smile showing her small and beautiful teeth, bewitched those who approached her. The nose was unusually small and turned up slightly, and the complexion was decidedly ruddy, perhaps too much for one so young, but it gave the idea of perfect health and strength." Lady Paget found Vicky's voice delightful, with its slightly foreign accent (in English as well as German). If there was any fault in Vicky's face it lay in "the squareness of the lower features" and "a look of determination about the chin."

A more dangerous fault, according to Lady Paget, was the fact that Vicky was "no judge of character, and never became one, because her own point of view was the only one she could see." So powerful were many of Vicky's enthusiasms that no one dared contradict her. If a word of warning or criticism did reach her, Vicky's enthusiasm, if anything, grew stronger. "She often mistook a real friend, who blamed, for an enemy," wrote Lady Paget, "whilst she trusted a fawning hypocrite. She never understood proud or sensitive natures, and her own want of moral courage in not telling her friends what displeased her in them has been the cause of many heartaches and disappointments."

Vicky's affection and devotion to her family and theirs for her were so strong and so obvious to all (and especially to Fritz, whose own family relations were cold, distant and formal) that even the excitement of dances and her trousseau could not ease the pain of leaving home. Lady Paget, her beloved Wally, wrote that "even before she left England I never saw anyone so entirely attached to her home and her belongings and consciously appreciating them—a thing very rare in one so young." And the American ambassador remarked that Vicky had "an excellent head" and "a heart as big as a mountain."

The wedding was fixed for January 25, 1858, in the Chapel Royal, St. James's. On her last visit to Balmoral, Vicky tried to distract herself from her tortured fear of the "unknown" in Germany by translating a difficult German author! As ever, Fritz was tender and full of consideration. The Prussians, among the large numbers of foreign royalty and guests, were surprised at the enthusiasm shown by the British people for their royal family.

On the day itself Vicky wore white moiré, trimmed with Honiton lace, with white roses fastening her bridal veil, and her hair worn smooth in the German fashion. Although she could never have been thought a leader of fashion, her trousseau was suitably elaborate. As a compliment to Ireland, it included a dress of emerald green, richly embroidered with gold shamrocks. Irish embroidery was also chosen for collars and sleeves. A month after the wedding Queen Victoria wrote to her, "I hear from all sides how your dresses and toilettes are admired, so I take a good deal for myself, as I took such pains with your dresses." (This from someone who was capable of wearing truly horrific toilettes at times, as on a visit to Saint-Cloud in 1855, when she sported a huge reticule embroidered with a gold poodle.)

Londoners were dazzled by the pomp and ceremony and the astonishing concentration of royalty—more than at the Congress of Vienna, some said. Albert had been created Prince Consort by Queen Victoria to dispel his foreignness, and now his English daughter was becoming a German.

Fritz gave Vicky a string of enormous pearls, the largest she had ever seen, as a wedding gift. The Queen and Prince Albert gave a magnificent set of crystal candelabra. The Duchess of Kent's gift of a dressing case in gold and coral was particularly admired. The Emperor Napoleon III and the Empress Eugénie gave splendid jewelry, as did the Prussian royal family. The King of Prussia had also ordered the Royal Porcelain Manufactory in Berlin to create a rich service of sixty covers as a present for his future niece. Vicky had been actively encouraging a taste for British porcelain at home, and by her numerous gifts to foreign courts she created a similar fashion abroad.

The ceremony itself was choked with emotion, and afterward the cheers were loud and warm for the bridal pair and both sets of parents as they stood on the balcony of Buckingham Palace. After the wedding breakfast Vicky, enchanting in white velvet and fur, left with Fritz for a brief two-day honeymoon at Windsor.

A week later, after endless sobbing farewells, Vicky left her beloved papa at the pier at Gravesend and sailed with Fritz on the *Victoria and Albert* across the Channel.

Germany

Mid-nineteenth-century Germany was still a semifeudal society, deeply conservative, with the people's patriotism directed to their local princely house. Throughout the 1850s the internal politics of Prussia became less and less liberal, while Germans in general increasingly abandoned the old traditions represented by Austria and based their hopes on the aggressively rising new star, Prussia. It was Prussia now, not Austria, which led the princely states away from their peaceful agricultural way of life—the breeding grounds of poetry and philosophy— and pushed them into the highly industrialized, unified state which, with Bismarck and the Emperor Wilhelm II at its head, was feared and respected by the rest of Europe.

When Vicky married Fritz, there were four elderly brothers and their families at the head of the Prussian royal house. They lived in close proximity in their Berlin palaces in winter, moving to their Potsdam palaces in summer. The Prussian king was childless and he suffered from an arterial disorder which affected his reason. His brother, the Prince of Prussia, Vicky's father-in-law, in spite of his splendid authoritative appearance, was a rather weak character. Of his two younger brothers he observed that but for their high birth, "Charles would have gone to prison and Albrecht would have become a drunkard." With little cultural education and largely only military interests, these difficult and considerably older relatives were to be Vicky's new world. Hardly an ideal place for the highly intelligent and carefully educated product of the greatest monarchy in the world to flourish.

Lady Paget wrote of an incident en route to Berlin that was the first of many tactless occasions which hurt Vicky. At Hanover a great court banquet awaited the party, and they saw to their horror the long table groaning under the famous golden dinner service which had been for so many years, with other heirlooms, the subject of a lawsuit between Queen Victoria and the King of Hanover, and which the English crown lawyers had given in his favor. The princess recognized the dinner service at once, "and was much hurt; but she was there, as through the whole journey, gentle, charming, but affable; not for one moment relaxing her endeavour to make the best impression."

But there were lighter moments on the journey, as when old Field Marshal Wrangel, "the most daredevil and original of Prussian generals," got into the train to compliment the royal couple. The citizens of Wittenberg had just presented Vicky with one of their renowned and most succulent apple tarts which she had put away on a seat, when Wrangel sat down plump on top of it. "The tart clung to its position tenaciously," recorded Lady Paget, "whilst the Princess, shrieking with laughter, tried with pocket-handkerchiefs and napkins to disengage the old hero from its sweet embrace."

Once they reached their new home, there was much to annoy Vicky. Lady Ponsonby (maid of honor to Queen Victoria at the time of the marriage) wrote that Vicky had difficulty restraining her English feelings: "Small things got on her nerves, like German boots, the want of baths, the thin silver plate, and the terrible amount of etiquette."

These petty annoyances were aggravated by the fact that Vicky's future home, Babelsberg, outside Potsdam, was not yet ready. She and

Fritz had to live in the old *Schloss* where her apartment was vast but gloomy, with smoky chimneys and rattling, drafty windows. There was neither hygiene, nor heating in the stone staircases, and "endless dark corridors connected huge mysterious looking rooms, hung with large pictures of long forgotten Royal personages." Used to Victorian inventions and innovations, Vicky tried hard to make the apartments comfortable. This was not easy as Fritz's grandfather had died there and the "death room" could not be touched, and Vicky had to pass through it to reach her bedroom or dressing room from her library. The door had the eerie habit of opening by itself which, especially on cold winter evenings, had an unnerving effect, made worse by tales of a ghost called "the White Lady." Each year on the anniversary of King Frederick William III's death Vicky's room was converted into a mausoleum for a family service in his memory. Several years later she wrote to her mother that once again her room was filled with "horrid musty old furniture" for this purpose, making her extremely cross. "I must say I think it is so inconsiderate" she told Queen Victoria; "besides, it spoils our things which have to be taken down and shifted and taken to pieces every year for this whim. It really is time this barbarous custom should cease." Vicky hated being alone there and Fritz, who was no longer in the army, rarely left her; but despite her entreaties he refused to give up his walk alone in the streets for an hour each evening.

Vicky's household in Berlin was nonetheless substantial. She wrote to her mother in April 1859 that when almost the whole of her household went to Holy Communion, with footmen, grooms, servants, maids and cooks the total was forty-two. In addition Queen Victoria sent Mrs. Innocent to Berlin as a nurse and Mrs. Hobbs as a maid. (Known as "Hobbsy," she is said to have taught Kaiser Willy English.) The queen also engaged a personal maid for Vicky called Miss Bennett, who was "exceptionally quiet and of very peaceful, unassuming disposition, handy and quick in dressing—dresses hair well and evidently is a thoroughly experienced lady's maid."

Yet despite the size of Vicky's household they were battling against almost insurmountable odds. As well as the lack of heat, smoky chimneys and rattling windows, there were no cupboards for Vicky's clothes, which had to remain in boxes. Not surprisingly the maids complained when the chosen dress was found, full of creases and with no maids' pantry nearby. They then had to rush down endless corridors to find an iron in the kitchen. Several such walks a day did not improve tempers.

The old *Schloss* in Berlin was without lights, baths or "closets," and a week after her arrival Vicky saw to her dismay signs of chilblains on her fingers. The problem seemed to be that rooms were either stifling hot or freezing cold. Shortly after her marriage Queen Victoria had warned her daughter about the dangers of going from overheated rooms to icy corridors in Berlin: "Pray don't forget putting on something warm whenever you go out into the passages and don't think you are here; have a wadded cloak or thick shawl always by you for that." Victoria considered that a hot room was one of the quickest roads to an early grave. Early visitors to Vicky in Berlin were constantly horrifying the queen on their return with accounts of how the German stoves were kept. Vicky herself commented once: "We give a large party tomorrow and another on Friday; I tremble at the thought of it. To prevent the stifling atmosphere—between 80 and 90 Fahrenheit which is in all ball and concert rooms in Berlin—I have had two large panes taken out of every window and flannel put in instead and the panes above made to let down with strings so I hope we shall not be smothered."

Fritz was used to "going without." It never occurred to him to recreate the luxury of Queen Victoria's court and he bore Vicky's complaints philosophically. Others did not. Vicky's continual comparisons of life in Germany with life in Britain endeared her to few. "There can be no doubt that the Princess from the first compared life at Berlin disadvantageously with her English homes, but at that time certainly without any bitterness," wrote Lady Paget. Since the prince adored his bride, he failed to warn her of the bad impression she was making. Even Lady Paget, a German brought up by English nurses and governesses, with English ideas and English prejudices, thought Vicky quite in the right, and only wondered when some of those surrounding her took umbrage at what appeared to her to be only natural.

The Prussians found the natural affection between Fritz and Vicky hard to understand, just as Vicky regarded it as "doubly painful" to see the Prussian royal family all together "with only the mere outward appearance of mutual affection." She found it "very sad to see husbands and wives and parents and children unable to respect one another as they ought." By April 1860 she had realized that her new family regarded her own behavior in this respect as particularly odd, even offensive. It was considered "a sin" to drive in a closed carriage, she told her mother, worst of all with one's wife. "All the princes drive with their gentlemen in a carriage with two horses and the princesses drive with their ladies and four horses. We are the only ones that drive and walk together; even to church and to the railway station the others drive separately." Vicky's own determination not to abandon what the Prussians regarded as an absurd singularity was strengthened by the approval of her mother. "I am delighted to hear that people stare at seeing husband and wife together!" wrote Queen Victoria.

At first Vicky seemed tolerant of the daily ritual of the Prussian court. "I take great pains to remember names and faces and to talk to people and remember their place." But even then it was beginning to irritate her. "At twelve every day we have received deputations and addresses and presents from different towns, it becomes very tiresome at last; they all make long speeches, and poor Fritz has always to answer them which he does quite wonderfully. He has such a command of the language. I have never heard him hesitate once." She loved to get away. "As soon as the business is over," she continued, "we drive out of town and then walk in the places where we are least tormented by being run after." Eight years later the tedium of it all had become almost insufferable. "I have so many ladies to see and audiences to give which is the greatest bore I know," she wrote to her mother; "it makes me feel so stupid talking about the weather etc., that I get quite absent, and nearly go to sleep before the ladies. Most ladies are bores; I suppose that is what makes the exception so charming and valuable."

In the spring of 1858 Fritz and Vicky toured some of the smaller German courts and encountered conditions which to her seemed appallingly primitive: "it meant seeing life as it was a hundred years ago with all its restrictions and discomforts." The complete lack of baths, carpets and writing tables astonished the English princess, "but the beds were wonderful to behold and fearful to sleep or rather to lie awake in, for huge feather beds insisted upon either suffocating one or tumbling upon the floor." When Victoria learned of Vicky's spartan apartments in Weimar, she wrote, "How terribly disagreeable to be lodged in that way: nobody would dream in England of such a thing." At Gotha, Vicky wrote to her mother, "I must tell you they gave us the same *vaste machine* which is called in England a bedbath which was made for you and has never been used since."

As for the palace in Berlin, Lady Paget called it an ugly structure with not a good room in it. Vicky furnished it in "much the taste of Osborne which she has been brought up to admire." In an attempt to make the best of things, Vicky was determined to try to improve her own room in Berlin. She put matting and a few old Oriental rugs on the floor. She picked up bits of old furniture in Italy and Paris as well as Germany. "I have made it as pretty as I can," she told her mother. "It is not near so full of furniture, pictures and knick-knacks as those of my relations; and perhaps you wouldn't like the colour of the walls that are only distempered a soft sage green to show off my few good pictures (mostly old ones) and the curtains are only plain green merino." And she filled the room with flowers.

But some disagreeable aspects could not be changed. The room looked out onto hideous dirty old walls, so that Vicky tried to block out the view with panes of old stained glass in her windows. It was noisy and, worst of all, a virtual passage for anyone who needed to pass from one part of the *Schloss* to another.

Sadly, too, it seemed that she was seeing less and less of her beloved Fritz. Early in her marriage Vicky spent her mornings painting and attending to her correspondence, writing almost daily to her parents. Just before luncheon she took a short drive with her husband, and another in the afternoon. She seldom went to the theater or opera, and always retired very early.

Two years later her daily routine had changed, at least as regards her husband. "I see him at breakfast and then usually not again until five— our dinner hour. I go out at one always—and his business is never over till two, except sometimes, when he goes out with me, usually however we take a ride every day, and then a good walk, so I see very little of him. The evenings when we do not go to the theatre or parties are very happy hours but they have been very rare lately."

In the same year Vicky wrote to her mother from Das Neue Schloss: "We shall not stay here longer than a day or two, but I cling to my rides and walks with Fritz, as when we are at Berlin he has hardly ever leisure to go with me, and walking round and round the horrid old Tiergarten with one of my ladies—two footmen at my heels to keep off the troop of dirty little boys, is no great amusement, and this will be my lot until May or June next year. I shudder at the thought." The idyll that she had looked forward to seemed to have disappeared: "Here at Berlin we see each other so little, and our rooms are so far from each other with the whole house between them we might just as well not be married at all." She did not even know whether or not he was in the house. Vicky never publicly complained, but she did write plaintively to her mother: "Fritz hardly ever breakfasts with me now or takes walks and drives with me as he used."

Palaces, Domesticity and Gossip

In May 1858 the royal couple finally moved to Babelsberg, a pretty Gothic château outside Potsdam. It was here that Prince Albert and Queen Victoria came to visit their daughter. They were horrified at the poky and cramped conditions. Vicky's bedroom was situated over the huge kitchen range, which was always lit and made her rooms unbearably hot. The furniture was heavy, with the looking glasses and screens framed by hothouse plants.

Everywhere the Prince of Prussia's personality pervaded the rooms. However hard Vicky tried, filling her rooms with family photographs and souvenirs from Windsor Castle and Buckingham Palace, as well as her own paintings, nothing could make her feel at home—it seemed as if everything conspired to remind her of her strained relationship with her parents-in-law.

The Neue Palais was a different story. Prince Albert came upon it while visiting old buildings with Vicky on that first visit in June 1858, and he instantly felt that this vast rococo masterpiece would make an ideal home for Fritz and Vicky. Built by Frederick the Great between 1763 and 1769—to impress his enemies and show them that war had not exhausted his exchequer—the Neue Palais comprised 200 rooms. Fritz had been born there, and the place badly needed restoration—two further reasons that captured Vicky's heart. As she and her father walked around the neglected garden, he showed her how to restore and reclaim flower beds and paths, and how to bring to light long-dormant plants and shrubs. Her passion for restoration was born.

But the first sight of her new home was not too promising, especially for an eighteen-year-old. The Neue Palais was a rabbit warren of apartments for long-retired and forgotten ladies-in-waiting and old retainers, and Vicky had to wait until each one died before expanding her own apartments. Everything had been neglected. Frederick the Great's beautiful silver furniture was tarnished black; the walls were covered by blanched tapestries full of moths, and by torn and faded silk coverings; the once beautiful Savonnerie carpets on the floors were faded by the sun and eaten by mice. Vicky found "thousands of dead bats," and all the beds crawled with lice. Water came from a pump in the courtyard, and there were neither lavatories nor bathrooms—on the rare occasions when someone wanted a bath, one was borrowed from a nearby hotel.

But the rooms were beautifully proportioned, with painted ceilings, elegant columns and wonderful carved chimneypieces. The large windows allowed these rooms to be flooded with light throughout the day, and it was said there were no ghosts! As for the windowpanes, all of them original and intact, Lady Paget remembered that they were "the most lovely shades of pale amethyst, not two of them being alike." She also remembered that they used to dine "in a room panelled with celadon blue, and ornamented with a kind of Chippendale device in silver. The effect on a hot day was delicious."

Until Fritz and Vicky came to live in the Neue Palais not one of his family had shared Frederick the Great's appreciation of the arts. Vicky involved herself in every detail of the work of restoration, as she did in all her houses. And restoring the garden offered her another link with England. She asked her mother to send roses "as they are both scarce and dear here." Primroses were unknown in Germany, and in response to her daughter's request Victoria sent a boxful from Osborne. She also sent violets, which Vicky had been unable to grow in Prussian soil. Vicky even telegraphed the head gardener at Osborne to send her milk pans for her tiny dairy, as she found the milk and butter in Germany inedible and decided to improve the standard with the gardener's six cows and two of her own. She wrote happily to her mother that she had put up "a swing, a see-saw and a giant strides . . . for little and big children." She had also set out "a crocket [sic] ground."

Fritz renamed the Neue Palais "Friedrichskron," though the old name reverted after his death. It had been his favorite home as a small boy and it became his favorite home as a married man; and it was here that he died. Years later Vicky was encouraging her daughter Sophie to cope with the same problems in Greece as she had encountered at Friedrichskron: "It took me over 30 years by degrees to get that old Palace into working order, and then I had to leave it, and had spent much of my own money on it." Getting the old palace in order partly meant making it more like the palaces she had known as a child in Britain. "I am shut out of my sitting-room," she wrote to her mother, "because there is a man from London setting a grate and fender—an English fireplace altogether, in one of our large empty chimney-pieces. It will serve as a pattern for others later; it is copied from Bertie's* fireplace in his hall at Marlborough House." Five years later she asked Queen Victoria, "Is it indiscreet if I ask for a drawing and the measurements of the meat larders (out-of-doors) at Osborne and Balmoral? Here there are no such things, and I am afraid to trust alone to my description."

Lord Ronald Gower and his mother visited Fritz and Vicky at Potsdam in 1864 and he described the Neue Palais as Vicky had so far transformed it. Their rooms were near the entrance, and his mother slept in the immensely high state bed with plumes at the top where the Crown Prince had been born. The walls were covered with yellow silk, on which Chinese figures were embroidered. His room, he added, had gilded brackets halfway up the painted walls, with porcelain statues in them of Hercules and Omphale. Since these were multiplied all round the room there were, reported Lord Ronald, "about two dozen Hercules and Omphales there."

He also described the room where they dined, with walls of blue silk, fringed with gold lace. "After dinner we went to the Crown Princess's sitting room; the furniture there is covered in Gobelin tapestry—a gift of the Empress Eugénie's. Here are some of the Princess's own paintings, lately finished, representing Prussian soldiers."

Yet no matter how enthusiastically Vicky restored and renovated Friedrichskron, the stifling atmosphere of court life and of her Prussian in-laws made her long for a country retreat, away from Berlin and Potsdam, where she could play the country wife and Fritz the squire. The closest she got to this dream was in a charming but decaying farmhouse, with grounds, a church and a village, at Bornstedt, almost on her doorstep in

*Bertie was Prince Albert Victor, the Prince of Wales and Vicky's younger brother, the future Edward VII.

Potsdam. Its simplicity delighted her, though everything was in appalling condition. She set about doing up the farmhouse with white wallpaper and very plain furniture. "I think it will look, if not very pretty, yet fresh and neat and clean," she observed. "I hope to surprise Fritz with it when he comes home."Vicky also turned her attention to the dilapidated state of the rest of the village. "The school was a disgrace, the church too, and the churchyard was scandalous," she later recalled; "all the graves trodden over, the monuments broken and thrown down, one tangle of weeds and nettles. We put all that in order again."

Bornstedt offered Vicky and her husband the chance to lead a simple life away from both the cares of state and the backbiting of the court. "We can go and take our meals there whenever we like," she rejoiced, "and put up a visitor or two." She needed the escape. All her life criticism surrounded her. She was vivacious, attractive and spontaneous, impulsive, generous, easy to hurt and envied by many for her position. Nor was tact her strongest quality, though she later learned from experience to bite her tongue. In the early years she was often indiscreet, telling her Prussian ladies how much better everything was "at home," and mocking German customs and whatever seemed to her to be a primitive way of life. She insisted on going everywhere she chose in Berlin, often on foot, wrongly thinking herself incognito, full of curiosity about the everyday lives of the inhabitants. Why was there no art gallery or museum or public library in Berlin? What of the hospital? No matter how hard she tried, and Vicky did try, she clashed constantly with Fritz's family. Tittle-tattle was spread about her. Inevitably she made mistakes but most were the mistakes of her youth, and her enemies never took her youth into consideration. Cleverer than they were, Vicky possessed all the qualities that would irritate jealous, stubborn older people.

Soon she realized that she needed to escape not only tittle-tattle but also organized spying. She made it a rule never to disclose her inner thoughts to anyone. "I cannot be too careful here, where the Royal Family is the perpetual topic of stories and criticisms, alas too often true, but still exaggerated sometimes," she told her mother. "An unguarded word is repeated and of course distorted." Vicky told her astonished mother that each prince had in his household "a person who is a sort of spy—and repeats all over the town what the prince or princesses say and do." She resolved above all to keep silent on two topics, her husband and her parents-in-law. Vicky was not imagining all this out of some sort of paranoia. As Princess Feodora Hohenlohe-Langenburg confided in a friend, "The Princess is so young and inexperienced in the world, and Berlin is a hotbed of envy, jealousy, intrigue and malicious knavery."

Even so, Vicky's character would not allow her to be dispirited. Amazed at the ignorance of Fritz's family, she made herself a new circle of friends, including scientists, painters, historians and literary figures. They taught her and she entertained them, unaware that such a breach of protocol shocked her relatives and distanced her even more from them. Fortunately Fritz sympathized with her thirst for knowledge. He arranged for his former mathematics tutor, Professor Schellbach, to teach her. She greeted him with the cry, "I love mathematics, physics and chemistry," and told him how in Britain she had been taught by Faraday and Hoffman. Through Schellbach she met many of the learned men of the day, and happily sat at their feet.

She also had her children to comfort and distract her. She adored them, and was terribly hurt by Prussian criticism of her as a mother—all part of Bismarck's campaign to discredit her for political reasons. Vicky felt that her mother-in-law interfered in the education of her children, especially with William, her eldest, who was difficult, volatile and proud. He suffered a great deal at the hands of doctors attempting to improve his withered arm—the result of a difficult breech birth, and an added lifelong complication to his relationship with his mother. By contrast Vicky was always on good terms with her four daughters, Charlotte, Victoria, Sophie and Margaret.

The Victorian ideal to which Vicky steadfastly adhered brought her into conflict with German customs for bringing up babies which she thought barbaric. One such custom was the use of "dribbling bibs." They shocked her English principles; dribbling bibs belonged, she felt, "to the swaddling clothes and baby-binder and the rest of the antediluvian apparatus the poor little Germans are stuffed into shortly after their appearance in this vale of tears."

Even more infuriating was her doctors' refusal to allow William or the other children to bathe in the sea (save in the Baltic, which was scarcely salty and lacked tides or sand), because it "excited their nerves." Vicky had taken William bathing at Osborne, on the Isle of Wight, and felt it had done him a world of good. "It does annoy me so much," she lamented at the doctors' attitude; but she was powerless to overrule them.

She also hated the Prussian conventions surrounding baptism, as did her mother. Dating from the time when babies were baptized at three weeks, it was traditional for mothers to stay in bed at the child's christening. Queen Victoria found it absurd. "Let German ladies do what they like, but the English Princess must not," she fulminated. But even against her wishes Vicky was obliged to conform. "It would seem strange if a German Princess married in England and insisted on having a christening there with the same customs observed as in her home," she explained. The absurd convention was exacerbated for Vicky when her son Henry's baptism was postponed. "She had been out and about for two weeks, it was traditional for mothers to lie down at the child's childbed again."

Philanthropy and Sufferings

Of her four sons only Willy, the eldest, and Henry survived. Waldemar (Waldie) died of diphtheria at the age of eleven. And her beloved Sigismund died horribly of meningitis on June 19, 1866, aged only twenty months. Their two deaths affected Vicky terribly. After Sigi died, she seems to have experienced some kind of breakdown. She had placed such hopes in this child, "my pride, my joy, my life," and she poured out the pain in her heart to her mother: "The sorrow is greater than I can bear." But bear it she did, recalling her father's solution to all problems and distracting herself in hard work. In her despair she painted a portrait of Sigi from memory, holding his favorite ball, which still hangs in her bedroom at Friedrichshof. In Berlin she kept an even more tragic reminder of her loss—a locked nursery, and in the child's cot a marble figure of her baby which she had sculpted herself. When Waldemar died of diphtheria thirteen years later, Vicky poured her energy and grief into an attempt to find a scientific explanation for the disease. Mourning was for her "the last sign of respect for a loved relation," and she consulted her mother as to how long she could continue to wear her black crêpe.

To sink her grieving in good works was second nature to a woman as philanthropic as Vicky. "I could not live as the rest do here, in busy idleness." Possibly Vicky's greatest contribution to German life was in her hospital work. She had never forgotten her meeting with Florence Nightingale before her marriage. On Christmas Day 1868, Florence Nightingale wrote: "I have a fresh neophyte, in the person of the Crown Princess of Prussia, [who] is cultivating herself in knowledge of sanitary (and female) administration for her future great career. She comes alone like a girl, pulls off her hat and jacket like a five-year-old, drags about a great portfolio of plans and kneels by my bedside* correcting them."

In April 1869 Vicky wrote to her mother, "If wars are to continue and their art to be studied, surely all the ingenuity the human mind possesses ought to be set to work to mitigate their horrors? And this ought to be done without delay." The following year, at the outbreak of the Franco-Prussian War, she begged for the help of a Nightingale-trained matron. The remarkable Miss Florence Lees was sent to organize three large German war hospitals. In Miss Lees's judgment, "Perhaps not the least good thing Her Royal Highness did in this war—although she devoted herself untiringly to visiting, and in a thousand ways helping, the sick and wounded—was the battling against the prejudice of German medical men with respect to fresh air and a strengthening diet for the sick, two things generally spoken of as 'English ways.'"

Initially this battle seemed lost. Neither nurses nor patients were willing to carry out the wishes of the Crown Princess with regard to ventilation. Fritz, commanding the Third Army at the front, sadly confided to his diary that "all her endeavours and offers of help in the matter of tending the sick were contemptuously rejected—presumably on account of the anti-British feeling." However, when Vicky moved near the frontier to organize hospital work, much of the criticism died down. In the early autumn of 1870 she went to live in the old *Schloss* at Homburg, so as to be near the battlefields. Here she turned the old military barracks into a modern hospital. She built new wards at her own expense, and her husband was gratified to learn how generally her efforts were appreciated.

Even though support for Vicky's schemes brought him unpopularity, Fritz loyally backed her attempts to found training schools for nurses. She was fascinated by her visit to the nursing school which Miss Lees

---

*Florence Nightingale had become bedridden in 1861 at Christmas.

had set up in London in 1875, and sent a German woman there for training, and consequently founded her own Victoria Haus school for nurses on similar lines. It was (as she told her daughter Sophie) "uphill work"; but she was determined to institute good nursing in Prussia. In 1883, as a silver wedding present, the people of Berlin collected 180,000 marks, to be used in her Victoria Haus, and a further 820,000 marks was collected throughout Germany. Vicky immediately applied over a third of it to the training of her nurses. Nor could she resist helping with hospitals elsewhere in Germany besides Berlin, and she assiduously promoted what she called "the newest plans" from England.

Vicky was also deeply committed to raising the standard of life in ordinary homes and was the guiding spirit of the Society for Promoting Health in the Home, set up in Berlin in 1875. This society fostered house-to-house visiting of the poor, encouraging them in industry and cleanliness and instructing them in household management. Naturally enough Vicky was especially delighted with the success of such work in her beloved Bornstedt. She and Fritz had started their kindergarten with only a handful of ragged children, but by the 1890s, when it took in eighty-six children, Vicky was able to open a new wing. "My Bornstedt *Kinderheim* does so well now that people are going to imitate it in other parts of Germany," she delightedly wrote in 1896. "It answers the purpose of a combined crêche and kindergarten, and is invaluable for those poor little children who would otherwise be neglected while their parents are busy or out at work." The mothers learned from the Victoria sisters how to wash, dress and look after their children properly, though Vicky despaired at the opposition from some of them who were "obstinate and ignorant to a fearful degree."

Nor was the church neglected in Vicky's philanthropic efforts. She was anxious to have a richly appointed English church in Berlin, and (as a true daughter of Queen Victoria) managed to raise money from an unlikely source. Learning that a Jewish banker named Bleichröder seemed willing to contribute, having already made "a magnificent donation" before the cornerstone was laid, she wrote asking whether he had any specific sum in mind. Would he like to give the organ, perhaps ("one could affix a dedicatory plaque to it")? Bleichröder graciously obliged, and the church was opened, amidst a great fanfare, on Vicky's birthday.

Vicky's determination to improve the education of girls was "uphill work" too. It is easy to see why she had outraged Berlin from her earliest days when one remembers the position of women in nineteenth-century Germany. The country was so backward, both socially and politically, that the general consensus of opinion was that to educate women was unnecessary as they had no role outside the domestic sphere. Creative and talented women did exist, but their only outlet seemed to be in the arts; even then society regarded them as eccentric. Until the turn of the century universities in Germany admitted no female students except those that came from abroad. Vicky, with her intelligence and extraordinary level of education, as well as her tendency to speak her mind, was a phenomenon completely unknown in the Germany of her day.

But she was determined to inspire others like herself. Not only did Vicky believe women needed to be far better educated; she was also conscious of her own unique position in furthering this aim. She founded three schools to provide higher education for girls. Naturally the schools caused resentment, especially as the most important had an Englishwoman as headmistress. Worse, Vicky encouraged physical training and outdoor exercises for the girls in her schools. Incredible as it may seem, gymnastic exercises had long been banned in Prussia and even in the 1860s were considered unseemly for boys. Bismarck could not bring himself to let his sons take part in any such thing at their school. That girls (considered by some to be indecently dressed) might be seen taking part in outdoor sports so outraged Prussian society that it alienated some of those who were otherwise prepared to support the Crown Princess.

Yet Vicky persisted. She wanted to start what she called "a *real* Ladies' College, rather like Newnham or Girton or Holloway." She told Sophie of her belief that "If women remain only a sort of upper servant, the whole of the nation *must* suffer," adding that "*selfish* men are silly enough to think that they can trample more easily on *ignorant* women." So she agreed to be patroness of the Pestalozzi-Froebel House in Berlin, whose first principal was Froebel's great-niece and one of the last students he trained. Here girls were taught kindergarten methods and domestic science, and teachers were trained, as well as future governesses and mothers' helps. The school was so highly regarded that pupils began to come from as far away as Scotland as well as from England.

This was perhaps no credit to Vicky in the eyes of Berliners, since the

British inspiration behind much of the Crown Princess's activities ran-
kled so much. On one visit to Britain she was intrigued by the high
standard of education at the school set up by the Prince and Princess of
Wales at Sandringham. She was enthralled by Alexandra's "little techni-
cal school, where the children are taught to make charming things in
wood and iron-work and brass and copper." As soon as she returned to
Germany she started a similar school, teaching boys carpentry, carving
and bookbinding as well as other such crafts. Her account of this to Sophie is predictable. The school, said Vicky, "has really good results,
though it met with great opposition at first."

Another of Vicky's plans inspired by Britain was the erection of a museum and school of art and industry on the same principle as Prince Albert's museum at South Kensington (now the Victoria and Albert).
Needless to say, there was again much opposition, but this eventually sub-
sided and the museum opened in January 1868. Her school alongside it
made slow progress, but the shop or bazaar for women's work had a
greater success. She wrote to enlist the help of her mother: "How kind
you would be if you could once send them a little order, it would help
them so much—anything in the way of linen, drapery, or embroidery, or
knitting—which you might wish to give away. I only ask for a small order
because I do not think it fair to your subjects to ask for money for a foreign charity though it will be my own special undertaking."

Although such a forward-looking Crown Princess enraged diehards,
nothing made Fritz happier than when people were being won round,
whether by Vicky's medical work or her many other charitable endeav-
ors. "It is with intense joy that I learn from various sources that my
wife's presence in the hospitals at Homburg, Frankfurt and in the Rhine
province is properly appreciated, and also that officials and physicians
declare that they are astonished at the wide range of her knowledge.
Certainly I would have looked for nothing else, yet it is with unspeak-
able satisfaction that I hear the fact acknowledged, for it is high time
that my wife should win the grateful recognition she has long deserved."

Fritz was oversanguine. Although in some circles his wife won a
grudging respect for her reforms and innovations, it seemed that she
would receive the recognition she had long deserved only when she became empress.

Tragically, when that time came, Fritz was a dying man. He became emperor in 1888 and survived for only three more months, while his terminal throat cancer was treated to the accompaniment of bitter, undignified fighting on the part of the doctors. Just when at last the chance had arrived for Vicky and Fritz to fulfill everything they had planned for so long, he was taken from her. Vicky did all she could to boost his spirits and keep him alive. No sooner was he dead than her son Willy surrounded the Neue Palais with his guards to "prevent all important papers from leaving." (In fact the new kaiser found nothing; Fritz had taken three boxes of papers for safekeeping to Windsor when he and Vicky visited Britain for Queen Victoria's Golden Jubilee the previous year.) Heartbroken, Vicky moved out of the Neue Palais to make way for her son.

The Widowed Empress

In the year following Fritz's death she bought 350 acres of land in the Taunus Mountains near Kronberg, a few miles from Frankfurt. The court architect was sent to inspect all the well-known castles in France and England. He built Vicky a castle dedicated to the name and memory of her late husband, "Friedrichshof," in the "later Gothic" style of most castles and many country houses in Britain. Early German Renaissance in parts, it had interior details borrowed from Venetian, Italian, Dutch and French originals.

A large and comfortable house, Friedrichshof was known as the most modern in Germany. Ten years earlier Vicky had visited the International Electrical Exhibition in Paris. It greatly inspired her, with its "marvellous telephones and phonographs and many different specimens of lighting up by electricity" and she incorporated many of the new inventions at Friedrichshof. Visitors would comment delightedly on the beautiful light fittings installed by Vicky. Like her father she had a passion for details, each of which bore the stamp of her own individuality, and she lavished as much attention on the drains as on the drawing room. At last she was able to utilize her many original ideas, developed over many years of study.

Friedrichshof was built of bluish Taunus slate, with the moldings, windows, ornamentation and cornerpieces in light sandstone. No surface was plastered or painted. All the materials of the doors and mountings were left in their original color and texture. Furnished with carefully chosen antiques and countless art treasures, the new house nonetheless exuded "an atmosphere of modern comfort." "I know every piece of furniture," she wrote, "every one of which represents for me a part of history, and my heart belongs to it."

Here she created for her dead husband what she had done for her beloved Sigi: a permanent memorial. Her library at Friedrichshof contained every scrap of paper Fritz had written on, once his voice had failed him; indeed, Vicky devoted the whole house to his memory.

Since the age of ten Vicky had bought books with her pocket money; these now filled her library. She had no books that she had not read or studied—influential works on politics and economics, political history and biography—and she had them carefully protected from heat and dust. She also possessed a remarkable library of mid-nineteenth-century books on the arts. She had even read Karl Marx during his own lifetime. No wonder she told visitors, "I am very proud of my library." Her letters to Queen Victoria often discuss her reading matter, which was far too highbrow for her mother, and she would often ask for books from Britain. Both the *Edinburgh Review* and (after 1879) the *Daily Telegraph* were sent to her. As well as books, the library housed Vicky's collection of photographs in 300 folios, and a large collection of autographs of celebrated men and women from the fifteenth century onward. She also used the library to display her collection of medals and coins and an interesting set of old works on genealogy.

Friedrichshof was always full of flowers, often gathered by Vicky herself. A deep knowledge of plants and horticulture, which she had partly derived from her father, enabled her to plan most of the park and gardens herself. She loved roses, and planted a remarkable terraced rose garden, using a hedge of red and white roses to hide the park enclosures. Any royal visitor was asked to plant a tree, usually a "pine of noble species." There were fountains and shady groves of beech trees where Vicky and her guests would relax, reading or painting when the weather was warm enough.

The stables at Friedrichshof also incorporated new ideas, including a bath for the horses, and she sent to Britain for carriages and stable fittings. There was a dairy, and greenhouses full of the rarest orchids and fruit.

Even before she went into mourning for Fritz, it was generally thought that when it came to fashion Vicky could have made more of herself. Her mother had designed her trousseau, and the princess tried to keep Queen Victoria abreast of the new trends in clothing, describing in minute detail what various ladies wore at the great court functions. More often than not she disapproved, observing that she supposed it was the German fashion. Even when dining alone with her aunt in Berlin, Lady Paget would never appear without her gloves—"It would have been considered the crassest ignorance, or worse, vulgarity, to wear anything but Swedish leather, and it was only at balls or large dinner parties that white or yellow kid were allowed." But she also recalled that in England no such rules were followed: "I am now speaking of continental habits: English women had quite different fashions."

But some English fashions had spread to Germany. Lady Paget remembered the rage for "Mrs. Brown's hats—all the *jeunes élégantes* had them." These were black or brown, with two long feathers, one on each side, with a flounce of jetted lace hanging over the brim. The fashion for red underskirts also came from England, though Britain on the whole lagged behind Europe in fashion. Before Vicky's wedding Queen Victoria told the German ladies not to bring their crinolines, as that fashion had not yet arrived in Britain. (Actually she was wrong; it had.) Inevitably foreign beauties tended to despise the fashions adopted by Queen Victoria's court and the ladies of English society. Lady Paget felt they had no notion of how to flatter physical beauty: "English clothes were so peculiar, and no importance was attached to figure, hands and feet."

In her early fifties when Fritz died, Vicky gave up the glamorous colors of contemporary haute couture. Thereafter she wore only perfectly plain and simple black dresses. For jewelry she wore no more than a gold chain around her neck carrying a miniature of Fritz, and two gold rings, one set with a ruby, the other with a sapphire flanked by diamonds, and her eyeglasses hung on a long, thin gold chain dotted with tiny round amethysts.

In spite of the deep loss she felt after Fritz's death, such an intense and spirited woman could never settle for a life of quiet widowhood. She had loved to ride since childhood, and could do so for hours, whether in hot sunshine or a sharp wind, without seeming to notice or becoming tired. As a widow she continued to ride each morning from eight till ten. She was fearless on horseback, and even at sixty would jump tricky fences and ditches on the most difficult and spirited horses she could find.

Like her mother she adored cats, and both of them would put a collar with their royal monogram on their pets. Once a cat belonging to her son Waldie was shot by a keeper in her garden and hung from a tree with her nose cut off. Vicky was distraught, remembering how her little cat had always shared her morning tea, lying on the bed, purring and rubbing her head against Vicky's cheek. "People are so brutal here with poor dogs and especially cats," she complained to her mother, but she received no sympathy from her eldest son, Willy, who praised the keeper for doing his duty, "as cats might harm pheasants." Vicky seems to have had little influence on her eldest son with regard to pets, or anything much else for that matter.

Between Vicky and her mother there was an endless exchange of animals. They exchanged carriage horses and Vicky even sent to England for carriages. When Henry was born in 1863 Vicky asked Queen Victoria for donkeys for milk, as she could get none in Germany, even by advertising, and she judged Prussian cows' milk to be "shockingly bad." When she set up her farm at Bornstedt, she asked her mother for a boar and two sows and a ram and two ewes. German mutton, she wrote, was very indifferent, and she declared she had not seen a good pig since she left England. Vicky offered to buy these animals from Windsor "at not too high a price," but her mother was happy to send them as Christmas gifts. The queen described them as beauties, adding that the four ladies were "in hopeful shape." A few years later it was the queen's turn to beg one or two of her daughter's much admired red and black dachshunds, "as I have given you a sheep and a collie," and Vicky promptly sent the puppies to England by messenger. She loved dachshunds—"they are capital watch dogs"—as they would savage ill-dressed or dirty-looking people who (in the dachshunds' opinion) ought not to be about the place, while treating their masters with great affection, and they helped to console her after her husband's death.

She also continued to paint, building a studio at Friedrichshof and sometimes visiting one of the local painters. Like her mother, Vicky had a real talent for painting, and what she lacked in imagination she made up for in skill and observation. Working chiefly in watercolors, she imitated the work of Millais and Alma-Tadema, both of whom she very much admired. In her widowhood her style became influenced by more modern artists whose work she had seen in Rome and London. She experimented with light and shade, form and structure, and her household thought this new and bolder work "very strange." Apart from landscapes, Vicky was also very successful with flowers, still-lifes and portraits of children. She enjoyed painting in company, often with someone reading to her while she worked. Nor was music neglected at Friedrichshof. Her favorite composers were Bach, Handel, Gluck and Beethoven, whereas she found Wagner "dull and tiresome and heavy—and fatiguing to listen to."

Vicky filled her house with guests, and often had cause to complain about them. "Alas, very few servants of any of my guests take the least care of things, and are very messy and untidy in their rooms," she lamented. Some guests were so deplorably untidy that she was obliged to put up fresh wallpaper in their rooms, and others completely spoiled the new blotting books and inkstands she had brought from England. "I have to have my eyes everywhere," she said. "I know what a privilege it is to have such a nice home, and am anxious to keep it so, I can assure you," she wrote to her mother. But if she had cause to complain, so did her guests. Vicky allowed smoking only in the one smoking room. When Sir Frank Lascelles stayed with her, not only did he have to remove his shoes in his room so as not to scratch the beautiful parquet flooring, but whenever he wanted to smoke he could do so only by spreading a copy of *The Times* on the floor, kneeling on it, and smoking up the chimney!

Friedrichshof cost immense sums to build. Even so, Vicky continued to accede generously to the almost infinite demands made on her purse, and she was very adept at raising money for the needy. One bazaar she organized on behalf of the widows of soldiers, their orphans and the war wounded brought in 85,000 thalers, after all expenses had been paid. "Nothing approaching it was ever known in this country," Vicky proudly announced. In spite of her dislike of Berlin, she continued to spend a part of each winter there, particularly to keep an eye on her numerous charitable institutions and, where possible, to extend their work. She continued to visit her friends and the interesting professors, politicians, artists, writers and foreign visitors who delighted her sharp mind. She also promoted the work of the painters von Angeli, Passini, Leighton and Alma-Tadema throughout Europe.

In the autumn of 1898 Vicky had an accident. She fell awkwardly from her horse, which then stood on her hand. It seems she was never really well afterward and began to suffer from "lumbago"; cancer of the spine was subsequently diagnosed. Vicky took the news calmly, keeping her illness a secret until it could no longer be hidden. She met her final, terrible, lingering sufferings with great courage, and died at Friedrichshof in August 1901. Her will carefully disposed of her possessions, and her funeral, at her own request, was relatively simple. She is buried in the Friedenskirche, Potsdam, and her effigy on the tomb is of the finest Pentelic marble.

Vicky's tragedy was being an enemy alien—a highly cultured, cultivated and intelligent Englishwoman in a backward (by English standards) society. Quite early in her marriage she wrote to her mother, "I cannot do the simplest thing without its being found to be an imitation of something English, and therefore anti-Prussian." Brought up to see herself as absolutely English and liberal, she acquired by her marriage the conflicts of a dual loyalty—to her mother and England on the one hand, and to Fritz and Germany on the other. As she told her daughter Sophie, who had married the Duke of Sparta, heir to the Greek throne, she was hated, abused and persecuted, "as the old Prussian conservative party did *not want* the influence of the liberal-English wife, and opposed it at every turn."

Vicky never really learned discretion when it came to politics. As late as 1898 she visited Versailles, Saint-Cloud and the battlefields of the Franco-Prussian War, supposedly incognito but inevitably stirring up bitter memories of France's defeat by Prussia twenty years previously. During the Schleswig-Holstein affair, she openly came out against Bismarck, and her public outbursts against him included the taunt that he was either planning to become King of Prussia himself or intending to set up a Prussian republic. Bismarck had distrusted her from the start; she felt, as she put it, trodden down under his iron heel for long years; and the intrigues he fostered against her were "purgatory."

No one could have foreseen that her husband would be kept from the throne by the long reign of Wilhelm I. Vicky and Fritz spent almost all their married life waiting in the wings, full of promising ideas and constructive changes that they were not in a position to implement. As

Vicky sadly expressed it, "When the time came for us to be of real use to the country, death snatched all away." After Fritz's death she was deeply hurt that her influence over their son Willy was not stronger; yet throughout her trials she kept up her own spirits and those of everyone around her, and her enthusiasm and energy were an inspiration. Vicky's philosophy was simple: "Example is better than precept, and people who have never seen how things ought to be cannot be expected to know," she told Sophie, adding, "If you only manage to have a *little* centre of civilization around you, and show how things ought to be, it will be *spread*."

7

Alexandra and Minnie

PRINCESS ALEXANDRA OF DENMARK/
QUEEN OF GREAT BRITAIN

PRINCESS DAGMAR OF DENMARK/
EMPRESS MARIE FEODOROVNA OF RUSSIA

1844–1925/1847–1928

*B*ritish society was mourning the death of Prince Albert, and Queen Victoria in her melancholy wore only black. During his lifetime Albert had frowned on Society (then always spelled with a capital), and Society disapproved of him. In consequence neither he nor the queen had ever held the center of the social stage, but true to their calling both had kept up appearances, attending important social functions and giving them as well. Once Albert was dead, even this minimal social duty ended for the queen.

Society needed a leader. For some time before his unexpectedly early death, the prince and the queen had been preoccupied with the vexing problem of finding a bride for the Prince of Wales. Bertie had an eye for a pretty woman, and for a marriage to succeed he would have to be strongly attracted to the chosen candidate. Since only seven or eight European princesses could be considered potential brides, for him to fall in love with one of them would be a near miracle.

Politically both Victoria and Albert favored a German wife. Their eldest daughter, Vicky, the Princess Royal, was—as Crown Princess of Prussia—admirably placed to give a sound opinion on the matter and found none of the German candidates at all suitable. However, the eldest of the Danish princesses was said to possess charm, beauty and gentleness; but for the heir to the throne to accept a Danish bride might imply that Britain took Denmark's part against Germany over the Schleswig-Holstein affair. Alexandra of Denmark was therefore considered politically unsuitable.

Bertie himself was also a problem. He was fun-loving, wild and cared little for restraint or for the strictures of his father and was the despair of his mother. Again and again, it appeared to all those seeking a bride for the Prince of Wales that the only royal paragon of beauty, virtue and modesty who might make him happy was the ravishing Princess Alexandra of Denmark. Bertie's happiness was genuinely a major political consideration: an unhappy heir might make an unstable king, who could damage his country and disturb the peace of Europe. Even against their most shrewd political judgments, it was agreed by Vicky and Queen Victoria that the delightful Alexandra was after all the right choice.

Victoria invited the seventeen-year-old girl to stay alone with her at Osborne and, showing no apparent signs of nervousness or fear, Alexandra surpassed all expectations. The formidable British queen fell under the spell of the girl's charm and was completely enchanted with her. To everyone's relief, so was Bertie. A date was set, and Britain would soon have a Princess of Wales who was to become one of the best-loved queens in its history.

Denmark

Alexandra had been an ugly baby, very plump and even violent as a child. At the time of her birth on December 1, 1844, her father, Prince Christian of Schleswig-Holstein-Sonderburg-Glücksburg, seemed a man of neither fortune nor prospects. Married to Princess Louise of Hesse-Cassel, he inhabited a grace-and-favor residence, the Yellow Palace in Copenhagen, which in spite of its grandiose name was little more than a large town house with its front door opening directly onto the street.

When little Alexandra reached her eighth birthday, her status changed. There was no direct heir to the Danish throne. Her mother was the niece of King Christian VIII (who had died in 1848) and thus the natural heiress, as the new king, Louise's cousin Frederick, was childless. In 1852 the European powers—England, France, Russia, Austria, Prussia and Sweden—signed a protocol agreeing, that so long as Frederick produced no male heir, the crown of Denmark would pass to Prince Christian and Princess Louise.

Although the fact that their father would now become the next King of Denmark undoubtedly helped the marriage prospects of his children, it did little to improve their financial situation. With no money available for governesses or tutors, Alexandra and her five brothers and sisters were educated at home, largely by their parents. They learned English from their English nurses and from the British chaplain at Copenhagen. Alexandra spoke the language fluently (though all her life with a strong Danish accent) and somehow also picked up French and German. Her mother passed on to all her children her love of music as well as giving them sound instruction in religion, and her father taught them gymnastics, sport and drawing. They were all good-looking, outgoing and athletic and particularly loved riding with him. However, intellectually Prince Christian had little to offer them. A decent, honest and affectionate man, he himself had almost no education and was not particularly intelligent. Nonetheless he was a stern disciplinarian and stressed the value of learning. It was Princess Christian who dominated the home, with her lively personality and strong character. The parents were devoted to one another and to their children (and the children felt the same). Life at home was full of laughter and childish pranks, and as Prince Christian was now known as the Prince of Denmark the family moved to an eighteenth-century royal hunting lodge in the country a few miles outside Copenhagen. Bernstorff was an elegant white stucco house set in a large park with woods—an ideal summer playground for this merry band of children, their horses and dogs.

By the time Alexandra was fourteen her looks had greatly improved. Now her complexion, her rosy cheeks, her deep-set violet eyes and her soft brown hair, together with her height and newly slender figure, transformed the former ugly duckling into a beauty. Few could resist her smile or the sweetness of her expression. She was kind, affectionate, honest, sincere and sympathetic and possessed a wisdom far beyond her years. With all that, she was also stubborn and quick-tempered, as well as being incredibly unpunctual, in spite of her parents' best efforts.

Of her five brothers and sisters, the closest to Alexandra was her sister Dagmar, who was known as Minnie. Alexandra was always acknowledged as the beauty of the family, while Minnie, who was shorter than Alexandra but very pretty, was the only one of the children to show the slightest interest in books and literature. She also had Alexandra's sense of fun. Because the Yellow Palace was so cramped the two sisters had shared a room—and their confidences. Only at sixteen was Alexandra given a room of her own, along with a dress allowance of £20 a year.

There were no bathrooms and the only concession to cleanliness was to sit in a tub once a week. But if their education was not intellectual, at least it was practical. Lack of space and cash was matched by a paucity of servants. On the staff's night off the children took turns to wait at table and help in the kitchen. The girls learned to sew and make their own clothes. If a girl without a personal maid does not wish to spend hours brushing the mud off her hems or ironing her petticoats, she quickly learns to avoid puddles, to sit straight so as not to crease her skirts, and to fold her clothes carefully before putting them away. Even in later years, when Alexandra had as many maids as she could want, she always remained extremely tidy.

The children rarely appeared at court functions. Their uncle the king had married morganatically an actress who for years had been his mistress, and it was felt that the atmosphere at court was not suitable for innocent princesses. Society had ostracized the king's wife, and as Prince and Princess Christian refused to call upon her or receive her, their children had little experience of court life—although they did know something of court intrigue. Princess Christian was deeply concerned lest any of her pretty daughters became as coquettish as their cousin Mary of Cambridge, and she firmly told them that if they showed any such signs, she would slap their faces.

This was the background of the young girl who so delighted Victoria's daughter Vicky. "I never set eyes on a sweeter creature than Princess Alex," she wrote to her mother; "she is lovely. Her voice, her walk, carriage and manner are perfect, she is one of the most ladylike and aristocratic looking people I ever saw . . . I never saw a lady since the Empress Eugénie who made such an impression upon me." Although Vicky had charm, she looked like the young Hanoverian matron she was, and was praised for her brains rather than her beauty. That Alexandra had few if any intellectual accomplishments made no difference to Vicky's appreciation of her obvious goodness, simplicity and unaffected ways.

Before even meeting Alexandra, Queen Victoria was convinced she was "a pearl not to be lost." After meeting her at Osborne, the queen confided to her journal that "a gleam of satisfaction" shone into her heart, and noted that she was "so pretty to live with." What worried her was the Danish princess's reaction to her eldest son. Queen Victoria herself found Bertie "sallow, dull, heavy, blasé" and a "very unpleasant element in the house." Although it was generally assumed that a penniless princess would be only too grateful to marry the heir to the British throne, Victoria had justifiable fears that Alexandra might not accept him. To add to her anxiety, Bertie showed a marked reluctance to propose to Alexandra after meeting her, in spite of his mother's wishes. Soon the reason was clear: Bertie had fallen in love with an actress called Nelly Clifden.

As a nineteen-year-old army officer he was behaving in much the same way as his fashionable contemporaries, but the news shocked his father. Despite the accepted immorality at the court of his own German family, Albert was totally inflexible on this question. He severely reprimanded his son, who relented and apologized for yielding to temptation, assuring his father that the affair was over. Prince Albert visited his son at Cambridge for a reconciliation and returned to London feeling drained, he confessed, by the whole episode. A few days later he collapsed with typhoid fever. Within two weeks he was dead.

In the depths of her despair, Queen Victoria unreasonably blamed the Prince of Wales for his father's death. As her beloved Albert had approved of the marriage to Alexandra, she was now determined that it should go ahead. But with the death of the Prince Consort everything seemed in flux and Princess Christian, who also knew of the Nelly Clifden affair, feared the marriage might not take place. Moreover, as Alexandra's beauty and goodness were now known of throughout the courts of Europe, the young tsarevich was making overtures to her. And yet, despite Alexandra's virtues and obvious personal suitability, there were many factions that did not want the marriage to go ahead for political reasons. The Germans had their eyes on Schleswig-Holstein and a Danish Princess of Wales could influence popular opinion against Germany. Enemies of the match with England spread scandalous stories about the young girl, suggesting for instance that a scar on her neck had been caused by scrofula and that she was possibly barren. Although this was quite untrue, Alexandra wore her hair in ringlets to cover the disfigurement and later, when fashion decreed that hair should be piled on top of the head, she popularized the choker, or dog collar, which effectively concealed the ugly scar.

In spite of everything, Bertie fell under her spell and proposed. His father's death had been a shock and understandably he needed a little time to adjust at first. Now he eagerly looked forward to his marriage and even started to buy jewelry and trinkets for his future wife. He was captivated with her beauty, and the warmth and affection she showed him filled a great need in his life. He was impressed by her skilled horsemanship and iron nerve, and when she played the piano and sang in her sweet, true voice he appeared enchanted.

Although Alexandra had little to say about the plans for her future, she seems to have made no objections. Indeed, as many women were to discover, when the Prince of Wales wanted "to be charming," he was the most irresistible of men. He was also the world's most eligible bachelor, so it is not surprising that Alexandra loved him. But the fact that she was good and virtuous did not mean that she did not have a mind of her own. Queen Victoria's great fear that her son would dominate his wife and impose his ideas and "fast" way of life on her proved groundless, and she was pleased to hear Prince Christian say Alexandra was "a good child, not brilliant, but with a will of her own."

The question of language was important to Queen Victoria, and in order to show respect to Albert, Victoria instructed Bertie and Alexandra to write to one another in German. Alexandra was dutiful in every way, and determined to place her new country's interests and considerations before her own, but the one area where she would never give way all her life was in her loathing of Germany and all things German. That Queen Victoria wanted to promote the German element out of respect for her husband was only natural, but Alexandra had been brought up by parents who had always promoted the English element—and both Queen Victoria and Prince Albert jointly and most vehemently disliked the Danish element. In order to avoid Alexandra sharing confidences and chatting away in a language that her husband did not understand, the queen would not allow her to have a Danish maid or lady-in-waiting. Alexandra should come to England totally alone and start her life and relationships anew. The bride-to-be returned to Denmark to spend her eighteenth birthday with her family and to prepare for her wedding on March 10, 1863. Churchmen objected to a royal marriage in the middle of Lent, but Queen Victoria would hear none of it—marriage was a "solemn holy act not to be classed with amusements." Nor did she think Bertie should be made to wait till June for his bride; and according to family superstition May was a bad month for royal weddings—and Princess Alice's first baby was due in April.

Alexandra's wedding party sailed from Copenhagen to Hamburg and then on to Brussels. The journey became a royal progress, with crowds turning out everywhere to welcome and cheer the bride of the Prince of Wales. After the royal yacht reached Gravesend a late but ecstatic Bertie ran up the gangway to embrace his future wife.

Britain and Russia

If Bertie's welcome was enthusiastic, it was more than matched by that of the people. She was a "sea-king's daughter from over the sea," already known as a gracious and legendary beauty, but best of all, she wasn't German. Not since the Empress Eugénie had come with her husband on a state visit some seven years before had the British people been so totally and effortlessly charmed by a foreign princess. It seemed as if half the country had turned out to greet her. Despite the bitter cold in March 1863, the Thames estuary was full of boatloads of people with cheering, happy faces, and the streets were packed. The new network of railways made it possible for people to travel from all over the country to see Alexandra and they bought tens of thousands of postcards with her picture. As well as her beauty, people were immediately struck by her simple and natural manner and behavior, her kindness and warmth. Brought up in the protocol-free atmosphere of life at her father's court, this peculiarly Danish ease with all classes would lie at the root of her universal popularity throughout her life.

As the court was still in mourning for Prince Albert, after fifteen months of wearing black and no festivities the prospect of a royal wedding came as a great relief to Society. Nonetheless, the wedding would be small and largely private, in St. George's Chapel, Windsor. Feeling cheated of a great spectacle, the people were determined to catch at least a glimpse of Alexandra on her arrival. Although the queen gave permission for the invited guests to wear colors, her family were only permitted a slight relaxation to half-mourning. Two days after her arrival at Windsor Castle—in those days, cold and drafty, with few loos and notoriously bad drains—the wedding took place.

From the moment Alexandra set foot on English soil at Gravesend, everything about her was the subject of admiration and close scrutiny. The impact of her beauty was overwhelming—she was simply a delight to the eye—but she also brought with her the much-needed aura of glamour. It was the time of the sweet Dickensian heroine; wearing pale gray and violet half-mourning for Prince Albert, a white bonnet edged with pink roses she had made herself, Alexandra, with her innocent expression, epitomized this ideal. At eighteen, and with only a small dress allowance until her engagement, she could hardly have as yet completely formed her own taste. But unlike her new sisters-in-law, she had the great advantage of a supremely elegant mother and a very slim figure—"flat as a board," according to Queen Victoria. Her clothes from that first day were always to be admired, envied and copied. There were some adverse comments about her trousseau, but there were few good dressmakers in Copenhagen and even fewer fashionable materials to chose from. Victoria's uncle King Leopold wanted to give her a wedding dress of exquisite Brussels lace, but at the last minute, a more patriotic choice of an English-made dress of silver tissue and Honiton lace in a pattern of roses, shamrocks and thistles was chosen. The skirt was draped with garlands of orange blossom, and more flowers were twisted with diamonds in her hair. Just as Alexandra's ravishing beauty was remarked on, unfortunately so was the acknowledged ugliness of her eight English bridesmaids! Nor could Queen Victoria's daughters have been at their best—they were all red-eyed from weeping when the chorale composed by their father was sung. The lavish wedding gifts were on show, and although Alexandra had never owned anything like the splendid jewels she received from European royalty as well as from her husband and mother-in-law, she remained her natural self and not in the least overwhelmed.

The key to her personal style was simplicity, and there can be no doubt this sprang from her impecunious Danish childhood. On Alexandra's first visit to Osborne, Queen Victoria remarked on the jackets she wore. "I like them," Alexandra answered, adding, "and then, you see, a jacket is so *economical!* You can wear different skirts with it, and I have very few gowns, having to make them all myself." To wear a shirt of one color and a skirt of another was quite an innovation at that time, as the two-color division had for centuries been a masculine prerogative. Her height and slimness made dressing much easier, but in an age of fussiness and profusion of detail in clothes, Alexandra always relied on color and line. Her elegance came to her naturally and not by the usual way of trial and error. She was graceful and moved beautifully, and very soon was considered able to hold her own with those other two great beauties of the time, the Empress Elizabeth of Austria and the Empress Eugénie of France. Unlike Eugénie, who sometimes wore an evening dress only once, she was never accused of extravagance. Nor did the lessons of childhood ever leave her. Her maids were asked to darn her stockings and her handkerchiefs, and several sofas and chairs at Sandringham were re-covered with the fabric of six brocade dresses.

The Princess of Wales was not a fashion leader like Eugénie, and wore the same general style of dress all her life. For patriotic reasons she used English dressmakers, but she had the occasional shopping spree in Paris. Like Eugénie, Alexandra's sister Minnie dressed exclusively at Worth, and although Alexandra also bought there, she was more inclined to favor a variety of houses in England and Paris. She did make several innovations, particularly in sports clothes. She popularized the boater, attractive sailor suits for sailing at Cowes and the chic small toque worn at an angle, and she saw the common sense of wearing a sweater. Worth himself christened her dresses with long tight-fitting bodices *les robes princesses,* and she launched the fashion for tight-fitting jackets, buttoned and frogged like a hussar's. She also popularized the tailored suit, a way of dressing becoming to everyone, as well as being comfortable. Her mannish, simple, tailored clothes would have been considered unfeminine on anyone else, but as she wore them with such grace and style, soon everyone was following her lead. It was not long before Britain led the world with a combination of practical and elegantly tailored sports clothes. Alexandra learned early in her youth to wear clothes suitable to the occasion, and this ability was one of the secrets of her elegance.

After a short honeymoon at Osborne, the Prince and Princess of Wales returned to London and the social whirl began. Queen Victoria and Prince Albert were never lionized by Society and were thought of as "respectable" rather than "smart"—as the Waleses instantly became. Queen and consort had made only rare sorties into Society, and since Albert's death, Victoria had retired from it completely. Alexandra remained the Princess of Wales for thirty-eight years—and considered the title her own to the extent that when she became queen it was with great reluctance that she eventually allowed her son and daughter-in-law to use it. But if she was not yet crowned, she was the undisputed Queen of Society. As a result of her marriage, the London Season was brilliantly revived. By tradition, the country's situation politically, economically and socially was a direct reflection of the life of the sovereign. If Society was dull and morose, as it was after the death of Prince Albert and the queen's total withdrawal—and it had never been brilliant while he lived—this attitude permeated all social strata. If there was no Season, and great balls were not given, thousands of craftsmen and women would not be engaged in creating the clothes, the decorations, the jewelry, the food; the rich gentry would not come to London from their estates and spend money and visitors would not come from abroad. Alexandra's arrival changed all that. Britain was increasing in prosperity and prestige, and the enthusiasm and splendor which characterized social life after Alexandra's marriage was a clear indication of the nation's pride not only in its ruling family, but in itself.

Poor Bertie had nothing whatever to do. He lived for parties, for people, for entertaining and being entertained. His new wife loved this extravagant social life; she revelled in her beautiful clothes and jewels, and above all in the adulation she received. Overnight she was imitated and copied and guests would stand on chairs at receptions simply to catch a glimpse of her. When, after her illness and the birth of her second child, she was left with a stiff leg and a slight limp, the ladies of Society even copied that when they walked, as well as the exquisite parasols she chose to use in place of a stick.

In addition to the excitement of a new life, Alexandra also suddenly had two new homes: Sandringham in Norfolk and Marlborough House in London. Marlborough House had been given to the Prince of Wales on his eighteenth birthday as his London residence, and Alexandra loved it on sight. Christopher Wren's magnificent frescoed rooms, built in 1709 for the Duke of Marlborough, were decorated in the French taste of white and gold, with crimson silk curtains and upholstery. But contrary to the simple French classical arrangement of the rooms, here they were fashionably crowded with furniture and cluttered with unrelated objects. Potted palms stood in fireplaces and corners and every available surface was covered in trinkets and family photographs. Although the reception rooms had a certain elegance, the bedrooms and servants' quarters were appallingly crowded. As their family grew, the Prince of Wales's staff increased to 120. There was little enough room for the servants, but even the Waleses' three daughters shared the same small bedroom until they grew up. Since there were regular parties and receptions, furniture was constantly on the move and passages and corridors were lined and almost impassable with chairs, tables, sofas and packing cases. More valuable and fragile furniture had to be moved for storage to the stables (where the Prince of Wales kept sixty horses). The cellar was so hot and overcrowded that £1,500 worth of champagne was lost, either the heat or the damp ruining the wine. But worst of all was the plumbing, and as a result of the contaminated water supply typhoid fever swept through the household, affecting the children. The sewers under the house were rat-infested, and there was a real danger of fire, as rooms where furniture was temporarily stored were lit by gas and filled with the flammable litter used in the packing cases.

Because their home was classified neither as a palace nor as a royal lodge, the Prince of Wales had to pay for it all himself, apart from a small parliamentary vote for its upkeep. Since Bertie's income from the Duchy of Cornwall was so enormous, the government was reluctant to increase the state contribution to the costs of the royal residence. However, eventually Parliament relented and the house was at last made safe to live in.

Although there was a magnificent fifty-foot-long state dining room, the Waleses started the fashion for dining *à la Russe* in striped tents in the garden, sitting amid deep cushions on garden furniture placed on Oriental rugs. Footmen would serve the guests from a buffet, whereas until that time all the serving dishes had been placed on a central table. Here the meats would be carved and guests would help themselves and one another.

The beautiful state drawing room was white and gold with touches of pink. One of its features was a pair of grand pianos that stood side by side so that Alexandra and her daughters could play duets on separate instruments. If there were rats behind the panelling, inside the rooms the air was sweet all the year round with Alexandra's favorite flowers: lilies of the valley. These were grown especially for her in her greenhouses, and baskets were sent to London daily by train from Sandringham.

Old Sandringham House was extensively remodelled so as to be practical and comfortable rather than grand. The furniture was almost entirely contemporary, some of it "built in." There were no antiques, and instead of the usual royal portraits the pictures were modern. Here the Prince of Wales liked to imagine himself as an English country squire, although the impression he gave was really that of a successful industrialist. The three west-facing drawing rooms, which caught the evening sun, were decorated in pale blue, pink and cream, with the woodwork picked out in gold.

Alexandra loved the flat Norfolk countryside, for it reminded her of Denmark. She filled her boudoir at Sandringnam with her childhood mementoes, covering every table, shelf and inch of wall space with photographs, statuettes, programs, letters, lockets of hair and sketches that reminded her of past happiness, and paintings of the Yellow Palace and Bernstorff hung on the walls. Her husband crammed his own rooms with curios and trophies collected on his travels and on royal tours.

The guardian of the great hall was a fierce stuffed baboon holding a silver tray for calling cards. This "saloon" was the general meeting place, a room to relax in, write letters, play the piano, take tea or read the magazines and newspapers arranged on the side tables. But the entertainment center of the house was the billiard room and bowling alley. Furnished in a semi-Eastern style, with deep cushions, Oriental carpets and hookahs, both made excellent smoking rooms when not being used for their original purpose. The whole house gave a feeling of well-being and coziness, except perhaps the formal drawing rooms. The large amount of glittering glass—the luster chandeliers, the long mirrors fitted into the panelled walls and the tall glass cabinets with their mirrored backs and shelves—created an air of fragility and protocol.

For a woman who loved simplicity in all other things, Alexandra's taste in interiors was astonishingly ornate. Her bedroom at Sandringham was a maze of clutter, dominated by family photographs and mementoes. Her early religious training from her mother was echoed in a small replica of Thorwaldsen's statue of Christ, which she kept always by her bed. The bed curtains were draped from a carved cherub's head suspended from the cornice, and a crucifix hung just below.

At Sandringham, Alexandra built a dairy modelled on the Trifolium, the largest in Denmark. Its walls were lined with tiles brought back for her from India. The equipment for making butter was made of silver lined with porcelain, and scattered about the shelves and tables were little cows and calves made of silver, alabaster or terra-cotta. Here she introduced the Danish way of making butter, and she would often take tea in the dairy with her friends.

The gardens at Sandringham were another delight. Alexandra's taste in flowers was as simple in color and design as her taste in clothes, and she argued with her professional gardeners, "who preferred grand bedding-out displays to my poor innocent, inexpensive little flowers."

Although Sandringham was large and many bay windows flooded it with light, the accommodation, as at Marlborough House, was woefully inadequate. The bedrooms were tiny and two of Alexandra's sons slept in rooms no larger than a bathroom.

Yet the royal couple entertained constantly. Remembering the pleasure of his visits to Compiègne to stay with the Empress Eugénie and Napoleon III, Bertie carefully chose guests from all the professions, from industry, politics, diplomacy, and from the church. He invited musicians alongside members of the aristocracy, though curiously no writers or artists were invited, except for Lord Leighton. Although not intelligent herself, Alexandra enjoyed intelligent company and admired men who "did" something.

When Queen Victoria died, Alexandra was able to rearrange the rooms at Windsor, and apparently contrary to popular opinion did so very tastefully. Like a child opening presents, she delighted at finding wonderful pieces of furniture hidden away in dark corners and wrote touchingly to her son, the Duke of York, "I do not think even the Rothschilds could boast of anything better or more valuable." Her "clutter" included exquisite little trifles by Fabergé in the form of all the animals of the farm, even turkeys.

Minnie

Alexandra had been introduced to the work of Fabergé by her beloved sister Minnie. Their favorite brother, eighteen-year-old Willi, had been nominated George I of Greece, and in 1866 Minnie became the Grand Duchess Marie Feodorovna of Russia. A year after Alexandra's wedding she had become engaged to the Tsarevich Nicholas, but he died of tuberculosis the following year. On his deathbed Nicholas entrusted his fiancée to his brother with the words "She is worthy of your love, and you will make her happy." A year later they were married. By then Alexandra was expecting her second child and could not travel to Russia, but, eager to put her seal of approval on the match, she begged Bertie to go in her place.

Minnie seemed content with her gauche great bear of a husband, encouraging him to improve his sketchy education, his uncouth manners and his shy awkwardness in company. Minnie excelled on both private and public occasions, wearing her beautiful dresses and amazing jewels with great style and bearing. By the time she was thirty she had five children, and like her sister she was a natural and loving mother. She rarely interfered in politics—except, again like her sister, when her family's territories were involved—and concentrated on her husband, children and official duties. The Russian people instantly took this small, gay woman to their hearts, just as the British people adored Alexandra. Marie Feodorovna was both a witty and an intelligent conversationalist (unlike Alexandra, who at times could be a bit of a bore), and she shared her sister's charm and sympathetic kindness. Interested in everything and everyone, she undertook her duties with as much energy as she gave to her growing family, her husband, parties and dancing. Both sisters loved dancing, and when after her illness Alexandra was left slightly deaf as well as stiff, she still managed to move gracefully with the music, though with rather less enjoyment.

Although it was not politic for the sisters to meet on English soil—for British public opinion disapproved of the Russians' autocratic regime and particularly of their treatment of the Jews—Minnie and her husband did visit Alexandra and Bertie in 1873. London Society delighted in the sight of the two sisters, who often deliberately appeared dressed alike, whether on morning promenades in Hyde Park or at grand evening balls. On these occasions guests would gasp quite as much at the breathtaking size of Minnie's jewels as at Alexandra's beauty. Even as children, Minnie was considered the livelier and Alexandra the lovelier of the two, but both took the same childish delight in practical jokes.

In 1881, the Tsar Alexander II was assassinated and Minnie and her husband were crowned. The new Tsar Alexander III was as home-loving as his wife but made the transition to his public persona rather less well.

"The new Emperor is a very stay-at-home kind of person, devoted to his wife and fond of music . . . there is very little known about him," wrote the British ambassador, "probably because there is very little to know."

One of the richest men in the world, Minnie's husband was always trying to economize. He cut down on official entertaining, insisted on lights being turned off and was appalled when his wife paid £12,000 for a sable coat. Within a short time of his accession he had reduced his civil list by £2 million. His one great extravagance was the Fabergé Easter eggs he gave Minnie each year.

Eggs containing a hen and a "surprise" were not original to Fabergé. One was recorded in the Danish royal collection as early as 1743, and this may have inspired the tsarina. Each year the fantasies of the imperial jeweler surpassed his previous extravagances and the Fabergé eggs became more and more elaborate. Alexander presented Minnie with her first egg in 1886, and she continued to receive them each year until the Revolution.

Both Tsar Alexander III and his son Tsar Nicholas II were patrons of Fabergé. But according to Bainbridge (Fabergé's London agent at 48 Dover Street), in Europe "the lady to whom he owed everything was Queen Alexandra." Bainbridge's establishment was a treasury of precious *objets de vertu* in gold and enamel: boxes, cigarette cases, gold and enamel pencils, magnifying glasses and opera glasses with enamel and nephrite handles. Fabergé's workmen were particularly adept at carving nephrite, the soft translucent Siberian jade, into bowls and paper knives, handles for seals and parasols, and little pots, with or without lids—exquisite adult toys. Semiprecious stones were carved into the shape of animals, with tiny ruby or emerald eyes, or into models of peasants, often using two different-colored stones to simulate their clothes.

Royal Jewels

Alexandra had no desire to receive extravagant presents. Traditionally she was also unable to accept gifts of personal jewelry. As the objects were relatively inexpensive (ranging from £15 to £50), nothing gave her more pleasure than to receive on her birthday a small Fabergé animal, or a crystal vase carved to look as though it held water as well as a spray of flowers in enameled gold. As soon as a new shipment from Fabergé arrived at Bainbridge's, the king would insist on having the first choice for his wife; she would insist on seeing the collection first to choose presents for the king; and her friends would desperately try to buy for her something she had not already seen. In 1907, some of Fabergé's workmen came to Sandringham to model the royal animals—everything from the king's Derby winner Persimmon and his favorite terrier Caesar to the pigs and turkeys in the farmyard. The king and queen would inspect the wax models in the dairy at Sandringham, and these were then taken back to St. Petersburg to be carved in stone.

Both Minnie and Alexandra loved their clothes and jewels. They had beautiful sloping shoulders and Alexandra's long neck was ideal for the chokers she was to make so popular—they were to remain in fashion for the next fifty years. Most ladies have dresses made to suit their jewelry, but Alexandra preferred to subordinate her jewelry to her dresses. Later in her life she even bought quite a lot of paste jewelry in Paris, and wore some of it to the state opening of Parliament.

Alexandra's taste in jewelry and clothing was decisive and confident. "I know better than all the milliners and antiquaries," she declared when deciding on her coronation robes. "I shall wear exactly what I like, and so shall my ladies. Basta." Traditionally the color of a coronation robe for a British queen was violet shot with crimson, with blue for princesses. Alexandra wore hers woven in her own shade of purple (which Princess Louise christened "petunia"), and the princess wore violet. She also insisted on having all the royal emblems in her embroidery (although she was not really entitled to them). Alexandra placed great significance on the religious aspect of her coronation. Again she broke with tradition and had oil placed directly on her forehead by the archbishop, as otherwise it would only touch the toupee she wore as a fringe. She received as wedding gifts from her royal relatives jewels including not only a number of valuable "institutional" pieces but also extraordinary treasures from the maharajas in India. Using Indian diamonds, in 1904 Cartier created for her what must surely be one of the most beautiful necklaces of all.

Although Alexandra is usually seen in portraits and photographs festooned in ropes of pearls, with her dresses covered in brooches (sometimes all the way down to the hem), she actually wore very little jewelry during the day, and her favorite piece was a simple gold snake bracelet which twisted up her arm. She greatly admired the Empress Eugénie's jewelry and had her stones set in platinum to make the pieces look even lighter and more suitable to the delicate fabrics in fashion. As well as her choker, she wore as many as eight rows of pearls and diamonds around her elegant long neck. She popularized the sautoir, or long dangling rope necklace, and the huge brooch pinned centrally on the bodice known as the stomacher.

Her sister's fabulous jewelry came largely from the mines in Siberia. Her diamonds were huge, the center stone alone of one of her *rivières* weighing 32 carats. Minnie was very generous to her sister and would send her gifts of pearls, rubies, and sapphires. After Bertie's death, Minnie encouraged Alexandra to keep her jewelry as her own personal possession rather than passing it on as property of the crown, starting the permanent controversy over its division.

The Empress Marie Feodorovna

Tsar Alexander III's coronation in 1883, with all the gold and silver, the uniforms, the parades and the ceremonies, took its toll on the little empress and she was left quite exhausted. She even wore slippers under her robes, as her feet were so swollen that they could not fit any properly sized shoe. "It must be no joke to carry five yards of ermine and some lbs. of diamonds during several hours, while metallic popes drone and shuffle and wave candles and fling incense and bellow," remarked an English observer. Alexandra, who attended the coronation with Bertie, was deeply moved to observe the tender glances that passed between Minnie and her husband as he briefly held his massive crown on her head, replacing it with a smaller one topped by a huge sapphire. With her customary dignity Minnie then slowly rose and, suddenly breaking with formality, warmly embraced and kissed her husband.

Alexander and Minnie were extremely happy in their marriage. She could not introduce the unaffected ways of the Danish royal family into the Russian court, but her domestic life, away from all the pomp and splendor, was one of private, bourgeois coziness. On her marriage Minnie had found no difficulty in making the transition to her role in the Russian court, in spite of the many differences between the Russian royal family and her own. By tradition, Danish royalty was democratic in outlook and attitude, and the royal family mixed freely with the people. Danish subjects never felt a gulf between themselves and their sovereign, and anyone could come to the king with a problem. Russian court life was formal, theatrical and run with military precision.

Yet Minnie remained an unspoilt Danish princess. Her home, the Anitchkov Palace, was furnished with the same comfort and coziness as Marlborough House and Sandringham, and with the same clutter. Unlike her sister, she was an efficient, organized housewife, busying herself with the contents of the linen cupboard or the servants' accommodation and insisting upon open windows and fresh air.

Politically her attitudes were based on prejudice rather than informed judgment. For the most part she did not attempt to influence her husband, though she did succeed in turning him against Prussia, just as Alexandra did with Bertie.

All King Christian's children shared this same intense dislike of Prussia. Alexandra was only twenty-two at the time of the Schleswig-Holstein affair, but she never lost her bitter resentment of the humiliations then imposed by Bismarck on her family and country. One day at Wiesbaden, where she was seeking a cure at the baths for the rheumatic complaint that had partly crippled her, the King of Prussia sent a telegram offering to call on her at her own convenience. Alexandra dictated such a discourteous rejection of the offer that her secretary, Sir Francis Knollys, considered it best not even to write it down. Bertie insisted on a meeting whether she liked it or not. When Alexandra arrived for the meeting, leaning on her stick, Knollys, seeing how pale she was, asked her if she had caught a cold. Alexandra replied that if she was pale, "it is not from cold, but from anger at being obliged to see the King of Prussia."

Throughout her married life Alexandra was determined to put the interests of Britain before those of Denmark, but, try as she might, her youthful distrust of Germany never lessened. The British public's great love for their Danish princess turned the tide of feeling against Germany, despite Queen Victoria's pro-German opinions. Bertie took his wife's side and Queen Victoria was incensed. So was Vicky, who found Alexandra's behavior "neither wise nor kind." Yet whenever Queen Victoria saw Alexandra, her daughter-in-law's charms and sweetness would triumph and she would write to Vicky with her usual effusive praise of Alexandra's virtues.

By the time of World War I the descendants of King Christian of

Denmark sat on the thrones of Belgium, Britain, Denmark, Greece, Norway, Romania, Russia and Spain. Germany was effectively encircled by Danish royalty still burning with a desire to avenge the loss of Schleswig-Holstein. The fact that Russia and Britain were allied in 1914 owed a great deal to the fact that the dowager queens of both countries were loving sisters.

Hvidöre

Every year Alexandra returned to her father's house in Denmark for a family reunion. Even Bertie enjoyed these visits, where his in-laws gathered from all over Europe to relive the carefree days of their youth. When King Christian died, Alexandra and Minnie decided to buy a house of their own in Denmark, rather than impose on their sister-in-law. Their parents' house had always been "home" to them; now they needed a hideaway from the pressures of officialdom.

They bought Hvidöre, a white Italianate villa north of Copenhagen on the road to Elsinore; it overlooked the sea, with the white coast of Sweden clearly visible on the horizon. "Inside," wrote Alexandra, "it has all the comforts and beauties of an English House and outside is like an Italian Villa, with two charming verandahs and a small balcony in front of my bedroom covered with flowers." The grandest part was the hall, all white and gold, with a double staircase, gilt balustrade, giant pilasters and a columned gallery.

The two sisters tossed for which rooms they should have, and set about making them as cozy and unpretentious as possible. Both loved clutter, and they shared a sitting room, with twin writing tables and chairs, twin bookcases and a corner each for photographs. More photographs were scattered about the house in their Fabergé frames, together with the Danish porcelain. There was a billiard room, and the sisters ate in a charming trellised garden room. Everything was simpler and far more harmonious than in their great palaces. As Minnie put it, "What is the use of my four hundred rooms at Garchina? I never use more than two." Here they lived with three servants each and a shared page.

When the sisters began to redecorate Hvidöre, Minnie was ill and most of the alterations were left to Alexandra. The reception rooms, with their delicate molded plasterwork, were decorated in soft, pale colors. She made the house (in her own words) "bright and cheery," with "our bedrooms all chintzes and some silks in the drawing room downstairs." There was a garden around Hvidöre, and they built a tiny tunnel under the road to reach the beach. Alexandra brought Thomas Mawson from England to remodel these two acres by the sea into herbaceous borders and a rose garden. She found the result "delightful, full of nice old fruit trees, masses of pears and apples," with the strand garden, where "we sit basking ourselves in the sun," running right down to the sea and full of flowers.

Bertie had become king by the time these transformations were complete. He visited Hvidöre once and after the first night moved into a hotel! But he did arrange for a summerhouse to be erected by the shore, to the delight of his wife.

After her husband's death in 1910 Alexandra returned to Hvidöre for three more years, but after the war she felt too frail to make the voyage to Denmark. Two years after the Russian Revolution Minnie was finally persuaded to leave the Crimea, and Hvidöre became her home in exile. Here she would sit, surrounded by her photographs in their Fabergé frames, looking disbelievingly at the pictures of her murdered son and his family, her jewels which she had managed to bring with her in a box under the bed. Minnie became quite a drain on the financial resources of her Danish family, and they urged her to sell some of her treasures, until Bertie generously sent her a sizable allowance. After her death in 1928, Queen Mary "acquired" many pieces of her beautiful Russian jewelry, some of which were not paid for until 1968. Hvidöre was sold by her daughters and is now used as a nursing home.

Alexander had almost as little to do with the government as Bertie, owing to his disagreement with his father's liberal policies. Known in the family as "Sasha," he was a dear but stupid man, and as Minnie was only slightly more intelligent than he was, she had little interest in affairs of state. Unlike Alexandra's marriage, hers was a great success, as Sasha was devoted to his family and totally faithful. Surrounded at home by protocol and intense security, he took his greatest pleasure in the freedom of his family holidays in Denmark. The imperial family travelled with more than one hundred attendants as well as pets, and filled over twenty railway trucks with their luggage.

All Alexander's best qualities could be seen on these holidays. He was by far the most popular uncle as he romped with his nephews and nieces, as well as with his children, chopping down trees, shovelling snow and (to Minnie's horror) demonstrating his legendary strength by bending horseshoes and silver plates as if they were made of rubber. In such an atmosphere the imperial children were sensibly and lovingly raised. Minnie had always had the happy home life of her parents as a model, and she succeeded in passing on to her son Nicholas this Danish enjoyment of family life.

Alexandra and Bertie

Alexandra's first child, Prince Eddy, was born in 1864, and during the next five years she had four more children. Remembering the severity of his own upbringing, Bertie was determined that his offspring should have happy, carefree childhoods. Queen Victoria totally disapproved. "Bertie should understand what a strong right I have to interfere in the management of the children," she exclaimed. Heedless of her mother-in-law, Alexandra let the children run wild as she had done in her own Danish youth. A happy, high-spirited band, they inherited her Danish sense of humor and love of practical jokes, and displayed very little interest in study. They called Alexandra "darling mother dear," and she joined in their games as if she were one of them—even taking part in soda-siphon battles with her sons. Always childish by nature, in the isolation caused by her increasing deafness she returned to her own childhood by sharing that of her children.

Sadly, both Eddy and George proved to be weak and lethargic (a weakness mirrored in Minnie's son Nicholas). Eddy was engaged to be married in 1892, the year before his death. After Christmas he went shooting with his father at Sandringham and came back shivering. Influenza duly developed into pneumonia and on January 13, 1893, he died, as Alexandra despairingly wiped the sweat from his face and neck. "Gladly would I have given my life for his," wrote Bertie to Queen Victoria.

Bertie's relationship with his wife was far from ideal. Both were immature and unintellectual, and although they enjoyed clothes and spending money, they had little else in common. Alexandra depended on informed, intelligent conversation as a compensation for her lack of education. As her growing deafness made this impossible, she retreated more and more into those areas where she felt comfortable: her children, her homes, her dogs, her horses. Another reason for this retreat was Bertie's unfaithfulness. In a frantic effort to dispel the boredom of having no real role to play in government, and as Alexandra's socializing decreased, he added to his list of mistresses.

The public saw only the benign and gentle side of his restless and irritable character. Bertie could not have been an easy man to live with, but he was always courteous and kind to Alexandra. She never complained, although she must often have felt neglected and humiliated by his infidelities. Alexandra despised jealousy, and whenever she met one of her husband's mistresses she never failed to be gracious. A number of anecdotes have survived which do reveal her inner feelings, however. She nicknamed Miss Chamberlayne, the pretty American with whom her husband dallied, "Chamberpots." Another time she watched through a Sandringham window the buxom Mrs. Keppel and her portly husband, and could not resist inviting her lady-in-waiting to join in her laughter at the two tubby lovers as they trundled by.

Animals proved more faithful and both Minnie and Alexandra loved them. Minnie took her dog Beauty with her to Russia, but when Alexandra arrived in England she brought only two white turtle doves, given to her as a girl. On her first visit to Ireland the women of Dublin gave her another white dove, which she cherished for years. Once her love of animals became known, they came in a constant stream of gifts, until she possessed at Sandringham a menagerie of monkeys, bears, tigers and parakeets—so many that they eventually had to be sent to a zoo. One of her Sandringham parrots, Cocky, was over a hundred years old. She taught him to take a piece of sugar from her mouth and croak, "God save the Queen." Another of her menagerie was a long-tailed black ram, which she brought back from a trip to Egypt. Tethered on the deck as they sailed down the Nile, he was to have been the lunch, but he chewed through his rope and found the Princess of Wales sitting in a deck chair. Laying his head in her lap he was instantly reprieved.

After her Sandringham menagerie had gone, Alexandra stuck on the whole to dogs and horses. She kept "indoor" and "outdoor" dogs, and loved them all. Her animals adored her in return. Indoors she kept at first pugs and then "Japanese spaniels" and Pekinese. These small dogs slept with her, and each evening at bedtime she would have a small supper tray of sandwiches left outside her room, in order to feed her dogs secretly in bed. Her outdoor dogs were St. Bernards, Newfoundlands,

Eskimo sledge dogs, basset hounds, chows and dachshunds. Her white Arctic dog Jacko was the first of that breed to be seen in Britain, and she had a magnificent slate-colored deerhound. She was the patron of the Kennel Club and would often exhibit her own dogs, frequently winning prizes. As well as having the dogs carved by Fabergé, Alexandra also had them painted in oils and some were even stuffed; many more were buried in the gardens of both Marlborough House and Sandringham. Alexandra could often be seen walking with as many as ten dogs leaping around her, each one obedient to her commands.

She exercised the same power over horses as she did over her dogs. During the drive to the Mansion House on her arrival in London for her wedding, one of her escort's chargers panicked and, plunging and kicking, caught a hind leg in the spokes of her carriage wheel. Without the slightest fear, Alexandra calmly leaned out and with her hand extricated the horse's hoof.

Her father had been Master of the Horse and taught all his children to ride beautifully. In the early days of Alexandra's marriage both she and Bertie rode to hounds in Norfolk, greatly to the queen's horror. Even after Alexandra's leg became stiff, she simply had the pommel switched on her sidesaddle and rode on the off side. She was a fearless rider and loved jumping—something Bertie did his best to avoid. Alexandra had a number of favorite horses: a brown mare called Violet, a horse called King Arthur, and her beloved Viva, who carried her for over twenty years. When Viva died, aged twenty-eight, Alexandra had her ears and forelock preserved in a case.

She was also an excellent whip, though rather dashing and often a little dangerous. She possessed a pair of Lipizzaners—rare at that time in England—which she drove with great skill in a phaeton, and Bertie gave her four Hungarian ponies when he left for India. She had a pair of bays called Mite and Puffy, which she drove in tandem, and she drove Bena, Beau and Belle in pairs in a little French carriage. Merry Antics she drove in a single harness. Alexandra liked to name all her horses herself. She preferred bays and chestnuts, in brown harness mounted in brass; and where nature did not provide her carriage horses with full, flowing tails, she added false ones. There are endless animal stories about Alexandra, but the chief result that her love of animals had was a far greater national awareness of their often sad conditions.

As for other sports, Alexandra fished and played croquet from childhood and continued to play even as a grandmother with young Prince Edward. But skating, the only form of winter sport possible in flat Denmark, was a favorite pastime, and she would glide over the ice for hours. The king had an elegant two-seater motorcar built especially for her, but Alexandra only rarely went out in the "Electric." Like the Empress Elizabeth of Austria, Alexandra used the gymnastics her father had taught her as a child to keep her figure; at the time of her coronation, when she was fifty-seven, she still had a twenty-three-inch waist. She also tried golf, but had no interest in tennis and converted the courts at Sandringham into a rose garden.

Both Alexandra and Minnie became enthusiastic amateur photographers. Their father had taught them drawing as children, but neither he nor his pupils showed the kind of talent possessed by Queen Victoria and her children. Alexandra continued to "dabble," as she called it, in both oils and pastels, but her artistic sense was better suited to the camera. She never tired of photographing her family and animals, and she and Minnie exchanged snaps constantly. Alexandra even had her pictures published in a Christmas Gift Book, which sold well for charity.

It was to Queen Victoria's despair that her daughter-in-law "never opened a book," but she did like the poetry of Tennyson and the stories of Rudyard Kipling. When she first met Tennyson, the Princess of Wales politely asked him to read aloud the "Ode of Welcome," which he had written for her wedding. She listened attentively for a while, then she caught the poet's eye and both collapsed in fits of laughter. Her favorite novelist seems to have been William le Queux—who is to prose what William McGonagal is to Scottish verse. It is a sad but true fact that the Danish cultural revival left Alexandra untouched; but she did appreciate beautiful porcelain, and collected Sèvres, Meissen and Worcester which, together with her fine collection of crystal ware, was displayed at Sandringham.

For all her beauty, elegance and grace, Alexandra is best remembered by the British people for her philanthropy. She chided the headmaster of Eton for flogging the boys with as much vehemence as she reproved a driver for ill-treating a horse. And the effects of her sweetness and affection could be seen in Queen Victoria herself, who mellowed under the influence of her daughter-in-law and changed from a middle-aged recluse into a benign old lady who smiled at the people and radiated goodwill.

Alexandra was a remarkably unsqueamish woman, which was useful when it came to helping the underprivileged of nineteenth-century Britain. She would walk the corridors of "her" hospital in London's East End, showing an interest in the patients' illnesses. She knew all the nurses, and was present during operations. On a visit to Denmark she was shown the Finsen lamp, an ultraviolet lamp for the cure of an ulcerous inflammation of the skin known as lupus; but back in England she found little enthusiasm for it among the staff of her hospital. Obstinate as ever, she persuaded the hospital to send two nurses and a doctor to Copenhagen to see the lamp in operation; in consequence a special Finsen unit was established in London, and for the next twenty years her lamps treated a hundred grateful patients a day.

Each morning her secretary would bring in a trayful of begging letters. She dealt with each one on its merits, and with a generosity that was the despair of her financial advisers. One of the most touching stories of her kindness concerns John Merrick, the "Elephant Man." An advanced case of a hideously deforming disorder, Merrick was put on display at fairs and shows all over Europe. When he was too ill to travel, his manager sent him back to London. Confused and lost, Merrick arrived at Paddington Station and sat huddled in a dark corner of the waiting room. People who saw him ran away screaming, and he fled. After being hunted like an animal through the streets of London, he was eventually brought into Alexandra's hospital. There the wretched man was segregated from the other patients. Young nurses lacked the strength to treat him. When Alexandra heard about Merrick, she immediately insisted on seeing him. She sat down and talked to him, looking fully at him and slowly giving him back some confidence. Each year until his death Merrick received a personal Christmas message from her.

In 1886 Alexandra founded the Soldiers' and Sailors' Families Association (forerunner of today's SSAFA) to give financial help to the dependents of servicemen who had lost their lives in battle. Another of her charitable ideas was Alexandra Rose Day, begun in 1913 to raise funds for London hospitals. Alexandra would drive in her carriage from Marlborough House to the Mansion House and back again, with women volunteers dressed in white selling artificial wild roses made by the disabled. This drive by the dowager queen became a great summer attraction, with thousands of Londoners crowding to cheer her. By 1920 Alexandra Rose Day had raised three-quarters of a million pounds.

Her charitable enthusiasm was boundless. To mark Queen Victoria's Diamond Jubilee in 1897, Alexandra gave a dinner to 40,000 poor people. In 1902 she instituted Queen Alexandra's Imperial Military Nursing Service (now Queen Alexandra's Royal Army Nursing Corps). At her coronation, 10,000 general maids were given a coronation tea at her expense in halls all over London. She visited each hall, and a brooch inscribed "From the Queen" was placed beside each plate. In 1906, through her inspiration, a quarter of a million pounds was raised for unemployed workmen.

Despite all the saccharine poured on Alexandra by her biographers, there is no doubt that her kindness was genuine and overflowing. Yet she could also be incredibly selfish. Although she truly loved her children, she made no effort to find husbands for her daughters, and quite deliberately kept Princess Victoria with her as (in the words of her cousin the Grand Duchess Olga) "a glorified maid." Even her son George, who was particularly close to his mother, considered her the most selfish woman he knew. She was a paradox. In spite of her care for the poor and for such unfortunates as John Merrick, her total lack of imagination rendered her incapable of putting herself in anyone else's place. As Sir Francis Knollys once commented, "How little she knows human nature."

And yet when she died at Sandringham in 1925, aged eighty, she was universally loved.

Bibliography

CATHERINE THE GREAT

Bartlett, R. *Human Capital: The Settlement of Foreigners in Russia, 1762–1804* (Cambridge, 1979).

Billington, James H. *The Icon and the Axe: An Interpretative Study of Russian Culture* (London, 1966).

Castéra, J. H. *The Life of Catherine II, Empress of Russia,* trans. W. Tooke (London, 1800).

Catherine II. *Memoirs,* ed. Dominique Maroget, with an introduction by G. P. Gooch, trans. Moura Budberg (London, 1955).

Cronin, Vincent. *Catherine: Empress of All the Russias* (London, 1978).

Cross, Anthony, ed. *Russia Under Western Eyes* (London, 1971).

Dashkova, Princess. *The Memoirs of Princess Dashkova,* ed. Kyril Fitzlyon (London, 1958).

Drage, C. L. *Russian Literature in the Eighteenth Century* (London, 1978).

Evans, Joan. *History of Jewellery 1100–1870* (London, 1953).

Garrard, J. G., ed. *The Eighteenth Century in Russia* (Oxford, 1973).

Gip, Bernard. *The Passions and Lechery of Catherine the Great* (Edinburgh, 1971).

Grey, Ian. *Catherine the Great, Autocrat and Empress of All Russia* (London, 1961).

Hamilton, George Heard. *The Art and Architecture of Russia* (London, 1975).

Haslip, Joan. *Catherine the Great* (London, 1977).

Horn, D. B. *Sir Charles Hanbury-Williams and European Diplomacy, 1747–1758* (London, 1930).

Hyde, H. M., ed. *The Russian Journals of Martha and Catherine Wilmot, 1803–1808* (London, 1934).

Kochan, Miriam. *Life in Russia Under Catherine the Great* (London and New York, 1969).

Madariaga, Isabel de. *Russia in the Age of Catherine the Great* (London, 1981).

Marsden, Christopher. *Palmyra of the North* (London, 1942).

Massie, Robert K. *Nicholas and Alexandra* (London, 1968).

Masson, C. F. *Secret Memoirs of the Court of St. Petersburg,* trans. from the French (London, 1801–1802).

Molloy, Fitzgerald. *The Russian Court in the Eighteenth Century* (London, 1905).

Oldenbourg, Zoé. *Catherine the Great* (London, 1972).

Oliva, L. Jay. *Catherine the Great* (Edgewood Cliffs, NJ, 1971).

Osborne, Harold, ed. *Oxford Companion to the Decorative Arts* (Oxford, 1975).

Polovtsoff, Alexander. *The Favourites of Catherine the Great* (London, 1940).

Raeff, M. *Catherine II: A Profile* (New York, 1972).

Richardson, William. *Anecdotes of the Russian Empire: In a Series of Letters, written, a few years ago, from St. Petersburg* (London, 1784).

Rogger, Hans. *National Consciousness in Eighteenth-Century Russia* (Cambridge, 1960).

Shcherbatov, Prince M. M. *On the Corruption of Morals in Russia,* ed. and trans. with an introduction and notes by A. Lentin (Cambridge, 1969).

Twining, Edward. *History of the Crown Jewels of Europe* (London, 1960).

Varneke, B. V. *History of the Russian Theatre* (New York, 1951).

Waliszewski, R. *The Romance of an Empress: Catherine II of Russia* (London, 1894).

Wren, Melvin C. *The Western Impact Upon Tsarist Russia* (Chicago, 1971).

Marie Antoinette

Adams, William Howard. *The French Garden, 1500–1800* (London, 1979).

Arneth, Alfred, and M. A. Geffroy. *Marie Antoinette: Correspondance secrète entre Marie-Thérèse et le Comte de Mercy-Argenteau.* 3 vols. (Paris, 1875).

Asquith, Annunziata. *Marie Antoinette* (London, 1974).

Belloc, Hilaire. *Marie Antoinette* (London, 1909).

Blaikie, Thomas. *Diary of a Scotch Gardener at the French Court at the End of the Eighteenth Century* (London, 1931).

Campan, Jeanne Louise Henriette. *The Private Life of Marie Antoinette* (London, 1887).

Castelot, André. *Marie Antoinette,* trans. Denise Folliot (London, 1957).

Cobban, Alfred. *A History of Modern France. Vol. I: 1715–1799* (London, 1981).

Crankshaw, Edward. *Maria Theresa* (London, 1983).

Cronin, Vincent. *Louis and Antoinette* (London, 1974).

Demuth, Norman. *French Opera: Its Development to the Revolution* (Sussex, 1963).

Genders, Roy. *A History of Scent* (London, 1972).

Gooch, G. P. *Louis XV: The Monarchy in Decline* (London, 1956).

Hearsey, John E. N. *Marie Antoinette* (London, 1972).

Honey, W. B. *French Porcelain* (London, 1950).

Honour, P. H. *Cabinet Makers and Furniture Designers* (London, 1969).

Huth, Hans. *Roentgen Furniture* (London, 1974).

Landais, Hubert. *French Porcelain* (London, 1961).

Lough, John. *An Introduction to Eighteenth-Century France* (London, 1960).

Moulton, Mayer. *The Tragic Queen: Marie Antoinette* (London, 1968).

Nolhac, Pierre de. *Marie-Antoinette Dauphine* (Paris, 1906).

Osborne, Harold, ed. *The Oxford Companion to the Decorative Arts* (Oxford, 1975).

Réau, Louis. *L'Europe française au siècle des lumières* (Paris, 1938).

Rohde, Eleanour Sinclair. *The Story of the Garden* (London, 1932).

Savage, George. *Seventeenth and Eighteenth Century French Porcelain* (London, 1961).

———. *French Decorative Art, 1638–1793* (London, 1969).

Seward, Desmond. *Marie Antoinette* (London, 1981).

Smollett, Tobias. *Travels Through France and Italy,* ed. Frank Felsenstein (Oxford, 1979).

Smyth, Lilian C. *The Guardian of Marie Antoinette: Letters from the Comte de Mercy d'Argenteau, Austrian Ambassador to the Court of Versailles, to Marie Thérèse, Empress of Austria, 1770–1780* (London, 1902).

Thrale, Mrs. *The French Journals of Mrs. Thrale and Doctor Johnson,* ed. Moses Tyson and Henry Guppy (Manchester, 1932).

Verlet, Pierre. *French Royal Furniture* (London, 1963).

————. *French Furniture and Interior Decoration of the Eighteenth Century* (London, 1967).

Vogt d'Hunolstein, Le Comte Paul. *Correspondance inédite de Marie Antoinette.* 3rd ed. (Paris, 1864).

Weiss, Gustav. *The Book of Porcelain* (London, 1971).

Wraxall, N. William. *Memoirs of the Courts of Berlin, Dresden, Warsaw, and Vienna.* Vol. II (London, 1806).

Zweig, Stefan. *Marie Antoinette: The Portrait of an Average Woman* (London, 1933).

Maria Carolina

Acton, Harold. *The Bourbons of Naples, 1734–1825* (London, 1956).

Bearne, Mrs. *A Sister of Marie Antoinette: The Life-Story of Maria Carolina, Queen of Naples* (London, 1907).

Colletta, Pietro. *History of the Kingdom of Naples* (London, 1858).

Collison-Morley, Lacy. *Naples Through the Ages* (London, 1925).

Corti, Egon Caesar. *Ich, eine Tochter Maria Theresias* (Munich, 1950).

Hersey, George L. *Architecture, Poetry, and Number in the Royal Palace at Caserta* (Cambridge, MA, 1983).

Jeaffreson, John Cordy. *The Queen of Naples and Lord Nelson.* 2 vols. (London, 1899).

Johnston, R. M., ed. *Mémoire de Marie Caroline, Reine de Naples* (Cambridge, MA, and London, 1912).

Millar, Lady Anne. *Letters from Italy.* Vol. II (London, 1776).

Novotny, Fritz. *Painting and Sculpture in Europe 1780–1880* (London, 1961).

Seward, Desmond. *Naples: A Travellers' Companion* (London, 1984).

Tresoldi, Lucia. *La Biblioteca privata di Maria Carolina d'Austria Regina di Napoli* (Rome, 1972).

Wilmot, Catherine. *An Irish Peer on the Continent, 1801–1803,* ed. Thomas U. Sadleir (London, 1924).

Woolf, Stuart. *A History of Italy, 1700–1860* (London, 1979).

Leopoldina

Azevedo, Fernando de. *Brazilian Culture* (New York, 1950).

Bradford Burns, E. *Perspectives on Brazilian History* (New York and London, 1967).

————. *History of Brazil* (New York, 1970).

Calogeras, João Pandiá, *A History of Brazil* (Chapel Hill, NC, 1939).

Costa, Sergio Corrêa da. *Every Inch a King: Dom Pedro I, First Emperor of Brazil* (New York, 1950).

Dalbian, Denyse. *Dom Pedro, empereur de Brésil, roi de Portugal* (Paris, 1959).

Ferrez, Gilberto. *O Veilho Rio de Janeiro Através das Gravuras de Thomas Ender* (São Paolo, 1968).

Freyre, Gilberto. *The Mansions and the Shanties* (New York, 1963).

Graham, Maria. *Journal of a Voyage to Brazil and residence there during 1821–3* (London, 1824).

Grande Enciclopédia portuguesa e brasileira. Vol. XVI (Lisbon, 1936–1960).

Guimarães, A. C. D'Araújo. *A Côrte no Brasil* (São Paolo, 1825).

Harding, Bertita. *Amazon Throne: The Braganzas of Brazil* (New York, 1941).

Haring, C. H. *Empire in Brazil: A New World Experiment with Monarchy* (Cambridge, MA, 1969).

Luccock, John. *Notes on Rio de Janeiro and the Southern Parts of Brazil* (London, 1820).

Martius, C. F. Phil. von, and J. B. von Spix. *Travels in Brazil in the Years 1817–20.* 2 vols. (London, 1824).

Oberacker, Karl Heinrich. *La imperatriz Leopoldina* (Rio de Janeiro, 1975).

Turnbull, Patrick. *Napoleon's Second Empress* (London, 1971).

Williams, M. W. *Dom Pedro the Magnanimous* (London, 1937).

Worcester, Donald E. *Brazil: From Colony to World Power* (New York, 1973).

EUGÉNIE

Bac, Ferdinand. *Intimités du Second Empire*. 3 vols. (Paris, 1931).

————. *La Cour des Tuileries* (Paris, 1934).

Barthez, E. *The Empress Eugénie and Her Circle* (London, 1912).

Bellesort, A. *La Société française sous Napoléon III* (Paris, 1932).

Bertavt, J. *L'Impératrice Eugénie et son temps* (Paris, n.d.).

Bury, J. P. T. *Napoleon III and the Second Empire* (London, n.d.).

Corley, T. A. B. *Democratic Despot: A Life of Napoleon III* (London, 1961).

Filon, Augustin. *Recollections of the Empress Eugénie* (London, 1920).

Fischel, Oskar, and Max von Boehn. *Modes and Manners of the Nineteenth Century* (London, 1927).

Fleury, Comte, and Louis Sonolet. *La Société du Second Empire.* 4 vols. (Paris, n.d.).

Gooch, G. P. *The Second Empire* (London, 1960).

Gregorietti, Giulio. *Jewellery Through the Ages* (London, 1976).

Guériot, Paul. *Napoleon III* (Paris, 1934).

Guest, Ivor. *The Ballet of the Second Empire* (London, 1974).

Jerrold, Blanchard. *The Life of Napoleon III*. Vol. III (London, 1877).

Kurtz, Harold. *The Empress Eugénie, 1826–1920* (London, 1964).

La Gorce, Pierre de. *Histoire du Second Empire*. Vol. I (Paris, 1935).

Paléologue, Maurice. *The Tragic Empress: Intimate Conversations with the Empress Eugénie* (London, 1928).

Praz, Mario. *An Illustrated History of Interior Design* (London, 1964).

Ridley, Jasper. *Napoleon III and Eugénie* (London, 1979).

Sencourt, Robert. *The Life of the Empress Eugénie* (London, 1931).

Simpson, F. A. *Louis-Napoleon and the Recovery of France* (London, 1931).

Taisey-Chatenoy, Marquise de. *A la Cour de Napoléon III*. 3 vols. (Paris, n.d.).

Vicky

An Anecdotal Memoir of Her Royal Highness the Princess Royal of England from Her Birth to Her Marriage, by a Lady (London, 1858).

Balfour, Michael. *The Kaiser and His Times* (London, 1964).

Barkeley, Richard. *The Empress Frederick* (London, 1956).

Bennett, Daphne. *Vicky: Princess Royal of England and German Empress* (London, 1971).

Bunsen, Marie von. *The World I Used to Know,* ed. and trans. Oakley Williams (London, 1930).

Carr, William. *A History of Germany, 1815–1945* (London, 1969).

Corti, Count Egon Caesar. *The English Empress* (London, 1957).

Craig, Gordon A. *Germany 1866–1945* (Oxford, 1978).

Dacre Craven, Mrs. [Florence Lees]. *Servants of the Sick Poor* (London, 1885).

————. *A Guide to District Nurses and Home Nursing* (London, 1889).

Duff, David. *Alexandra: Princess and Queen* (London, 1980).

Eyck, Eric. *Bismarck and the German Empire* (London, 1950).

Fischel, Dr. Oskar, and Max von Boehn. *Modes and Manners of the Nineteenth Century.* 4 vols. (London, 1927).

Fulford, Roger, ed. *Dearest Child: Letters Between Queen Victoria and the Princess Royal, 1858–1861* (London, 1964).

————, ed. *Dearest Mama: Letters Between Queen Victoria and the Crown Princess of Prussia, 1861–1864* (London, 1968).

————, ed. *Your Dear Letter: Private Correspondence of Queen Victoria and the Crown Princess of Prussia, 1865–1871* (London, 1971).

————, ed. *Darling Child: Private Correspondence of Queen Victoria and the Crown Princess of Prussia, 1871–1878* (London, 1976).

————, ed. *Beloved Mama: Private Correspondence of Queen Victoria and the German Crown Princess, 1878–1885* (London, 1981).

Gould Lee, Arthur, ed. *The Empress Frederick Writes to Sophie* (London, 1955).

Gower, Lord Ronald. *My Reminiscences* (London, 1895).

Lees, Florence. "The Crown Princess's Lazareth for the Wounded" and "In a Fever Hospital Before Metz," *Good Words* (London, 1873).

Leinhaas, G. A. *Reminiscences of Victoria, Empress Frederick* (Mainz, 1902).

HRH Princess Marie Louise. *My Memories of Six Reigns* (London, 1956).

Paget, Lady Walburga. *Scenes and Memories* (London, 1912).

————. *Embassies of Other Days* (London, 1923).

————. *The Linings of Life* (London, 1930).

Ponsonby, Magdalen, ed. *Mary Ponsonby: A Memoir, Some Letters and a Journal* (London, 1927).

Reischach, Hugo von. *Under Three Emperors* (London, 1927).

Röhl, John G., and Nicholaus Sombart, eds. *Kaiser Wilhelm II: New Interpretations* (Cambridge, 1982).

Russell, George W. E., ed. *Letters of Matthew Arnold, 1848–1888,* Vols. 1 and 2 (London, 1901).

Sagarra, Eda. *A Social History of Germany, 1648–1914* (London, 1977).

Seaman, W. A. L., and J. R. Sewell, eds. *The Russian Journal of Lady Londonderry 1836–7* (London, 1973).

Stern, Fritz. *Gold and Iron: Bismarck, Bleichröder, and the Building of the German Empire* (London, 1977).

Van der Kiste, John. *Frederick III: German Emperor 1888* (Gloucester, 1981).

Woodham-Smith, Cecil. *Florence Nightingale* (London, 1976).

ALEXANDRA AND MINNIE

Adburgham, Alison. *A "Punch" History of Manners and Modes* (London, 1961).

Andrew, Christopher. *Secret Service* (London, 1985).

Anronson, Theo. *A Family of Kings* (London, 1976).

Bainbridge, H. C. *Peter Carl Fabergé* (London, 1949).

Battiscombe, Georgina. *Queen Alexandra* (London, 1969).

Beaton, Cecil. *The Glass of Fashion* (London, 1954).

Brooke, Iris, and James Laver. *English Costume of the Nineteenth Century* (London, 1964).

Buchanan, Meriel. *Victorian Gallery* (London, 1956).

Burdett, H. C. *Prince, Princess, and People, 1863–89* (London, 1889).

Chelwood, Viscount Cecil of. *Queen Alexandra: A Pictorial Biography, 1844–1925* (London, 1925).

Cooper, Nicholas. *The Opulent Eye: Late Victorian and Edwardian Taste in Interior Design* (London, 1976).

Cunnington, C. W. *The Art of English Costume* (London, 1948).

———. *The Perfect Lady* (London, 1948).

Crawford, T. S. *A History of the Umbrella* (London, 1970).

de Marly, Diana. *The History of Haute Couture* (London, 1980).

Dictionary of National Biography, 1922–1930 (London, 1937).

Downs, Brian W. "Anglo-Danish Literary Relations 1867–1900," *Modern Language Review,* vol. XXXIX, no. 3 (Cambridge, 1944).

Duff, David. *Alexandra, Princess and Queen* (London, 1980).

Farr, Dennis. *Oxford History of English Art, 1870–1940* (Oxford, 1979).

Flower, Margaret. *Victorian Jewellery* (London, 1951).

Foster, Vanda. *A Visual History of Costume in the Nineteenth Century* (London, 1984).

Hartnell, Norman. *Royal Courts of Fashion* (London, 1971).

Judd, Denis. *Edward VII: A Pictorial Biography* (London, 1975).

Jullian, Phillipe. *Edward and the Edwardians,* trans. Peter Dawnay (London, 1967).

Laver, J. *The Age of Optimism: Manners and Morals 1848–1914* (London, 1966).

———. *A Concise History of Costume* (London, 1969).

Madol, Hans Roger. *The Private Life of Queen Alexandra* (London, 1940).

Magnus, Philip. *King Edward the Seventh* (London, 1964).

Massie, Robert K. *Nicholas and Alexandra* (London, 1968).

Middlemas, Keith. *The Life and Times of Edward VII* (London, 1972).

Nowell-Smith, Simon, ed. *Edwardian England* (London, 1901–14).

Rowe, John G. *Queen Alexandra the Beloved* (London, 1925).

St. Aubyn, Giles. *Edward VII Prince and King* (London, 1979).

Saunders, Edith. *The Age of Worth* (London, 1954).

Snowman, A. Kenneth. *Fabergé, 1846–1920: Silver Jubilee Catalogue* (London, 1977).

———. "Carl Fabergé in London," *Nineteenth Century* (Summer 1977), pp. 50–55.

Tisdall, E. E. P. *Unpredictable Queen: The Intimate Life of Queen Alexandra* (London, 1953).

Trowbridge, W. R. H. *Queen Alexandra* (London, 1921).

Villiers, Elizabeth. *Queen Alexandra* (London, 1925).

Wakeford, Geoffrey. *Three Consort Queens* (London, 1971).

Waterfield, Hermione, and Christopher Forbes. *Fabergé: Imperial Eggs and Other Fantasies* (London, 1978).

Williamson, David. *Queen Alexandra: A Biography* (Edinburgh, 1919).

———. *Queen Alexandra* (London, 1926).

Index

Illustration Credits

PAGE 1

Catherine the Great in coronation robes, NOVOSTI (London)

Archduchess Marie Antoinette Habsburg-Lotharingen, by Martin van Meytens, Schloss Schönbrunn, Vienna, Austria/www.bridgeman.co.uk

PAGE 2

Maria Carolina Bonaparte as Queen of Naples with her daughter Laetitia Murat, 1807, by Louise Élisabeth Vigée-Lebrun, Château de Versailles, France, Lauros/Giraudon/www.bridgeman.co.uk

Archduchess Leopoldina of Austria, by Josef Kreutzinger, Schloss Schönbrunn, Vienna, Austria/www.bridgeman.co.uk

PAGE 3

Empress Eugénie, c. 1852, by Edouard Louis Dubufe, Château de Versailles, France, Lauros/Giraudon/www.bridgeman.co.uk

Queen Alexandra, by François Flameng, The Royal Collection © 2005 Her Majesty Queen Elizabeth II

PAGE 4

The Empress Frederick of Germany as Crown Princess of Prussia, 1882, by Heinrich von Angeli, © Wallace Collection, London, UK/www.bridgeman.co.uk

Catherine II and Peter III, 1756, by Anna Rosita Lisiewska, Nationalmuseum, Stockholm, Sweden

PAGE 5

Portrait of Prince Gregory Orlov, Michael Holford

Portrait of Prince Grigory Aleksandrovich Potemkin, c. 1790, by Johann Baptist Edler von Lampi, Hermitage, St. Petersburg, Russia/www.bridgeman.co.uk

Equestrian Portrait of Catherine II the Great of Russia, by Vigilius Erichsen, Musée des Beaux-Arts, Chartres, France/www.bridgeman.co.uk

PAGE 6

The Château de Versailles and the Place d'Armes, 1722, by Pierre-Denis Martin, Château de Versailles, France/www.bridgeman.co.uk

Royal château at Marly, author's collection

PAGE 7

Marie Antoinette in hunting dress, Kunsthistorisches Museum, Wien oder KHM, Vienna

Queen Marie Antoinette with her children in the park of Trianon, 1785, by Adolf Ulrich Wertmüller, Nationalmuseum, Stockholm, Sweden/www.bridgeman.co.uk

PAGE 8

Two hairstyles, author's collection

The execution of Louis XVI, January 21, 1793, Musée de la Revolution Française, Vizille, France/Visual Arts Library, London, UK/www.bridgeman.co.uk

PAGE 9

Frances XXI with his wife, Marie-Therese, and their children, by School of Meytens, Château de Versailles, France/www.bridgeman.co.uk

Lady Hamilton as Bacchante, mezzotint, c. 1790, by John Raphael Smith after a painting by Sir Joshua Reynolds, akg-images

Caserta from the cascade, Edwin Smith/RIBA Library Photographs Collection

PAGE 10

Coronation of Dom Pedro, Rio de Janeiro, Brazil, December 1, 1822. Lithograph by Thierry Frères after Jean-Baptiste Debret. *Voyage Pittoresque et Historique au Brésil,* Imperial Museum, Petrópolis, Brazil

Arrival of Carolina Leopoldina, 1817. Engraving by Simon Pradier after Jean-Baptiste Debret, Imperial Museum, Petrópolis, Brazil

PAGE 11

Contemporary engraving of Rio de Janeiro, from *Journal of a Voyage to Brazil, and residence there, during part of the years 1821, 1822, 1823,* by Maria Graham, Library of Congress/National Library of Brazil

A slave market in Rio de Janeiro, from *Journal of a Voyage to Brazil, and residence there, during part of the years 1821, 1822, 1823,* by Maria Graham, Library of Congress/National Library of Brazil

PAGE 12

Empress Eugénie of France, by Franz Xavier Winterhalter, Château de Versailles, France, Giraudon/www.bridgeman.co.uk

Eugène-Louis Napoleon Bonaparte, 1874, by Jules Joseph Lefebvre, Château de Versailles, France, Lauros/Giraudon/www.bridgeman.co.uk

PAGE 13

The Imperial Family on Horseback, engraving, French School, Château de Compiègne, Oise, France, Lauros/Giraudon/www.bridgeman.co.uk

Empress Eugénie surrounded by her ladies-in-waiting, 1855, by Franz Xavier Winterhalter, Château de Compiègne, Oise, France, Giraudon/www.bridgeman.co.uk

PAGE 14

Sketch by Victoria of Vicky, TLP/Getty Images

The Crown Prince and Crown Princess of Prussia with some of their children, August 1874, by Hills and Saunders, The Royal Archives © 2005 Her Majesty Queen Elizabeth II

Victoria, Crown Princess of Prussia, Berlin, January 18, 1883, by Reichard and Lindner, The Royal Archives © 2005 Her Majesty Queen Elizabeth II

PAGE 15

Queen Alexandra when Princess of Wales on Viva, outside Sandringham House, with her dogs Plumpie, Joss, Tip, Lassie and Rover, 1885, by Jean-Edouard Lacretelle, The Royal Collection © 2005 Her Majesty Queen Elizabeth II

Alexandra on the royal yacht, Hulton/Getty Images

PAGE 16

Empress Marie of Russia and her sister Alexandra, Princess of Wales, wearing matching dresses, hats and fur stoles, late 1870s, by Bergamasco, The Royal Archives © 2005 Her Majesty Queen Elizabeth II

Tsar Alexander III and Empress Marie Feodorovna, c. 1890, by Levitsky, The Royal Archives © 2005 Her Majesty Queen Elizabeth II

ALSO BY HER ROYAL HIGHNESS PRINCESS MICHAEL OF KENT:

An international bestseller in its initial publication, the fascinating account of five of history's most famous royal mistresses…

and the epic tale of King Henri II, Catherine deMedici, and Diane de Poitiers — the extraordinary love triangle that forever changed the face of France.

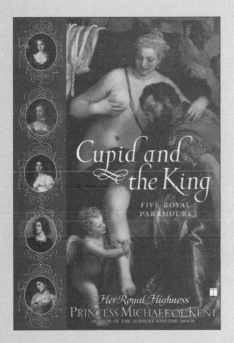

0-7432-7086-X

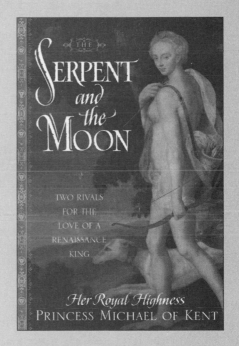

0-7432-5104-0 (hardcover)
0-7432-5106-7 (paperback)

Now available from Touchstone
Wherever books are sold or at www.simonsays.com

TOUCHSTONE
A Division of Simon & Schuster
A CBS COMPANY